TABLE OF CONTENTS

Secret Key #1 - Time is Your Greatest Enemy

Pace Yourself

Wear a watch. At the beginning of the test, check the time (or start a chronometer on your watch to count the minutes), and check the time after every few questions to make sure you are "on schedule."

If you are forced to speed up, do it efficiently. Usually one or more answer choices can be eliminated without too much difficulty. Above all, don't panic. Don't speed up and just begin guessing at random choices. By pacing yourself, and continually monitoring your progress against your watch, you will always know exactly how far ahead or behind you are with your available time. If you find that you are one minute behind on the test, don't skip one question without spending any time on it, just to catch back up. Take 15 fewer seconds on the next four questions, and after four questions you'll have caught back up. Once you catch back up, you can continue working each problem at your normal pace.

Furthermore, don't dwell on the problems that you were rushed on. If a problem was taking up too much time and you made a hurried guess, it must be difficult. The difficult questions are the ones you are most likely to miss anyway, so it isn't a big loss. It is better to end with more time than you need than to run out of time.

Lastly, sometimes it is beneficial to slow down if you are constantly getting ahead of time. You are always more likely to catch a careless mistake by working more slowly than quickly, and among very high-scoring test takers (those who are likely to have lots of time left over), careless errors affect the score more than mastery of material.

Secret Key #2 - Practice Smarter, Not Harder

Many test takers delay the test preparation process because they dread the awful amounts of practice time they think necessary to succeed on the test. We have refined an effective method that will take you only a fraction of the time.

There are a number of "obstacles" in your way to succeed. Among these are answering questions, finishing in time, and mastering test-taking strategies. All must be executed on the day of the test at peak performance, or your score will suffer. The test is a mental marathon that has a large impact on your future.

Just like a marathon runner, it is important to work your way up to the full challenge. So first you just worry about questions, and then time, and finally strategy:

Success Strategy

1. Find a good source for practice tests.
2. If you are willing to make a larger time investment, consider using more than one study guide- often the different approaches of multiple authors will help you "get" difficult concepts.
3. Take a practice test with no time constraints, with all study helps "open book." Take your time with questions and focus on applying strategies.

4. Take a practice test with time constraints, with all guides "open book."
5. Take a final practice test with no open material and time limits

If you have time to take more practice tests, just repeat step 5. By gradually exposing yourself to the full rigors of the test environment, you will condition your mind to the stress of test day and maximize your success.

Secret Key #3 - Prepare, Don't Procrastinate

Let me state an obvious fact: if you take the test three times, you will get three different scores. This is due to the way you feel on test day, the level of preparedness you have, and, despite the test writers' claims to the contrary, some tests WILL be easier for you than others.

Since your future depends so much on your score, you should maximize your chances of success. In order to maximize the likelihood of success, you've got to prepare in advance. This means taking practice tests and spending time learning the information and test taking strategies you will need to succeed.

Never take the test as a "practice" test, expecting that you can just take it again if you need to. Feel free to take sample tests on your own, but when you go to take the official test, be prepared, be focused, and do your best the first time!

Secret Key #4 - Test Yourself

Everyone knows that time is money. There is no need to spend too much of your time or too little of your time preparing for the test. You should only spend as much of your precious time preparing as is necessary for you to get the score you need.

Once you have taken a practice test under real conditions of time constraints, then you will know if you are ready for the test or not.

If you have scored extremely high the first time that you take the practice test, then there is not much point in spending countless hours studying. You are already there.

Benchmark your abilities by retaking practice tests and seeing how much you have improved. Once you score high enough to guarantee success, then you are ready.

If you have scored well below where you need, then knuckle down and begin studying in earnest. Check your improvement regularly through the use of practice tests under real conditions. Above all, don't worry, panic, or give up. The key is perseverance!

Then, when you go to take the test, remain confident and remember how well you did on the practice tests. If you can score high enough on a practice test, then you can do the same on the real thing.

General Strategies

The most important thing you can do is to ignore your fears and jump into the test immediately- do not be overwhelmed by any strange-sounding terms. You have to jump into the test like jumping into a pool- all at once is the easiest way.

Make Predictions

As you read and understand the question, try to guess what the answer will be. Remember that several of the answer choices are wrong, and once you begin reading them, your mind will immediately become cluttered with answer choices designed to throw you off. Your mind is typically the most focused immediately after you have read the question and digested its contents. If you can, try to predict what the correct answer will be. You may be surprised at what you can predict.

Quickly scan the choices and see if your prediction is in the listed answer choices. If it is, then you can be quite confident that you have the right answer. It still won't hurt to check the other answer choices, but most of the time, you've got it!

Answer the Question

It may seem obvious to only pick answer choices that answer the question, but the test writers can create some excellent answer choices that are wrong. Don't pick an answer just because it sounds right, or you believe it to be true. It MUST answer the question. Once you've made your selection, always go back and check it against the question and make sure that you didn't misread the question, and the answer choice does answer the question posed.

Benchmark

After you read the first answer choice, decide if you think it sounds correct or not. If it doesn't, move on to the next answer choice. If it does, mentally mark that answer choice. This doesn't mean that you've definitely selected it as your

answer choice, it just means that it's the best you've seen thus far. Go ahead and read the next choice. If the next choice is worse than the one you've already selected, keep going to the next answer choice. If the next choice is better than the choice you've already selected, mentally mark the new answer choice as your best guess.

The first answer choice that you select becomes your standard. Every other answer choice must be benchmarked against that standard. That choice is correct until proven otherwise by another answer choice beating it out. Once you've decided that no other answer choice seems as good, do one final check to ensure that your answer choice answers the question posed.

Valid Information

Don't discount any of the information provided in the question. Every piece of information may be necessary to determine the correct answer. None of the information in the question is there to throw you off (while the answer choices will certainly have information to throw you off). If two seemingly unrelated topics are discussed, don't ignore either. You can be confident there is a relationship, or it wouldn't be included in the question, and you are probably going to have to determine what is that relationship to find the answer.

Avoid "Fact Traps"

Don't get distracted by a choice that is factually true. Your search is for the answer that answers the question. Stay focused and don't fall for an answer that is true but incorrect. Always go back to the question and make sure you're choosing an answer that actually answers the question and is not just a true statement. An answer can be factually correct, but it MUST answer the question asked. Additionally, two answers can both be seemingly correct, so be sure to read all of the answer choices, and make sure that you get the one that BEST answers the question.

Milk the Question

Some of the questions may throw you completely off. They might deal with a subject you have not been exposed to, or one that you haven't reviewed in years. While your lack of knowledge about the subject will be a hindrance, the question itself can give you many clues that will help you find the correct answer. Read the question carefully and look for clues. Watch particularly for adjectives and nouns describing difficult terms or words that you don't recognize. Regardless of if you completely understand a word or not, replacing it with a synonym either provided or one you more familiar with may help you to understand what the questions are asking. Rather than wracking your mind about specific detailed information concerning a difficult term or word, try to use mental substitutes that are easier to understand.

The Trap of Familiarity

Don't just choose a word because you recognize it. On difficult questions, you may not recognize a number of words in the answer choices. The test writers don't put "make-believe" words on the test; so don't think that just because you only recognize all the words in one answer choice means that answer choice must be correct. If you only recognize words in one answer choice, then focus on that one. Is it correct? Try your best to determine if it is correct. If it is, that is great, but if it doesn't, eliminate it. Each word and answer choice you eliminate increases your chances of getting the question correct, even if you then have to guess among the unfamiliar choices.

Eliminate Answers

Eliminate choices as soon as you realize they are wrong. But be careful! Make sure you consider all of the possible answer choices. Just because one appears right, doesn't mean that the next one won't be even better! The test writers will usually put more than one good answer choice for every question, so read all of them. Don't worry if you are stuck between two that seem right. By getting down to just two remaining possible choices, your odds are now 50/50. Rather than wasting too much time, play the odds. You are guessing, but guessing wisely, because you've been able to knock out some of the answer choices that you know are wrong. If you are eliminating choices and realize that the last answer choice you are left with is also obviously wrong, don't panic. Start over and consider each choice again. There may easily be something that you missed the first time and will realize on the second pass.

Tough Questions

If you are stumped on a problem or it appears too hard or too difficult, don't waste time. Move on! Remember though, if you can quickly check for obviously incorrect answer choices, your chances of guessing correctly are greatly improved. Before you completely give up, at least try to knock out a couple of possible answers. Eliminate what you can and then guess at the remaining answer choices before moving on.

Brainstorm

If you get stuck on a difficult question, spend a few seconds quickly brainstorming. Run through the complete list of possible answer choices. Look at each choice and ask yourself, "Could this answer the question satisfactorily?" Go through each answer choice and consider it independently of the other. By systematically going through all possibilities, you may find something that you would otherwise overlook.

Remember that when you get stuck, it's important to try to keep moving.

Read Carefully

Understand the problem. Read the question and answer choices carefully. Don't miss the question because you misread the terms. You have plenty of time to read each question thoroughly and make sure you understand what is being asked. Yet a happy medium must be attained, so don't waste too much time. You must read carefully, but efficiently.

Face Value

When in doubt, use common sense. Always accept the situation in the problem at face value. Don't read too much into it. These problems will not require you to make huge leaps of logic. The test writers aren't trying to throw you off with a cheap trick. If you have to go beyond creativity and make a leap of logic in order to have an answer choice answer the question, then you should look at the other answer choices. Don't overcomplicate the problem by creating theoretical relationships or explanations that will warp time or space. These are normal problems rooted in reality. It's just that the applicable relationship or explanation may not be readily apparent and you have to figure things out. Use your common sense to interpret anything that isn't clear.

Prefixes

If you're having trouble with a word in the question or answer choices, try dissecting it. Take advantage of every clue that the word might include. Prefixes and suffixes can be a huge help. Usually they allow you to determine a basic meaning. Pre- means before, post- means after, pro - is positive, de- is negative. From these prefixes and suffixes, you can get an idea of the general meaning of the word and try to put it into context. Beware though of any traps. Just because

con is the opposite of pro, doesn't necessarily mean congress is the opposite of progress!

Hedge Phrases

Watch out for critical "hedge" phrases, such as likely, may, can, will often, sometimes, often, almost, mostly, usually, generally, rarely, sometimes. Question writers insert these hedge phrases to cover every possibility. Often an answer choice will be wrong simply because it leaves no room for exception. Avoid answer choices that have definitive words like "exactly," and "always".

Switchback Words

Stay alert for "switchbacks". These are the words and phrases frequently used to alert you to shifts in thought. The most common switchback word is "but". Others include although, however, nevertheless, on the other hand, even though, while, in spite of, despite, regardless of.

New Information

Correct answer choices will rarely have completely new information included. Answer choices typically are straightforward reflections of the material asked about and will directly relate to the question. If a new piece of information is included in an answer choice that doesn't even seem to relate to the topic being asked about, then that answer choice is likely incorrect. All of the information needed to answer the question is usually provided for you, and so you should not have to make guesses that are unsupported or choose answer choices that require unknown information that cannot be reasoned on its own.

Time Management

On technical questions, don't get lost on the technical terms. Don't spend too much time on any one question. If you don't know what a term means, then since you don't have a dictionary, odds are you aren't going to get much further. You should immediately recognize terms as whether or not you know them. If you don't, work with the other clues that you have, the other answer choices and terms provided, but don't waste too much time trying to figure out a difficult term.

Contextual Clues

Look for contextual clues. An answer can be right but not correct. The contextual clues will help you find the answer that is most right and is correct. Understand the context in which a phrase or statement is made. This will help you make important distinctions.

Don't Panic

Panicking will not answer any questions for you. Therefore, it isn't helpful. When you first see the question, if your mind goes blank, take a deep breath. Force yourself to mechanically go through the steps of solving the problem and using the strategies you've learned.

Pace Yourself

Don't get clock fever. It's easy to be overwhelmed when you're looking at a page full of questions, your mind is full of random thoughts and feeling confused, and the clock is ticking down faster than you would like. Calm down and maintain the pace that you have set for yourself. As long as you are on track by monitoring your pace, you are guaranteed to have enough time for yourself. When you get to the last few minutes of the test, it may seem like you won't have enough time left, but if you only have as many questions as you should have left at that point, then you're right on track!

Answer Selection

The best way to pick an answer choice is

to eliminate all of those that are wrong, until only one is left and confirm that is the correct answer. Sometimes though, an answer choice may immediately look right. Be careful! Take a second to make sure that the other choices are not equally obvious. Don't make a hasty mistake. There are only two times that you should stop before checking other answers. First is when you are positive that the answer choice you have selected is correct. Second is when time is almost out and you have to make a quick guess!

Check Your Work

Since you will probably not know every term listed and the answer to every question, it is important that you get credit for the ones that you do know. Don't miss any questions through careless mistakes. If at all possible, try to take a second to look back over your answer selection and make sure you've selected the correct answer choice and haven't made a costly careless mistake (such as marking an answer choice that you didn't mean to mark). This quick double check should more than pay for itself in caught mistakes for the time it costs.

Beware of Directly Quoted Answers

Sometimes an answer choice will repeat word for word a portion of the question or reference section. However, beware of such exact duplication – it may be a trap! More than likely, the correct choice will paraphrase or summarize a point, rather than being exactly the same wording.

Slang

Scientific sounding answers are better than slang ones. An answer choice that begins "To compare the outcomes..." is much more likely to be correct than one that begins "Because some people insisted..."

Extreme Statements

Avoid wild answers that throw out highly controversial ideas that are proclaimed as established fact. An answer choice that states the "process should be used in certain situations, if..." is much more likely to be correct than one that states the "process should be discontinued completely." The first is a calm rational statement and doesn't even make a definitive, uncompromising stance, using a hedge word "if" to provide wiggle room, whereas the second choice is a radical idea and far more extreme.

Answer Choice Families

When you have two or more answer choices that are direct opposites or parallels, one of them is usually the correct answer. For instance, if one answer choice states "x increases" and another answer choice states "x decreases" or "y increases," then those two or three answer choices are very similar in construction and fall into the same family of answer choices. A family of answer choices is when two or three answer choices are very similar in construction, and yet often have a directly opposite meaning. Usually the correct answer choice will be in that family of answer choices. The "odd man out" or answer choice that doesn't seem to fit the parallel construction of the other answer choices is more likely to be incorrect.

Top 20 Test Taking Tips

1. Carefully follow all the test registration procedures
2. Know the test directions, duration, topics, question types, how many questions
3. Setup a flexible study schedule at least 3-4 weeks before test day
4. Study during the time of day you are most alert, relaxed, and stress free
5. Maximize your learning style; visual learner use visual study aids, auditory learner use auditory study aids
6. Focus on your weakest knowledge base
7. Find a study partner to review with and help clarify questions
8. Practice, practice, practice
9. Get a good night's sleep; don't try to cram the night before the test
10. Eat a well balanced meal
11. Know the exact physical location of the testing site; drive the route to the site prior to test day
12. Bring a set of ear plugs; the testing center could be noisy
13. Wear comfortable, loose fitting, layered clothing to the testing center; prepare for it to be either cold or hot during the test
14. Bring at least 2 current forms of ID to the testing center
15. Arrive to the test early; be prepared to wait and be patient
16. Eliminate the obviously wrong answer choices, then guess the first remaining choice
17. Pace yourself; don't rush, but keep working and move on if you get stuck
18. Maintain a positive attitude even if the test is going poorly
19. Keep your first answer unless you are positive it is wrong
20. Check your work, don't make a careless mistake

Counseling, Assessment and Diagnosis

Mental Health Counseling

Historical impact on therapeutic interventions

Therapeutic interventions require the use of foundational models incorporating philosophy, theory, and practice methodologies. The disadvantage of applying past solutions is their tendency to hinder the application of unconventional solutions not found in old psychotherapy treatment manuals. Unconventional solutions may work for the individual who has not had success with a conventional method, though it may have previously worked for another patient. Mental health care has undergone a progressive development throughout time. Therapeutic trends have become part of the accepted model for mental health care. Institutions of the past have been replaced with community treatment centers that have had an innovative impact on mental health. Treatments have become more psychoecologically based as patients' surroundings have become a factor. Psychologically-trained and educationally-trained counselors have begun to specialize.

Counseling and psychotherapy

Some practitioners use the terms counseling and psychotherapy interchangeably to indicate the same service. However, those practitioners who believe these terms are not identical state the difference lies in the class of client that receives treatment. Other substantive differences in terminology include: The kind of therapy received; degree and nature of illness; clinical work setting or environment in which treatment is received; and the training received by the therapist. Counseling is a treatment that allows the client to express emotions while the therapist provides support, education, and feedback. However, psychotherapy is a remediation process that involves getting to the root cause of the problem. Neither counselor nor psychotherapist can make these divisions in treatment, as there is a distinctive overlap when talking with the patient.

Kant, Leibnitz, and Locke

A number of philosophies, assumptions, and applied theories govern mental health practice. One theory holds that human beings gain knowledge from their experiences in life. Another theory holds that the environment impacts knowledge. Inherited factors also contribute to this schema. Plato and Aristotle contributed to philosophical beliefs in mental health practice. Leibnitz was a philosopher who believed in personology, which states that a person can change when his or her perceptual awareness is changed. Leibnitz's Theory of Mind is based on subjective reality -- how a person perceives things to be within his or her own mind. John Locke held a more empiricist viewpoint, believing the human brain absorbs environmental events and sensory inputs from its surroundings in an effort to form meaning and knowledge, so studying only nature and the environment unlocks a person's mental health needs.

Kant held the assumption that reality is based on subjective observations drawn from a person's objective reality or environmental events. Kant's theories are based on interactionism. Freud found

- 12 -

Kant's interactionism offered a starting point for his psychoanalytical work. Leibnitz's theory of personology evolved into humanistic psychology, resulting in a counseling model known as Rogers' Person-Centered Psychotherapy. John Locke's empiric theories evolved into Behavior Therapy and Behavioral Counseling. Despite the differences in philosophies, the goal of each of these psychotherapy models is the same. Each works to transform a person's thought patterns to affect the way that person handles emotional responses and behaves.

Theory development

The five stages of theory development are:
- Stage 1: The Original Paradigm, in which Freud's psychoanalysis, client-centered therapy, and behavior therapy are found
- Stage 2: Paradigm Modification by Jung, Adler, Patterson, and Bandura
- Stage 3: Paradigm Specificity by Berne, Jourard, Genlin, Beck, and Krumboltz
- Stage 4: Paradigm Experimentation by Strupp, Mitchell and Aron, Ellis, Beutler, Wexler, and Lazarus
- Stage 5: Paradigm Consolidation by Lazarus, Seay, and Beutler

According to Rychlak, psychotherapy can be broken down into three basic motives. Motives correspond to purpose, ethics and healing. Scholarly motive is one of the three motives of psychotherapists noted by Rychlak. Rychlak believed this rationale for performing psychotherapy was best characterized in the works of Freud, where the psychotherapist is a scientist who records the inner workings of the mind, instinctive drives and actions, and analyzes the data. Ethical motive is the counselor's desire to help the client grow and express strong feelings and opinions about his or her life problems. Curative motive is when the psychotherapist wants to initiate the healing process for the patient by engaging in such a way as to help modify those behaviors detrimental to the patient's success in society.

In Stage 2, the Modification Stage, Jung, Adler, Patterson, and Bandura adapted Freud's Original Paradigm. Adaptation was necessary because the Original Paradigm of development theory did not adequately answer all of the questions raised. Jung had a more restrained viewpoint regarding Freud's bisexual theories. Adler had a more social viewpoint regarding Freud's theories. Modification Stage theorists worked to add to the developing paradigm without making revolutionary changes. In Stage 3, the Specificity Stage, changes to counseling tactics were initiated by Berne, Jourard, Genlin, Beck, and Krumboltz. Berne replaced Freud's superego, id, and ego with adapted terms referring to the parent, child, and adult. Berne's new nomenclature allowed Freud's work to remain intact, except for minor alterations in terminology.

In stage 4, the Experimentation Stage, Strupp, Mitchell, Aron, Ellis, Beutler, Wexler, and Lazarus initiated changes to the rules for conducting counseling sessions. Experimentation Stage theorists began making abstract structures, practices, and paradigm-linked procedures. Stages 1 to 3 of theory development were greatly altered. Old parameters were disregarded by radical behaviorists who accepted more humanistic, cognitive processing theories. Humanists adopted relaxation techniques common to the behaviorist theories. The models found in Stage 4 are inconsistent, without the foundational supports of previous paradigms, and are not reconciled with a philosophy. Stage 5, Paradigm Consolidation, is in its infancy. There are more developments along its horizon.

Theories that violate paradigm parameters

Cognitive-behavioral theory operates on a person's interaction with his or her surroundings. Environmental interaction is based on the person's cognitive abilities to organize information. The environment is also referred to as the non S-R. Cognitive-behavioral theory violates the paradigm parameters found in Lockean philosophy. Robert Carkhuff's affective-behavioral approach therapy reinterpreted Carl Rogers' work. Non-conformity or violation is known as technical eclecticism. Technical eclecticism is necessary if one is to achieve the next paradigm. Paradigms must be based on validated procedures, strategies, and applied techniques. Well defined theories find their roots in the beliefs that make up a foundational base. This belief system has to be kept intact if a violation of the paradigm's parameters is not to be the end result.

De-emphasis on theoretical dependency

Kuhn suggests psychotherapists adopt a single paradigm instead of the 250 paradigms already in place. Kuhn's suggestion was embraced in Lazarus' technical eclecticism, which allows more freedom of selection in choosing preferred or best theoretical models. Eclectic approaches allow for a mixture of different models. Some models find their basis in cognitive structures. One approach is to mix Freud's psychoanalytic approaches with Beck's Cognitive Theory. Models are founded on phenomenological knowledge structures, which incorporate

Rogers' Person-Centered Therapy. Some combine Wolpe's Behavior Therapy and behavior modification strategies. Model lines become indistinguishable when combinations of theoretical models cease to follow more structured guidelines. Abbreviations that demonstrate this blending are as follows: CB is a mixture of cognitive and behavioral standards; CA is a mixture of information processing structures with affective models; AB is a mixture of affective models with behavioral standards; CAB is a combination of all three.

Mental health counseling terms

The following terms are associated with mental health counseling:
- Community Psychology: The incorporation of psychological values and theories into publicly accessed areas within towns and neighborhoods.
- Mental Health Centers: Neighborhood and local community health services provided by psychiatrists, psychologists, and social workers. These centers originated out of legislation signed by President John F. Kennedy.
- Individual Therapy: Private counseling and psychotherapy sessions with a single client and a therapist. The initial session is designed to identity problems that require subsequent modification techniques. One of the three types of delivery systems.
- Group Therapy: Provides counseling and psychotherapy to a patient through group interaction and exchanges designed to help the individual to talk about personal issues in an atmosphere where the individual can gain active help and encouragement from other

- 14 -

members of the group. One of the three types of delivery systems.

- Family Therapy: Provides counseling and psychotherapy to a patient and his or her family through sessions with a therapist designed to help the patient identify problems in which the family can intervene and help to resolve or improve. One of the three types of delivery systems.
- Human Modalities: This term refers to the three classifications of models known as the Cognition, Affect, and Behavior. The Cognition model is abbreviated as (C). The Affect model is abbreviated as (A). The Behavior model is abbreviated as (B).

Humanistic Behavior

Humanistic Behavior was a three-stage model developed in 1969 by theorist Robert Carkhuff:

- First stage: Facilitation, where a relationship is cultivated between the client and therapist
- Second stage: Self-awareness, which allows the patient to find out more about the reasons behind his or her behavior through discussion with the therapist that expands on issues surrounding the understanding of self
- Third stage: Relates to the actions or measures that are to be taken

The Humanistic Behavior model incorporates client-centered therapy and behavior therapy. Client-centered therapy involves the client as the key person in the treatment. Humanistic Behavior is an (A) or affective model.

Personal Science

Personal Science was developed in 1977 by Michael Mahoney, based on the cognitive-behavioral (CB) approach. The acronym SCIENCE is used to explain the sequential steps through which the therapist guides the patient to solve a problem:

- S is for specification of the problem
- C is for collection of data or facts
- I is for identification of patterns or reasons for existing behaviors
- E is for examination of choices that can be used to modify behavior
- N is for narrowing the options and experimenting with possible modifications
- C is for comparing data or facts
- E is for expanding, modifying, or substituting unwanted behaviors for more preferred behaviors

Rational Behavior Therapy

Rational Behavior Therapy was developed in 1977 by Maxie C. Maultsby, Jr. It is a more direct method of dealing with a patient's emotional state than Ellis' Rational Emotive therapy from the mid-1950's. Maultsby was Albert Ellis' student. Rational Behavior is based on the cognitive-behavioral (CB) approach and has five steps, known as Emotional Re-education:

- Step 1: Self-analysis using rational thought helps the patient to gain intellectual insights
- Step 2: Changing actions or behaviors to reflect newly gained intellectual insights
- Step 3: Cognitive emotive dissonance is a refocus of attention that helps the patient bring feelings and thought patterns into alignment with each other
- Step 4: Rationalized feelings promote cohesive thought

patterns through consistent emotional insights
- Step 5: Habitual practice of newly gained insights develops new personality traits in the patient

Psychobehavioral Therapy and Cognitive-Client Therapy

Psychobehavioral Therapy was developed 1971 by George E. Woody. This is simply a combination of two psychoanalytic and behavioral techniques with a variety of eclectic approaches. Psychobehavioral Therapy is based on the cognitive-behavioral (CB) approach. Cognitive-Client Therapy was a cognitive-affective (CA) model designed by David Wexler in 1974. He used Information Processing Theory as the foundation for his beliefs concerning cognitive roles. Wexler postulated client-centered therapy is better established by combining affective experience with cognitive thoughts. Wexler's belief is similar to those of the cognitive-behaviorists. He believes that the client can gain control over his or her behavior through cognitive deliberations. Wexler also thinks that emotional experiencing can not be accomplished without a forerunner of cognitive thought processes.

Multimodal Behavior Therapy

Multimodal Behavior Therapy was invented in 1971 by Arnold Lazarus. This is a complex system that mingles client-conceptualization theories into all the human modalities of cognition, affect, and behavior that cannot be excluded from a patient's everyday life. Lazarus believed that there were exactly seven modalities. He used the acronym BASIC ID to explain each one:
- B is for behavior
- A is for affect
- S is for sensory
- I is for imagery

- C is for cognition
- I is for intrapersonal
- D is for drugs

Multimodal Behavior Therapy has no guide for which technique to choose for treatment, no set therapy process, or sequential steps to take. Multimodal Behavior Therapy identifies a theme, and then the therapist utilizes the BASIC ID techniques for treating the patient.

Brief crisis intervention therapy

Brief crisis intervention therapies help the client come to terms with a life event or societal change, for example:
- Debriefing after violence in the workplace
- Natural disasters (earthquake, tornado, flood)
- Sexual assault
- Criminal victimization
- Suicidal or homicidal ideation (telephone hot lines)
- Catastrophic illness or injury
- Drastic relationship changes, like divorce
- Reconciling gaps between our work values and the quality of our work due to technological advancements

Limited therapy sessions may be conducted because of:
- Insurance limitations
- The client's reluctance to engage in prolonged treatment
- A shortage of qualified mental health workers versus heightened public demand for mental health treatment

Short crisis intervention therapies promoted by Health Management Organizations (HMOs) emphasize the heavy cost of mental health services to the insurance system. HMOs affect how mental health care is delivered because they require traditional long term treatment models to change. Many short crisis intervention therapies incorporate:

- Short meeting times of 25 minutes or less, rather than traditional 60 minute sessions
- Restricted goal setting targeted at reaching short-term objectives, rather than consistent emotional insights
- Focused interviewing regarding the problem at hand
- Concentration on the here and now, rather than a detailed history
- Practical instruction about actions to be taken
- Diagnostic care that pinpoints the problem
- Flexible and varied choices of therapeutic tools to be utilized
- Prompt intervention strategies
- Inclusion of a ventilation practice
- Positive transfer of a therapeutic bond
- Selection of clients appropriate for short term crisis intervention therapies, rather than accepting all clients

Brief crisis intervention therapies often follow a six-step model developed by Small in 1979. The end result of these steps should be that the client feels that the therapist helped and provided a positive experience:

- Step 1: Identify and concentrate on the problem at hand
- Step 2: Assess the patient's personal history
- Step 3: Develop a therapeutic bond with the patient
- Step 4: Create a plan that uses an eclectic approach in selecting a wide range of intervention strategies
- Step 5: Work out a solution to the problem at hand

- Step 6: End therapy with an understanding between therapist and patient that the client can return whenever necessary

Solution Focused Therapy is another alternative that provides a productive atmosphere for the client, where the problem can be solved in a non-judgmental environment. The therapist in this situation discusses the pros and cons of that solution.

Assessments

Diagnostic and assessment procedures have gone through several transformations. One such transformation is the apparent disapproving attitudes that professionals have adopted towards psychological testing and assessments done in the past. Some therapists have moved away testing procedures entirely. However, the need for either a formal or informal diagnosis is still required so that treatment can begin. In the past, a patient could expect a medical exam, personal history assessment, projective tests, and paper-and-pencil assessment formats. Alternative methods of assessment include neuropsychological assessments, behavioral assessments, and thematic assessments. The purpose of neuropsychology is to make a connection between the brain's functioning ability and behaviors of the person. Neuropsychologists concentrate on diagnosis, care, and research. Behavioral assessment makes note of biological, physiological, and social behaviors of the patient. These areas help determine adaptive functioning levels in relationship with the desired outcome.

Thematic assessment appraises major themes that have happened over the lifetime of a patient. As the patient verbalizes the life events, the therapist makes notes of the themes or predominant topics that create a pattern. The predominant themes are then related to the assessment, which attempts to bring into focus a better understanding of what these themes mean. The assessment can be a paper-and-pencil type of test, behavioral charts, or clinical interview techniques. One type of paper-and-pencil test is the Minnesota Multiphasic Personality Inventory (MMPI). Behavioral chart assessments can be used to document a person's habitual, explosive angry episodes. Clinical interviews are used for cognitive imagery assessments. Methodological innovations are concerned with processes, strategies, and techniques which can be used to help a client change his or her behavior.

Cognitive techniques

Cognitive techniques modify misguided or erratic thinking and help a patient gain problem solving skills that are useful in making decisions. Some beneficial strategies involving cognitive theories are: Advanced therapy organizer; bibliotherapy; blow-up; cognitive imagery; cognitive rehearsal; cognitive restructuring; cognitive self talk; covert reinforcement; free association; graded task assignments; mastery and pleasuring; paradoxical intention; rational self-analysis; reality testing; distancing and centering; and repeated review. Affective techniques include: Affective focusing; body awareness; catharsis; emotional re-education; empathic responding; empty chair; evocative reflections; here and now focus; iconification of feeling; psychodrama; stress inoculation; ventilation; and warmth and acceptance. Behavioral techniques include: Assertiveness training; audiovisual feedback; aversive control; behavioral rehearsal; contracting; decision-making; escalation;

extinction; feedback; fixed role therapy; homework; hypnosis; minimal effective response; modeling; pain control; systematic sensitization; and contingency management.

Physiology of psychotherapy

The physiological foundation for psychotherapy is gaining momentum as research in this area advances. Biopsychological research is based on the notion that biological systems in the body are linked to human behaviors. Prescription drugs are used to alter brain chemistry to help the patient cope with imbalances in their biological systems. An alternative or supplement to drug therapy is exercise that releases endorphins and helps the patient to decrease feelings of depression. In the past, the person receiving psychological treatment was treated more like a casualty who was responsible for his or her own injured state. The mental health provider held to the belief that the patient's mental state, shortfalls involving relationships, and maladaptive behaviors were at the root of the patient's mental disorder.

Traditional and alternative treatment models

Traditional treatment models attempted to bring about a change in the client. This change was normally of short duration because when the patient returned to everyday life, old habits and behaviors resurfaced. Alternative treatment models have been put into place to bring about social reform in the mental health industry. However, the public has not been receptive to this social reform. One alternative treatment is referred to as the psychoecological perspective theory and is concerned with mental health and physical illness. It also makes note of delinquent members of society and criminal behaviors. Mental health providers apply strategies that relieve the client's stress and help them learn to cope with the community. A number of concurrent therapeutic treatments are employed that address the client's intrapsychic conflicts and interpersonal interactions. These concurrent treatments need to be furnished through an organizational model.

Organizational models for psychoecological delivery

The organizational models for psychoecological delivery were identified by Seay in 1983. Care can be delivered through direct preventive interventions, remediative, or aftercare systems. Direct preventive interventions are the Primary delivery target. Remediative care is the Secondary delivery target. Aftercare is Tertiary Prevention. These five areas are addressed: Residential; community; educational; business and political arenas; and the private sector. Services offered include: Individual psychotherapy; group psychotherapy; family psychotherapy; educational courses; synchronization of services; restructuring the patient's surroundings; making contacts within the community; advocacy; referral; ongoing professional instruction and training; psychodiagnostics; research and assessment; and financial support. The model contains: Counseling/psychotherapy; marriage counseling services; family counseling services; drug and alcohol therapy; environmental restructuring; funding; community health centers; and other approaches. This model should correct some of the organization deficiencies that are currently part of the mental health provider system.

Biological of Behavior

Neurons

The neuron, or nerve cell, is instrumental in thought processes and behavior. Most of the neurons that a human will ever have are present at birth. It is possible for neurons to regenerate throughout life. Most neurons have three basic components: dendrites, cell body (soma), and axon. The dendrites are like arms that receive information in the form of electrical impulses from other cells and relay it to the soma. The cell body (soma) then processes that information and passes it to the axon, which may then pass it along to other cells. Neurons typically have one axon which divides into a few branches, called collaterals. Axons are covered by a thin, fatty substance known as the myelin sheath, which accelerates the conduction of nerve impulses. The process through which electrical impulses are passed within a cell is called conduction; communication between cells is performed through the release of neurotransmitting chemicals between the cells (in a gap known as a synapse).

Neurotransmitters

Acetylcholine (ACh) is a neurotransmitter found in both the peripheral and central nervous systems. When it is released into the neuromuscular junction by the peripheral nervous system, it contracts the muscles. In the central nervous system, ACh is responsible for REM sleep, the maintenance of the circadian rhythm, and memory. The memory deficits associated with Alzheimer's disease and other illnesses result from the degeneration of ACh cells in the entorhinal cortex (EC) and other regions of the brain that communicate with the hippocampus. There are two sorts of receptor for these cells: nicotinic receptors are excitatory, while muscarinic receptors are inhibitory. Nicotine in tobacco products creates alertness by mimicking ACh at receptor sites.

The group of neurotransmitters known as the catecholamines includes norepinephrine, epinephrine (adrenaline), and dopamine. Catecholamines affect personality, mood, memory, and sleep. Dopamine is instrumental in regulating movement, and in reinforcing substance addiction. Elevated levels of dopamine in the mesolimbic areas of the brain are associated with the pleasant feelings engendered by stimulants, opiates, alcohol, and nicotine. Another important neurotransmitter (which is not a member of the catecholamines) is serotonin. Serotonin is inhibitory in general, and implicated in a broad range of serotonin disorders like depression, schizophrenia, and Parkinson's disease. Serotonin deficiencies have been one of the factors to blame for ailments such as anorexia, bulimia, obsessive compulsive disorders, migraines, social phobias and schizophrenia.

Gamma-aminobutyric acid, or GABA, is an inhibitory neurotransmitter that influences sleep, eating, seizure, and anxiety disorders. The development of Huntington's disease is in part due to the degeneration of the cells in the basal ganglia that are responsible for secreting GABA. Glutamate, on the other hand, is an excitatory neurotransmitter involved in learning and the formation of long-term memories. When glutamate receptors are overexcited, the result can be seizures and/or brain damage.

Endorphins are not neurotransmitters but neuromodulators; they have analgesic properties and are though to lower the sensitivity of postsynaptic neurons to neurotransmitters.

Spinal cord

The central nervous system contains the brain and the spinal cord. The spinal cord is composed of axons, dendrites, cell bodies, and interneurons. The job of the spinal cord is to carry information between the brain and the peripheral nervous system, coordinate the right and left sides of the body, and control all of the simple reflexes that do not involve the brain. The nerve fibers in the superior portion of the spinal cord carry sensory messages, while the nerve fibers in the inferior portion transmit motor messages. There are 31 sections to the spinal cord, divided into five groups; in order, from top to bottom, they are the cervical, thoracic, lumbar, sacral, and coccygeal.

When the spinal cord is damaged at the cervical level, the result is quadriplegia; when it is damaged at the thoracic level, the result is paraplegia. When a spinal cord injury is complete, there will be a total lack of sensation and voluntary movement below the site of the injury. When the injury is incomplete, some sensory and motor function below the level of injury will be maintained. If the flow of cerebrospinal fluid (CSF) to and from the four cerebral ventricles is obstructed, then a condition called hydrocephalus may develop in which fluid backs up and there is an enlargement of the ventricles, destroying brain tissue. A similar enlargement of the ventricles has been observed in individuals with schizophrenia.

Peripheral nervous system

The peripheral nervous system (PNS) is composed of nerves in distal parts, not in the spinal cord or brain. Its function is to transmit messages between the central nervous system and the sensory organs, muscles, and glands. There are 12 pairs of cranial nerves and 31 sets of sensory and motor nerves that link to the spinal cord. The PNS is divided into the somatic nervous system (SNS) and the autonomic nervous system (ANS). The SNS controls voluntary motions by relaying messages from the sense receptors to the CNS; the ANS is primarily concerned with involuntary motions, and connects the viscera to the CNS. The sympathetic branch of the ANS is associated with arousal and the discharge of energy, while the parasympathetic branch is concerned with relaxation and digestion.

Central nervous system

There are five basic stages in the development of the central nervous system:

- Proliferation, in which new cells are produced inside the neural tube; this begins when the embryo is about 2.5 weeks old.
- Migration, (8 weeks) in which the young neurons move to the appropriate place in the brain and begin to form structures.
- Differentiation, in which the neurons begin to develop axons and dendrites.
- Myelination, in which glial cells form an insulating and protective sheath around the axons of some cells.
- Synaptogenesis, in which the synapses form; this stage occurs at various periods, depending both on the brain's internal schedule, and factors of experience after birth.

Hindbrain

The medulla and the pons, which are located at the base of the brain near the spinal cord, combine with the cerebellum to form the hindbrain. The medulla regulates the flow of information between the spinal cord and the brain, and

coordinates a number of important processes like swallowing, coughing, sneezing, and the heart rate. The pons bridges the two halves of the brain, and is instrumental in coordinating movements between the right and left sides of the body. The cerebellum makes balance and posture possible, and contributes to the performance of coordinated and refined motor movements. Autistic individuals have been found to have smaller than normal cerebellums. A damaged cerebellum may result in ataxia, a condition involving slurred speech, tremors, and a loss of balance.

Midbrain

The midbrain is made up of the reticular formation, which extends from the spinal cord through the hindbrain and midbrain into the hypothalamus structure in the forebrain. It contains over 90 groups of neurons, with functions ranging from respiration, to coughing, to posture and locomotion. The reticular activating system (RAS) is essential to consciousness, arousal, and wakefulness. It regulates sensory input, especially during sleep. When it detects important information, it alerts other parts of the brain. If an individual suffers damage to his or her reticular formation, his or her sleep-wake cycle may be disrupted; it is even possible to fall permanently asleep as a result of damage to this area. Some anesthetics work by depressing the RAS so that sharp pains do not wake the person up.

Forebrain

The forebrain is composed of both cortical and subcortical structures. The subcortical structures are the thalamus, hypothalamus, basal ganglia, and limbic system. The thalamus takes sensory input (except for olfactory input) and directs it to the appropriate part of the brain. Korsakoff syndrome is associated with atrophy in the thalamus. The hypothalamus is linked to hunger, thirst, sex, sleep, body temperature, movement, and emotional reactions; if it is damaged, the emotions can be out of control. The hypothalamus also maintains homeostasis by regulating the pituitary and other glands. The suprachiasmatic nucleus is located in the hypothalamus; it controls the circadian rhythm.

The structure of the brain known as the basal ganglia includes the caudate nucleus, putamen, globus pallidus, and substantia nigra. The basal ganglia plan voluntary movements, and control the amplitude and direction of movement. The basal ganglia are also responsible for various facial movements that indicate emotional states, like smiling or frowning. Parkinson's disease, Tourette's syndrome, Huntington's disease, mania, depression, and psychosis all may stem from abnormalities in the basal ganglia. The amygdala directs motivational and emotional functions, and deals with emotionally-charged memories. The hippocampus processes spatial, verbal, and visual information, and consolidates declarative memories.

Cerebral cortex

The cerebral cortex, otherwise known as the neocortex, is the largest part of the brain; it is divided into a right and left hemisphere, each of which is further divided into four lobes. The frontal lobe includes motor, premotor and prefrontal areas. The primary motor cortex controls voluntary movements, while the premotor cortex contains the region known as Broca's area, which helps produce speech. Damage to Broca's area results in a condition called aphasia, in which a person cannot produce spoken or written language. The prefrontal cortex is involved in memory, emotion, self-awareness, and the so-called executive

(sophisticated cognitive) functions. Damage to the prefrontal cortex can cause pseudodepression, pseudopsychosis, and trouble with abstract thinking.

The parietal lobe of the cerebral cortex includes the somatosensory cortex, which controls the sensations of pressure, pain, temperature, gustation, and proprioception. If the parietal lobe is damaged, the individual may suffer spatial disorientation, apraxia (the inability to perform sophisticated motor movements), and somatosensory agnosia. This last condition includes tactile agnosia (the inability to recognize familiar items by touch), anosognosia (the inability to recognize one's own brain disorder), and asomatognosia (the inability to recognize parts of one's own body). If the right side of the parietal lobe is damaged, the individual may lose the ability to conceive of or control the left side of the body; if the left side is damaged, the individual may develop ideational apraxia, the inability to follow a simple set of directions

The temporal lobe of the cerebral cortex contains several parts. The auditory cortex processes audible sensations. If a person sustains damage to the auditory cortex, he or she may suffer auditory hallucinations, auditory agnosia, and other disturbances. Another part of the temporal lobe is called Wernicke's area; this region is responsible for the comprehension of language. Damage to Wernicke's area can cause a form of aphasia in which there are severe problems with language comprehension and production. There are other, smaller areas of the temporal lobe involved in the encoding, storage, and retrieval of long-term memories. Interesting studies have been performed in which electrical stimulation of these regions caused people to recall long-forgotten events.

The occipital lobe of the cerebral cortex includes the visual cortex, a region in which visual perception, visual recognition, and visual memory are managed. If an individual suffers damage to his or her occipital lobe, then he or she may suffer visual hallucinations, visual agnosia (the inability to recognize familiar objects by sight), or cortical blindness. In some cases, damage to the left occipital lobe can result in simultagnosia, or the inability to see either more than one thing or more than one aspect of a thing at a time. Individuals who suffer lesions at the intersection of the occipital, temporal, and parietal lobes may suffer from prosopagnosia, an inability to recognize the faces of familiar people.

Contralateral representation

Contralateral function refers to the fact that for almost all sensory and motor functions, the left side of the body is controlled by the right side of the brain, and vice versa. For example, all of the movements in the right leg are controlled by the motor cortex in the left hemisphere. There are only a few places in the brain where the two hemispheres are connected. One of these is a large bundle of fibers known as the corpus callosum. The fibers of the corpus callosum relay information that is sent from the body to both hemispheres. Fascinating studies have been made in which the corpus callosum is severed, causing the brain to act as two autonomous entities.

Hemispheric specialization

The two hemispheres of the brain are somewhat specialized in their functions. For almost all people, the right hemisphere manages spatial relationships, face recognition, and creativity, while the left hemisphere takes care of language, analytical thinking, and logic. Scientists first discovered this phenomenon in studies of so-called "split-brain" patients, individuals whose corpus callosum had been severed as a treatment for epilepsy. Besides greatly reducing the frequency of seizures, the procedure produced some amazing insights. Although the brain retained its levels of intelligence, memory, and motivation, in some areas it behaved quite differently. For instance, the patients were unable to say the name of a familiar object when it was placed in their left visual field, though they could do so easily when it was in the right visual field.

CAT scan and MRI

The procedure known as neuroimaging has vastly improved scientists' ability to assess the structure and function of living brains. The two most common techniques of neuroimaging are computed axial tomography (CT or CAT) and magnetic resonance imaging (MRI). In CAT scans, an x-ray is taken of various horizontal cross-sections of the brain. CAT scans are good for diagnosing pathological conditions like tumors, blood clots, and multiple sclerosis. An MRI is uses magnetic fields and radio waves to produce cross-sectional images. MRIs are able to produce more detailed images than are CAT scans, and MRIs can produce images from any angle, not just horizontally. MRIs are able to construct three-dimensional representations of brains.

PET, SPECT, and fMRI

Positron-emission tomography (PET) involves injecting the patient with a radioactive glucose tracer that is taken up by active brain cells. By analyzing images of brains that have been injected with radioactive glucose, doctors can gauge regional cerebral blood flow, glucose metabolism, and oxygen consumption, all of which correlate with the brain's level of activity. PET scans are often used by clinicians to assess the cerebral damage that has been done by cerebrovascular disease, dementia, schizophrenia, Alzheimer's disease, and other disorders. Researchers often use PET scans to determine which areas of the brain are active during certain functions. Single proton emission computed tomography (SPECT) and functional MRI (fMRI) are similar tests that are based on the PET and MRI exams, respectively.

Color vision and color blindness theories

There are two basic theories of color vision. Young-Helmholtz proposed a trichromatic theory, stating that there are color receptors for the three primary colors (red, green, blue). According to this theory, all other colors are based on variations and combinations in these three. The opponent-process theory of Ewald Hering proposed that there are three receptors, but they are red-green, yellow-blue, and white-black. Cells in these receptors are stimulated one way or the other, and the overall pattern in their stimulation creates differences in color perception. Neither trichromatic nor opponent-process theory adequately explains color perception, so the current consensus is that at the retinal level trichromatic theory holds, while the thalamus operates on an opponent-process model. Color blindness occurs when an individual has a recessive trait on the X chromosome; males are more likely than females to be colorblind.

Cutaneous senses

The cutaneous (skin) senses are pressure, warmth, cold, and pain. Sensory information is carried from cutaneous receptors to nerves and into the spinal cord. The place where the nerve enters the spinal cord is the dorsal root. The dorsal root of a particular section of spinal column is known as the dermatome. Adjacent dermatomes overlap, so when a nerve is damaged the result is typically diminished sensation, rather than the extinction of sensation altogether. Several kinds of stimulus cause pain: Heat, pressure, and cold. An individual's perception of pain may be amplified by depression or anxiety. The gate control theory, proposed by Melzack, suggests that the nervous system can handle a limited amount of information at any given time, and excess sensory information is blocked by cells in the spinal column. One way to reduce pain, then, is to apply more sensory input, like heat or cold

Synesthesia and psychophysics

Synesthesia is when the stimulation of one sensory modality triggers the stimulation of another sensory modality. Synesthetic individuals report being able to see the color of words or taste shapes. There is no clear understanding of the etiology of synesthesia, although many researchers believe that it is caused by "cross-wiring" in the brain. The study of the relationship between physical stimulus magnitudes and their corresponding psychological sensations is called psychophysics. An important part of psychophysics is the determination of absolute thresholds (minimum stimulation needed to produce a sensation) and difference thresholds (smallest unit of stimulus intensity needed to recognize a difference in stimulus intensity).

Weber's law, Fechner's law and Stevens' power law

Weber's law states that the more intense a stimulus, the greater will be the increase in stimulus intensity necessary for the increase to be perceived. Fechner built on Weber's law and was able to determine the exact relationship between the magnitude of a stimulus and the magnitude of the reaction. Fechner's law states that stimulus changes are logarithmically related to psychological sensations. Stevens determined that the work of Weber and Fechner was only good for studying stimuli of moderate intensity. In order to examine extreme stimuli, Stevens had to develop his Power law, which describes sensation as an exponential function of stimulus intensity. Stevens' work depended on a system of magnitude estimation, in which subjects assigned numerical values to the intensities of various stimuli.

Memory

Recent advances in neuroimaging have made it possible to locate specific areas of memory within the brain. The temporal lobes are involved in the encoding, storage, and retrieval of long-term declarative memories; the right temporal lobe is primarily engaged in nonverbal memory, while the left temporal lobe handles verbal memory. The hippocampus manages the consolidation of long-term declarative memory (that is, it transfers memories from short-term to long-term memory). The hippocampus also is involved in spatial memory. The amygdala is involved in fear conditioning and the formation of emotional memories. The prefrontal cortex helps with short-term memory, episodic memory, and prospective memory. The thalamus processes information and passes it along to the neocortex. The basal ganglia, cerebellum, and motor cortex all help with procedural and implicit (nonintentional) memory.

Scientists acquired much information about the neural mechanisms that affect human memory by studying sea slugs. One of the general insights is that short-term memory formation is shown by neurochemical changes at already existing synapses, while long-term memories necessitate the creation of more synapses and a change in the overall synaptic structure. Long-term potentiation (LTP) is the increased responsivity of a postsynaptic neuron to low-intensity stimulation for a while after it has been subject to high-frequency stimulation. LTP causes changes in the number and shape of dendrites, and increases glutamate receptors. Protein synthesis increases during memory formation. Genetic research has linked the apolipoprotein E gene (apoE4 on Chromosome 19) to Alzheimer's disease.

Emotion

Cross-cultural research has distinguished six basic universal human emotions: Fear, anger, happiness, disgust, surprise, and sadness. The James-Lange theory of emotion asserts that emotions are the body's reaction to changes in the autonomic nervous system caused by external stimuli. This theory is supported by the fact that quadriplegics report feeling less-intense emotions. The Cannon-Bard theory of emotion proposes that the body and emotions react to stimuli based on thalamic stimulation of the cortex and peripheral nervous system. The two-factor theory of Schachter and Singer proposes that emotions are the result of arousal, the cognitive interpretation of that arousal, and the environment in which the arousal occurs.

The amygdala helps perceive and express anger, fear, happiness, and sadness, among other emotions. One function of the amygdala is to determine the emotional significance of incoming information. If this area is given electrical stimulation, the individual will become afraid or angry. The hypothalamus helps convert emotion into a physical response by influencing the autonomic nervous system and the pituitary gland. The cerebral cortex is divided into two hemispheres. The left hemisphere controls happiness and other positive emotions, while the right hemisphere manages sadness, fear, and other negative emotions. The right hemisphere is typically in control of recognizing emotions in other people; and indeed, most people tend to express more facial emotion with the left side of their face.

Stress

There is a universal human response to stress, which was dubbed the general adaptation syndrome (GAS) by Selye. There are three stages to GAS response, which are managed by the adrenal and pituitary glands:

- Stimulation: The hypothalamus stimulates the adrenal medulla to release epinephrine (adrenaline). The glucose level rises and the heart and respiration rates increase as the individual becomes alarmed.
- Resistance: The body resists the stress by returning respiration and heart rates to baseline. The hypothalamus commands the pituitary gland to release ACTH, a hormone that causes the adrenal cortex to release cortisol, a chemical that maintains high levels of blood glucose.
- Exhaustion: The pituitary and adrenal glands fatigue, and the physiological processes break down. It is this sort of prolonged stress that is most destructive to health.

Hormones and sexual development

Hormones secreted during the prenatal period enable the formation of differentiated sex organs. There are two sources of sex hormones: The pituitary gland secretes gonadotropic hormones, while the gonads (ovaries, testes) secrete female (estrogen, progesterone) and male (testosterone and androstenedione, known as the androgens) hormones. All people produce both male and female sex hormones, though females produce more estrogen and males more androgens. At the beginning of fetal development, there is no differentiation in the gonads. Differentiation begins 6-8 weeks after conception. The initial stages of sexual development are motivated by the chromosomes, but without sex hormones, the process will not get very far. If there is a lack of androgen, for instance, both females and males will develop female sex characteristics.

The beginning of puberty is heralded by an increase in gonadal hormones, which stimulate the emergence of secondary sex characteristics. Basically, the hypothalamus secretes chemicals that instruct the anterior pituitary gland to release hormones, stimulating the production of testosterone and sperm in the male, and ovulation and the production of estrogen in the female. The age at which puberty begins is influenced by genetic and environmental factors like nutrition, exercise, and temperature. For humans, there is less connection between adult sexual behavior and hormones than there is for lower animals. In fact, research has shown that there is not a predictable relationship between estrogen and sexual interest in females, though there does seem to be some connection between testosterone and sex drive in males.

Dimorphism, spinal injuries and sexual activity

Sexual dimorphism is sex-based differences in appearance. The human brain is sexually dimorphic; males and females have differently-sized corpus callosa, hippocampi, and SCNs. Most researchers believe that these differences in brain structure are the result of varying exposure to androgens during the prenatal and early postnatal periods. Individuals who suffer spinal cord injuries are likely to retain sexual interest, and many are still able to have intercourse. Men that have complete lesions of the spinal cord, however, are unlikely to be able to ejaculate. Spinal cord injuries create even less of an obstacle to female sexual activity. Most women with spinal injuries report arousal and lubrication, though they have varying success reaching orgasm.

Sleep

Electroencephalograms distinguish five stages of sleep:
- Stage 1: The EEG is mostly composed of alpha waves, and is similar to that of a relaxed, awake person.
- Stage 2: The EEG is composed mainly of theta waves, indicating relaxation, though there are some bursts of activity known as K complexes or sleep spindles.
- Stage 3: The EEG mainly records long, slow delta waves.
- Stage 4: In deep sleep, delta waves continue to predominate with fewer interruptions from K complexes and sleep spindles. Muscle activity decreases from stage 1 to stage 3, and then increases markedly during stage 4 sleep. This is the period in which sleepwalking and night terrors may occur.

- Stage 5: Rapid eye-movement (REM) sleep occurs, the period of the most elaborate and vivid dreams.

Dreams are typically remembered if the individual is woken up during REM sleep, but if he or she is woken up just a few minutes after exiting this phase of sleep the dreams are likely to be forgotten. EEG readings taken during REM sleep are remarkably similar to those of stages 1 and 2, and indeed the physiological activity during REM sleep is almost identical to the wake state. Heart rate and respiration are both elevated, and sexual arousal may occur. Paradoxically, though, when individuals are in REM sleep they are almost entirely paralyzed. An individual typically runs through all five stages of sleep every 90—100 minutes and does this three or four times a night.

In the first 2 or 3 months of life, infants begin their sleep cycle in REM sleep, and slowly progress into non-REM, or NREM, sleep. Eventually, this sequence will reverse, and total sleep time will decrease. In these first couple of months, about half of all sleep time is spent in REM sleep, while as an adult only about 20% of sleep is REM sleep. It is a common fallacy that older people need less sleep; it is true, however, that they often have a harder time falling asleep and wake more often during the night. There are only mild adverse consequences of sleep deprivation lasting less than 48 hours; any more than that, however, can result in hallucinations, personality changes, and disorientation. When people are deprived specifically of REM sleep, they tend to have a harder time learning new information.

Language

Though the left hemisphere is typically dominant in the production and comprehension of language, there is increasing evidence that the right hemisphere also plays a role in these processes. Studies of patients who lost use of their left hemisphere indicate the right hemisphere will take over linguistic functions. Brain damage may result in a few different kinds of aphasia, impairments in the production and/or comprehension of language. In Broca's aphasia, an individual will only be able to speak slowly and with great difficulty. Individuals with this form of aphasia will often suffer from anomia, the inability to name familiar objects. Broca's aphasia, unlike other impairments, does not include a lack of self-awareness, so individuals are likely to become very frustrated by their deficits and impairments.

Wernicke's aphasia is caused by damage to the left temporal lobe. It is characterized by difficulty understanding and generating meaningful language. People with Wernicke's aphasia are capable of talking quite fluently, but will be unable to say anything consequential. Conduction aphasia is a condition that includes anomia and impaired repetition. Transcortical aphasia is caused by lesions that disconnect Broca's and Wernicke's areas from other parts of the brain. If Broca's area is isolated, then the patient labors to speak, may be unable to speak spontaneously, and may suffer from anomia. If Wernicke's area is isolated, the patient may have deficits in comprehension, anomia, and fluent but meaningless speech.

Injuries and disorders affecting mental health

Head injuries
An open-head cerebral trauma occurs when the skull is penetrated. A closed-head cerebral trauma (concussion) occurs when a severe impact damages the brain without penetrating the skull. A closed-head injury often includes damage both at the site of the impact and at the opposite side of the brain, as the brain was pushed against the skull wall. There may be bleeding (hemorrhage) and a buildup of fluid (edema). Transient loss of consciousness and/or coma associated with closed-head injury results from strain on the nerve fibers in the brain stem. Patients who wake from a coma are likely to endure a period of post traumatic amnesia (PTA), in which there are memory deficits, intellectual impairments, personality change, and motor deficit. If these problems last longer than 24 hours, then they are probably permanent.

Closed-head injuries often cause a small period of retrograde amnesia. Recovery from retrograde amnesia usually begins with the patient regaining the most remote memories. Patients who suffer severe closed-head injuries recover the most during the first three months post trauma. In most cases, it is easier to recover cognitive functions, rather than social adjustment and personality. Post concussional disorder is diagnosed in the presence of the following:
- A history of head trauma, including cerebral concussion.
- Disturbances in attention or memory.
- At least three of these symptoms: Fatigue; depression; affective liability; personality change; disordered sleep; apathy; and a lack of spontaneity.

Cerebral stroke

A stroke is a disruption in the supply of blood to the brain.

Stroke can have a sudden onset (aneurysm) or gradual onset (atherosclerosis). There are three major causes of stroke:

- An embolism is the sudden blockage of an artery by material from somewhere else in the blood stream
- A thrombosis is the gradual blockage of an artery by a blood clot
- A hemorrhage is bleeding from trauma or a congenitally weak-walled blood vessel.

Risk factors for stroke are: Hypertension (high blood pressure); atherosclerosis (hardening of the arteries); smoking; and diabetes. Symptoms of stroke are contralateral hemiplegia, hemianaesthesia of the face, arms, and legs, and contralateral visual field loss.

Epilepsy

Epilepsy is the most widely known seizure disorder. Seizures are caused by an electrical storm in the brain. The patient may have an aura (sight, smell, sound, or feeling denoting an impending seizure), then loss of consciousness, and finally, abnormal movement. A generalized seizure is one that occurs in both hemispheres of the brain and does not have a focal onset. Tonic-clonic (grand mal) seizures have three stages: Muscle contraction (tonic); rhythmic shaking of the limbs (clonic); and depression/confusion combined with amnesia (ictal). Absences (petit mal seizures) are brief attacks in which consciousness is lost without motor symptoms being present. A person undergoing an absence seizure stares blankly ahead. All other kinds of seizures are partial, beginning on one side of the brain and only affecting one side of the body. Simple partial seizures do not result in loss of consciousness; complex partial seizures do.

Psychophysiological disorders

Psychophysiological disorders are those in which the physical symptoms are initiated or amplified by emotional factors. Most of them only involve one system of organs, especially the autonomic nervous system. Hyperventilation is a psychophysiological disorder. The individual breathes rapidly from fear, anxiety or anger. Carbon dioxide levels in the bloodstream drop, which leads to respiratory alkalosis and cerebral hypoxia. An impending hyperventilation episode may be heralded by chest pain, tingling and numbness in the hands and feet, dizziness, impaired concentration, and tinnitus (ringing ears). For many people, anxiety is compounded by the fact that the symptoms of hyperventilation are quite similar to those of certain coronary conditions.

Optimal blood pressure is 120/80 mm/Hg. There are three kinds of hypertension (high blood pressure):

- Primary (essential) hypertension: The cause of the high blood pressure is unknown, but is linked to smoking, overuse of salt, stress, and old age. Primary hypertension has few symptoms and is often undiagnosed ("The Silent Killer").
- If primary hypertension is not treated, it can lead to malignant hypertension (diastole > 140 mm/Hg). Malignant hypertension causes blindness, strokes, heart failure, aneurysm, transient ischemic attacks (TIA), and kidney failure.
- Secondary hypertension: High blood pressure related to a known condition, such as diabetes or kidney disease.

Fibromyalgia is a non-specific condition characterized by general muscle aches, tenderness, stiffness, fatigue, and sleep disturbances. The condition is more common among women, and though it may have a physical cause it is often attributed to psychological factors.

Migraine headaches are severe, recurrent headaches that are usually restricted to one side of the head. Migraine headaches throb and are frequently accompanied by nausea, vomiting, diarrhea or constipation, and extreme sensitivity to light, noise, and odors. Any motion tends to make the headache much worse. A classic migraine begins with an aura, or focal onset, which alerts the individual that a migraine is about to occur. A common migraine does not have an aura, but may be preceded by gastrointestinal difficulties. The cause of migraines is unknown. Most research suggests that they arise out of problems with the constriction and dilation of blood vessels in the brain. NSAIDs, beta blockers, SSRI antidepressants, anticonvulsives, triptans, ergots, butalbital, Botox, antihistamines, and feverfew are used to treat migraines.

A *cluster headache* is characterized by excruciating, burning pain that occurs in clusters over a 2-3 month period. The pain is often centered behind one of the eyes, though it may spread to the face and/or temple. Tension headaches are characterized by nonpulsating pain on both sides of the head, at the back of the neck, and/or in the face. A tension headache may feel like a band of pressure around the head, almost like a tight hat. Although the traditional view was that tension headaches were caused by stress and muscle tension, it is now believed that they may also be caused by the dilation of blood vessels in the skull. The final kind of non-migraine headache is the sinus headache, which feels like pressure in the sinus cavity. This kind of headache may be caused by infection of the frontal sinuses.

Endocrine disorders
The endocrine system is composed of the ovaries, testicles, adrenals, thyroid, parathyroid, hypothalamus, pancreas, pineal, and pituitary glands. Endocrine glands are ductless and secrete hormones directly into the bloodstream, where they are carried to the various organs of the body. The exception is the pancreas, an exocrine and endocrine gland that has a duct. The pituitary gland secretes antidiuretic hormone (ADH) and somatotropic growth hormone. Deficiency of ADH causes excessive water loss from diabetes insipidus. Children who do not produce enough somatotropic hormone have dwarfism. Children who produce excess somatotropic hormone have gigantism. Adults who produce excess somatotropic hormone develop acromegaly, in which the hands, feet, and facial features become grotesquely enlarged.

The thyroid gland secretes thyroxine to maintain metabolism. If too much thyroxine is secreted, the result is hyperthyroidism, also known as goiter or Grave's disease. Patients with Grave's disease suffer accelerated metabolism, bulging eyes, pyrexia (high body temperature around 38°C), heat intolerance, rapid weight loss, nervousness, and tachycardia (accelerated heart rate). If the thyroid produces too little thyroxine, hypothyroidism results. Patients with hypothyroidism suffer slowed metabolism, low body temperature (less than 37°C), weight gain, depression, hair loss, fatigue, and impaired cognitive function (myxedema).

The pancreas secretes insulin, a hormone instrumental in taking up and using glucose and amino acids. If there is too much insulin, the blood sugar gets dangerously low (hypoglycemia). If the pancreas does not produce enough insulin, diabetes mellitus results.

Drug therapy

Antipsychotic drugs

Antipsychotic drugs are also known as major tranquilizers and neuroleptics. Traditional antipsychotics include phenothiazine, thioxanthene, and butyrophenone. These drugs help alleviate the positive symptoms of psychosis, especially in schizophrenia, but have severe side effects. Antipsychotics may also be used to treat major depressive disorders. They work by blocking dopamine receptors in the brain. This has led some researchers to speculate that schizophrenia is caused by overactivity at dopamine receptors. The fact that amphetamines and cocaine elevate dopamine levels and can also cause psychotic events gives some credence to this theory, though it is otherwise unsubstantiated by research.

Negative side effects common to the traditional antipsychotics are classified as either anticholinergenic or antipyramidal. Anticholinergic side effects include: Dry mouth causing teeth to rot, blurred vision, tachycardia, urinary retention, constipation, and delayed ejaculation. Anticholinergic symptoms usually disappear as the patient adapts to the medication over a few weeks. Antipyramidal side effects include: Parkinsonism, acathisia (extreme motor restlessness), acute dystonia (muscle spasms in the face, neck, and throat), and tardive dyskinesia (which has symptoms similar to Huntington's disease). Antipyramidal effects do not dissipate after two years of medication. One very rare but deadly side effect of antipsychotic medication is neuroleptic malignant syndrome (NMS), characterized by delirium, tremors, fever, rigidity, blood pressure swings, and encephalopathy.

The atypical (novel) antipsychotic drugs include dibenzodiazepine (clozapine), bensisoxazole, thienobenzodiazepine, and dibenzothiazepine. Atypical antipsychotics are used to treat schizophrenia and other psychotic symptoms. Atypical antipsychotics are unique in that they alleviate both the positive and the negative symptoms of schizophrenia; they are often successful in cases when traditional antipsychotics have failed. Atypical antipsychotics work by interfering with the receptors for dopamine, serotonin, and glutamate. The side effects are basically the same as for the traditional antipsychotics, with one important exception: Atypicals are less likely to cause tardive dyskinesia. However, atypical antipsychotics have been known to cause blood dyscrasias (imbalances) and NMS.

Antidepressants

The tricyclic antidepressants (TCAs) include amitriptyline, doxepin, imipramine, and clomipramine. Tricyclic drugs are usually effective in treating depressions that entail appetite loss, early morning waking, and psychomotor retardation. It usually takes a little under a month for these drugs to begin showing results. Tricyclics are also used to treat OCD, agoraphobia, bulimia, and enuresis. Tricyclics work by blocking the reuptake of norepinephrine, serotonin, and/or dopamine. The high level of success TCAs enjoy gives credence to the catecholamine hypothesis, which states that depression results from deficiency in the neurotransmitters dopamine and norepinephrine. Adverse effects include cardiovascular problems, confusion, drowsiness, fatigue, weight gain, and blood dyscrasia.

The selective serotonin reuptake inhibitors (SSRIs) include fluoxetine, fluvoxamine, paroxetine, and sertraline. These drugs are used to treat depression, especially of the melancholic variety. They may also be prescribed for OCD, bulimia, panic disorder, and PTSD. SSRIs work by blocking the reuptake of serotonin. SSRIs may lead to gastrointestinal disturbances, insomnia, anxiety, dizziness, anorexia, tremor, frequent urination, and sexual dysfunction. The most famous of the SSRIs is Prozac. The FDA warns that antidepressants can cause violent behavior and suicidal ideation in patients 18—24 in the first two months of treatment, and requires black box labels to that effect.

Monoamine oxidase inhibitors (MAOIs) include isocarboxazid, phenelzine, and tranylcypromine. These drugs are most helpful in treating non-endogenous and atypical depressions, like those entailing anxiety, reversed vegetative symptoms like hypersomnia and hyperphagia, and interpersonal sensitivity. MAOIs work by inhibiting the enzyme monoamine oxidase, which works to deactivate dopamine, serotonin, and norepinephrine. Side effects of MAOIs include: Anticholinergic effects; insomnia; agitation; dry mouth; confusion; skin rash; weight gain; edema; dizziness; hypertensive crisis, especially if MAOIs are taken with barbiturates, amphetamines, and antihistamines; and lethal interactions with tyramine in foods like sausage, fava beans, wine, soy, beer and cheese.

Bupropion (Wellbutrin) is a new form of antidepressant known as a norepinephrine dopamine reuptake inhibitor (NDRI). It has fewer anticholinergic side effects than the TCAs, and it does not have any association with sexual dysfunction. On the other hand, it

has been known to aggravate psychosis and seizure activity that already exists. Venlafaxine (Effexor) is a selective serotonin norepinephrine reuptake inhibitor (SNRI) that is frequently prescribed for major depression, OCD, and generalized anxiety disorder. Effexor patients have a decreased chance of overdose, and may obtain faster benefits. Another new class of antidepressants is the serotonin-2 antagonists/reuptake inhibitors (SARIs), which are used to treat major depression and the depressive phase of bipolar disorder. This group includes nefazodone (Serzone) and trazodone (Desyrel).

Mood-stabilizing drugs
Lithium was used from the mid-1800's to the 1940's to treat gout, diabetes, epilepsy, and mania. At present, lithium is most often prescribed for bipolar disorder, because it both suppresses mood swings and eliminates manic symptoms. Doctors are not entirely sure how lithium works, but its function is related to the reuptake of serotonin and norepinephrine. The potential side effects of lithium include: Nausea; fine hand tremors; polyuria; and polydipsia. The major danger posed by lithium is its toxicity to the kidneys. Patients must have their blood levels monitored at least monthly to avoid kidney failure. Overdoses may lead to seizures, coma, and death. Lithium levels are influenced by general salt levels. Bipolar patients who take lithium should monitor their intake of table salt, and should avoid caffeine, alcohol, and other diuretics.

Carbamazepine (Tegretol) is a drug formerly used as an anticonvulsant that now is often prescribed for mania. Tegretol is similar to valproic acid (Depakote) and clonazepam (Klonopin). Carbamazepine has proven useful as a treatment for bipolar disorder, particularly in cases where the patient has not responded to lithium. Some studies have indicated that it is more effective than lithium in treating cases of mania that entail rapid mood swings. The drug affects serotonin levels in some way, though its exact process of operations is not known. The adverse effects of carbamazepine include dizziness, ataxia, visual disturbances, anorexia, and nausea. Patients should develop tolerance to these side effects within a few weeks.

Sedative-hypnotics

The family of drugs known as the sedative-hypnotics includes barbiturates, alcohol, and anxiolytics. These drugs depress the central nervous system. The effects of sedative-hypnotics depend on the dosage. A high dose can lead to coma or death, while a low dose simply diminishes arousal and motor activity. In the period just after the drug is taken, the individual may feel a burst of energy because of the suppression of his or her normal inhibitions. When a person habitually uses sedative-hypnotics, he or she will become gradually tolerant of their properties and will come to physically depend on them. Abrupt withdrawal from the drug can lead to tremors, anxiety, and even hallucinations and seizures. These drugs are especially powerful (and deadly) when used in tandem; an anxiolytic in combination with alcohol or a barbiturate can be very deadly.

The family of drugs known as the barbiturates includes amobarbital, pentobarbital, secobarbital, and phenobarbital. Barbiturates were prescribed from 1912 to the 1960's as sedatives and anesthetic agents, but they are now infrequently prescribed because of their dangerous side effects. Barbiturates work by interrupting impulses to the reticular activating system. Adverse side effects associated with barbiturates include slurred speech, irritability, and impaired motor and cognitive performance. Sometimes barbiturates are prescribed to treat insomnia, but their soporific capabilities usually only last for a few weeks. Tolerance to barbiturates can be unequal across different body systems; for instance, the respiratory systems may continue to be impaired by the drug, even as it loses its sleep-inducing properties. Unequal tolerance leads patients to overdose.

Benzodiazepines are the most commonly prescribed form of anxiolytics (minor tranquilizers or anti-anxiety drugs). Benzodiazepines include diazepam, alprazolam, oxazepam, triazolam, chlordiazepoxide, and lorazepam. Benzodiazepines are mainly used to treat anxiety, though they are occasionally prescribed for sleep disturbances, cerebral palsy, and other disorders that include muscle spasms. They are routinely used in ER to stop seizures in poisonings, including alcohol withdrawal. Benzodiazepines work by inhibiting the neurotransmitter GABA. Side effects of benzodiazepines are drowsiness, lethargy, ataxia, and impaired psychomotor ability. The relaxation and sense of euphoria engendered by benzodiazepines leads many people to become physically and psychologically addicted to them. Azapirone (also known as buspirone) is the only anxiolytic that can reduce anxiety without sedation. According to all research so far, it is neither addictive nor subject to abuse. However, it requires a few weeks before its effects begin to appear.

Beta-blockers

Beta-blockers are used to treat high blood pressure, angina, tremors, migraine headache, and glaucoma. The most common beta-blocker is propanolol. Propanolol also reduces the symptoms of anxiety: Palpitations, tremors, and excessive sweating. Beta-blockers work by blocking beta-androgenic receptors, which normally respond to epinephrine and norepinephrine. The side effects of propanolol include bradycardia, shortness of breath, nausea, Raynaud's phenomenon (tingling or numb red and white extremities cause by insufficient blood flow), depression, and dizziness. Abrupt cessation of beta-blockers is linked to palpitations, sweating, headache, and tremors. Patients must be weaned off beta-blockers

Integrated Model of Psychotherapy

Therapeutic relationship

The therapeutic relationship between the patient and the counselor is the foundation for the counseling sessions. Patients must feel safe and comfortable in order to share the details of their lives with the therapist. The therapist must take on a role that demonstrates to the patient acceptance and compassion. The patient is encouraged to delve into secret agonies that need to be talked out. Carl Rogers instructed that the therapeutic relationship should have the following: An ability to understand and transfer your own feelings toward another person's situation; beneficial and positive concern for the client that demonstrates the therapist's unconditional acceptance; a non-judgmental attitude; and trust. This foundation of care leads to data collection on the life details of the patient. Another interviewing technique includes open-ended questions that begin with "how" or "what." Avoid using "why" questions as they can appear judgmental.

Rogerian tips on interviewing include paraphrasing the words of the patient. The therapist uses phrases that give confidence to the patient so he or she will reveal feelings for data collection that is

transferred into a plan of action. The data is monitored for patterns of behavior. Patterns can reveal constructive or damaging areas, strong or weak points, painful periods, a study of the mental illness' origin and progression, and any dysfunctional behaviors. Albert Ellis's Rational-Emotive Therapy and Aaron Beck's Cognitive Therapy both concentrate on the thought patterns for feelings which result in either a functional or dysfunctional behavior. The patient must prove a negative thought. The patient can not justify the negative thought. Therefore, the therapist using a cognitive approach furnishes a positive replacement thought for the negative one.

Behaviorism

Behaviorists anticipate that the patient can unlearn dysfunctional behaviors. Pavlov cultivated his theories from experiments where he conditioned dogs to salivate to different stimuli. Watson and Rayner experimented on a young boy by conditioning his response to white, furry animals; the young boy developed a phobia. This can be related to a person's development of a phobia after a negative experience. Some people become afraid of the water after a near drowning experience. Addictive cravings, anxieties, insomnia, and pain management may be improved with relaxation training and methodical desensitization techniques. B. F. Skinner's experiments involved operant conditioning, where he proposed that feelings and actions are reinforced and rewarded. Therefore, the way to stop a behavior is to take away the reinforcement. For example, a child who exhibits misbehaviors in school may be doing so to gain the teacher's attention.

Operant conditioning is based on feelings and actions that are reinforced and rewarded. The way to stop the behavior is to take away the reinforcement. An explanation for a client's pathological behavior is that it was reinforced. Behaviorists look for rewards that may cause their client to act out inappropriately. For example, a person who feels isolated may experience health problems out of a need to gain attention from hospital staff and or family. Token economy and contingency contractual agreements are the result of operant conditioning. Albert Bandura created Social Learning Theory in 1969, based on people learning from watching others. Violence on television has been linked to real life violent acts by Social Learning Theory. Proponents say a more functional TV model should be presented to replace the pathological behavior. Behaviorists use relaxation techniques, imagery, systematic desensitization, reinforcement contingencies, positive role modeling, and token economies.

Blending of cognitive and behavioral theory

The common ground between cognitive and behavioral theory is found in the following areas: Psychoeducational approaches; time-limitations; specifically targeted areas; and problems that can be measured for evaluation. Albert Ellis' Rational Emotive Therapy (RET) was blended with a behavior therapy called Rational Emotive Behavior Therapy (REBT). Beck's Cognitive Therapy (CT) develops into Cognitive-Behavioral Therapy (CBT). Mental health providers who use one of these therapies look for patterns of dysfunctional behavior that can be treated with an intervention from the Rational Emotive Behavior Therapy or the Cognitive-Behavioral Therapy. Arnold Lazarus applied a Multimodal therapy which involves a variety of techniques using the acronym, BASIC ID. B is for behavior. A is for affect. S is for sensations. I is for imagery. C is for cognitions. I is for interpersonal

relations. D is for drugs and biological causes.

Unconscious mind

Freud's theories involve getting at unconscious thoughts that cause behaviors. The client must come to terms with unconscious thoughts, does not bottle up those feelings, and thus deals with issues in a more functional manner. Psychodynamic theorists of today try to help the patient make a connection between the past and existing problems. However, a cognitive-behavioral approach may need to be supplemented with in-depth counseling. Some topics that may require further investigation are: The client's family and parental interactions; unresolved issues; unconscious practices; and defensive mechanisms. Freud believed pathological thinking was at odds with the id instincts of Eros and Thanatos. Eros stands for the life processes involving love and relationships. Thanatos stands for death processes involving negative emotions and the fighting response. The mind is trying to manage these forces, which causes anxiety and the client forms phobias or conversion disorders.

Freud's theories

Freud coined the word "super-ego" to make sense out of the rules imposed upon us by our parents. Rules involving parents, family, religion, and culture contribute to our sense of right and wrong. The problem arises whenever a rule has been imposed that is unrelenting and harsh. Freud linked this to his interview of female patients. Victorian women had difficulty accepting their sexual urges as a natural occurrence. This conflict of right and wrong caused the females to experience hysterical paralysis and other notable anxiety disorders. However, symptoms were alleviated when the patients gained insight and emotional release from their inner turmoil. Free association is the client's expression concerning secretive and painful thoughts, feelings, and memories in a non-judgmental therapy session. The therapeutic bond or relationship is imperative in this technique. Free association used in this way can still be beneficial today.

Object-Relations School

The Object-Relations School looks at the primary caregiver relationship in a child's early years of growth. A positive parental relationship leads the infant to understand about safety, security, self-worth, nurturance, and caring. The infant grows into a child with a positive self-identity and is better able to form healthy relationships with others. Those infants that have a negative parental relationship feel unloved, detested, valueless, insignificant, inferior, and shamed. These images form the person's personality and behaviors. The inner belief system is referred to as the schema in the cognitive therapy model. It is known as the incorporated object relation in the psychodynamic model. Object-relations take into account the Freudian theories regarding instinctive urges. These urges are the driving force to form either loving or destructive relationships. The client explores the repressed feelings in front of a counselor who has created a safe and trusted setting.

Blending of Freudian ideas with the Object-Relations School
Freud's concept of transference can be applied to the exchanges that take place between the modern client and counselor. The client's propensity is to behave toward the counselor as one would a key authority figure. The counselor can help the client understand this propensity and work to help the client alter this

unconscious transference to other people. Awareness of transference must become a part of the client's conscious thought. The client must be aware when this has happened and seek to change the behavior on a conscious level. Cognitive rethinking techniques and behavioristic role plays enable the counselor's efforts to get the client to work through a maladaptive behavior. The counselor can also use a variety of techniques to help the client internalize positive feelings and thought patterns.

Assessment and Diagnosis

Individual assessment

Mental health counselors hold to the belief that the individual has a specific blueprint of behaviors, genetic characteristics, and life circumstances that make up a unique and one-of-a-kind person. Counseling is designed to help the client gain a perspective on how he or she behaves. The client is also made to understand how genetics can influence a person's characteristics and behaviors. The client is encouraged to gain a perspective about circumstances that were negative influences in early life. Self-knowledge is used to help the client learn how to make better decisions and to take responsibility for his or her own actions. The client is also taught coping strategies to deal with unpleasant circumstances or memories. The counselor works to establish a rapport with the client and to develop the client's positive self-esteem.

Measurement and tests

The counselor develops a representation of the client through the collection of facts. Psychometric instruments are used to collect pertinent data on the client. Measurement is a numerical value that has been allocated to a mannerism, attribute, or characteristic on the instrument. The measurement used must be one that is commonly understood by the general population. A test is a task or series of tasks used to examine a psychomotor behavior or action that is indicative of a state of being. The state of being can be cognitively based or affective in nature. Answering written questions is typical test scenario. The student goes through the task of answering academically based questions to indicate that cognitive learning has been accomplished in an academic class. The teacher grades the test and makes the inference that the student has learned on a cognitive or affective level.

Evaluation and decision making

Evaluation is the process of accumulating data in order to improve a person's ability to make a decision based on reliable standards. The accumulated data is given careful consideration and appraisal by the evaluator to ensure that it is complete and accurate. The evaluator must make some kind of interpretation or inference about the data that has been collected. This inference is known as a value judgment, and is a common task for the mental health counselor. The counselor uses a methodical and well organized system to help make these value judgments. Decision making is a process in which the collected data has been weighed against possible consequences and test results. Decisions are made every day. Some lead to mistakes that need to be corrected. It is best to make decisions with confidence.

Assessment techniques

The first type of classification involves nonstandard procedures that are used to provide individualized assessments. Nonstandard procedures include observations of client behaviors and performance. There are three levels of observation techniques that can be applied. The first level is casual informational observation, where the counselor gleans information from watching the client in unstructured activities throughout the day. The second level is guided observation, an intentional style of direct observation accomplished with a checklist or rating scale to evaluate the performance or behavior seen. The third level is the clinical level, where observation is done in a controlled setting for a lengthy period of time. This is most often accomplished on the doctoral level with applied instrumentation.

Instruments used in observation

The following instruments can be used in an observation: Checklists; rating scales; anecdotal reports; structured interview; questionnaires; and personal essays or journals. The checklist is used to check off behaviors or performance levels with a plus or minus sign to indicate that the behavior was observed or absent. The observer is able to converse as the checklist is marked. The rating scale is a more complex checklist that notes the strength, frequency, or degree of a behavior exhibited. Likert scales are applied using the following ratings: 1. Never; 2. Rarely; 3. Sometimes; 4. Usually; and 5. Always. The evaluator of the behavior makes a judgment about whatever question has been asked on the rating scale. The anecdotal report is used to record subjective notes describing the client's behavior during a specified time or in a specified setting, and is often applied to evaluate a suspected pattern.

Assessment tools

The five standardized assessment tools or tests are the achievement test, the aptitude test, the intelligence test, the vocational preference instrument, and the personality test. The achievement test is used to measure what has been learned in academics, vocation, or other life experience. The aptitude test is used to make a prediction on the subject's future performance in a given field of study. The intelligence test predicts a person's academic performance in the future by determining the person's mental potential. The vocational preference instrument is used to discover a pattern of characteristics that describe the individual's preferences or inclination to do something in leisure, work and educational settings. The personality test describes the person's behavior, attitudes, beliefs, and values, and is used to diagnose psychopathology or in relationship counseling.

Using and selecting assessment tests

An assortment of tests is available to help the student make a decision process regarding future work. The selection category can include tests like the Graduate Record Exam (GRE) or the Law School Admissions Tests (LSAT). Selection tests may also include vocational preference tests or personality tests used in educational and occupational counseling. Placement tests are used to determine where a client belongs in a program. Colleges may use these tests to determine in which class a student should start a program of study. Diagnostic tests use a combination of psychometric techniques and tests to evaluate human performance levels, and incorporate the DSM IV diagnostic labels to determine a remediation program for a client. Many insurance carriers also require this DSM label before payment is released for services rendered. Individual progress incorporates psychometric instruments to help evaluate progress toward a goal.

Classification

Psychometric instruments can either be applied in group settings or in individual treatments. Group administered tests may be given by untrained proctors in a variety of settings. Typically, the group completes a paper-and-pencil test. Individuals may take a test under the supervision of an administrator. The administrator understands the complexities involved in giving the test, scoring the test, and interpreting the test results. Paper-and-pencil tests or performance tests are used to collect data about a behavior exhibited. The data is then evaluated. Paper-and-pencil tests are used to provide a fast, inexpensive, and objective grade. Test publishers develop most of the commercial grade paper-and-pencil assessment tests available. The administrator or proctor of the paper-and-pencil test will distribute materials, read the directions to the group, time the test, and collect the test.

Paper-and-pencil tests versus performance tests

Paper-and-pencil tests are used by a variety of test takers. One drawback is found when the client cannot read at the same level in which the test is written. The Minnesota Multiphasic Personality Test (MMPI) is suitable for illiterate clients, because it comes in an audio version that helps dyslexics, illiterates, and the blind. Performance tests are given with a verbal request. The verbal request elicits a response that measures whether the client can follow the instruction given. The Goodenough-Harris Drawing Test requires that a client draw a picture of a person. This is an intellectual functioning measurement that is assessed by an administrator who is trained in proper evaluation techniques. Optical scanners cannot be used for evaluating the Goodenough-Harris Drawing Test.

Norm-referenced, criterion-based, structured and unstructured tests

Tests can be norm-referenced tests or criterion-related tests. Both require that the test is graded with a raw score. The raw score indicates the number of right answers or a pattern found. The client's raw score is then compared to a group score. The raw score in a criterion-related test is compared to a criterion that can determine mastery or minimum competency levels within a subject. The difference found in a structured and an unstructured test is the range or degree of structure applied. For instance, the Strong Interest Inventory is a structured vocational preference test that only allows the client to give one of three possible answers. The Rorschach inkblot test allows the client to answer with any response that comes to mind.

Test selection

The counselor must primarily concern himself with his clients' needs and wants. Out of this consideration, the counselor makes an informed decision about which tests and psychometric techniques to apply. Suggest testing if there is a need to gain further information, but testing is not necessarily required. Your client may perceive the testing to be some kind of threat or manipulative tool. In that case, reassure and educate your client about the real purpose of the test. Consider your competency level when selecting, administering, measuring, and evaluating the test results, including legal issues involving a particular assessment. Also consider any ethical issues that may be associated with an assessment. You may require additional training in test procedures before giving and assessing a particular test.

The test-related issues that may impact the selection of a test include: Validity, reliability, and norm standards. The issue of validity in a test involves an effective examination that gives the desired results. Tests used within the mental health profession should have well founded, criterion-based content that measures what it is supposed to measure. Before using a test, make sure it received an independent appraisal from established sources, and is considered reliable, meaning that the test results should be able to stand up over a period of time. The test should give a precise and accurate score. The entire test should be evaluated for its reliability coefficient and standard of error measurement. The test may present a split-half reliability that measures internal consistency among other assessment instruments. The test should follow the norm-reference criteria for the client's age, sex, ethnic origin, culture, and socioeconomic status.

The Internet provides an excellent search tool for the mental health provider. Use the Internet to locate specific tests that are applicable to your client's needs and wants. Use the decision making model presented by Drummond in 1996 to help you select the most appropriate test. Evaluate the test for dimension, traits, and attributes. Make a decision based on what kind of information you think will be the most useful. This involves a thorough perusal of the information already available at hand. Use the internet to search through objective evaluations given by others. Appraise the test for its validity and reliability. The test and its results must provide you and your client with a practical use.

Communicating test results

Test results must provide the client and the counselor with information that will be of benefit to the client. This information should not add to the client's sense of bewilderment, embarrassment, unworthiness, or be perceived as critical in nature. The counselor should provide significant results to the client out of a sincere desire to help. The client should understand the reason for giving the test and what information will be gleaned from its results. Then, the results and the scores should be discussed in relation to the questions asked on the test. The client should be encouraged to make his or her own interpretation of the results discussed. This can alleviate an attitude of passive acceptance or a more defensive rejection concerning the outcome of the test. The client should be affirmed in the communication efforts of the counselor.

Ethical issues

Mental health providers should be thoroughly familiar with their Code of Ethics. The American psychological Association has issued the Ethical Principles of Psychologists and Code of Conduct. The American Counseling Association has issued the Code of Ethical Standards. There is some overlap in these documents. Recently, there has been need for revision to include computer applications. The computer has changed the construction, administration, scoring, and interpretation of tests used in the mental health field. The revisions also address validity in measuring ability levels of the client. Ethical issues address professional competence, qualifications, and confidentiality of the client. The ethical consideration given to professional competency involves graduate level training in the use of tests. Most tests require administration under the supervision of a licensed practitioner. Test publishers can only sell their tests to those who are legally qualified to administer it.

The client's information is handled with strict confidentiality throughout the entire process. Confidentiality can be compromised with the use of computers, so apply every protective precaution. Seek permission from the client before performing the test. Inform the client about how the information obtained will be stored and about what happens to the information after counseling has been completed. Keep in mind the potential for misuse of information and make sure that any test performed is absolutely necessary. Remain diligent in protecting the client's right to privacy. The client must sign a release before any information can be shared with other organizations or other professionals. Refer to the Code of Ethics whenever there is any question of how to proceed.

Computers

The computer has gained popularity over paper-and-pencil tests and has changed the field of assessment with a wide range of mechanically based scoring mechanisms. The analog computer has been incorporated in tallying the results score of the Strong Vocational Interest Blank developed by Elmer Hanks in 1946. Computer software capabilities have given way to school based vocational preference instruments. National testing organizations like the Educational Testing Service (ETS) uses computers to set in place multiple college-wide admissions tests like the GRE and to score that test. The computer is also used to administer and interpret some psychological instrument like the Rorschach and the MMPI tests.

Mental retardation

Mental retardation is defined as an intellectual disability mirrored by significant limitations in everyday functioning that are present early in life and before the age of 18. The Individuals with Disabilities Act states that all disabled individuals under the age of 25 need to be evaluated, and an individualized educational plan (IEP) needs to be developed for each child in order to provide education in the least restrictive environment. The case Larry

P. vs. Riles established that IQ tests can be racially discriminatory and should not be used to place African-Americans in special education classrooms. The Vineland Behavior Scales measure communication, daily living skills, and socialization, for the purpose of developing special education programs. The AAMR Adaptive Behavior Scales assess personal self-sufficiency, community self-sufficiency, personal-social responsibility, social adjustment, and personal adjustment.

Very few (approximately 5%) of all cases of mental retardation are hereditary. Hereditary forms of mental retardation include Tay-Sachs, fragile X syndrome, and phenylketonuria. Most retardation (about 30%) is due to mutations in the embryo during the first trimester of pregnancy. Down syndrome babies or those exposed to environmental toxins while in the uterus fall into this category. About 10% of mentally retarded individuals are so because of pregnancy or perinatal problems, like fetal malnutrition, anoxia, and HIV. About 5% of the mentally retarded have general medical conditions (like lead poisoning, encephalitis, or malnutrition) suffered during infancy or childhood. Approximately 20% are retarded because of either environmental factors or other mental disorders, for instance, sensory deprivation or autism. In the remaining 30%, etiology is unknown.

PKU
Phenylketonuria (PKU) is one cause of mental retardation. It occurs when an infant lacks the enzyme to metabolize the amino acid phenylalanine, found in high-protein foods and aspartame sweetener. PKU is a rare recessive genetic disorder diagnosed at birth by a simple blood test. It affects mostly blue-eyed, fair babies. Expectant mothers can reduce the hazard of PKU by maintaining a diet low in phenylalanine. Untreated PKU typically leads to some form of mental retardation. Some of the symptoms common to individuals with PKU are impaired motor and language development and volatile, erratic behavior. PKU can be treated if it is diagnosed in a timely fashion. Patients must monitor their diet to keep phenylalanine blood levels at 2—10 mg/dl. Some phenylalanine is required for growth.

Down syndrome
Down syndrome (Trisomy 21) occurs when an individual has three #21 chromosomes instead of two. Down syndrome causes 20%—30% of all cases of moderate and severe mental retardation (1:800 births). 80% of Trisomy 21 pregnancies end in miscarriage. Down syndrome children were formerly called Mongoloids. Classic physical characteristics associated with Down syndrome are: Slanted, almond-shaped eyes with epicanthic folds; a large, protruding tongue; a short, bent fifth finger; and a simian fold across the palm. Individuals with Down syndrome age rapidly. Medical conditions that often accompany Down syndrome and cause patients to have a shorter life expectancy than normal, or poor quality of life, include: Heart lesions; leukemia; respiratory and digestive problems; cataracts; and Alzheimer's disease.

Learning disorders

An individual will be diagnosed with a learning disorder when he or she scores substantially lower than expected on some standardized test. The expectation for the individual's score should be based on age, schooling, and intelligence, and the definition of "substantially lower" is a difference of two or more standard deviations. Learning disorders are frequently attended by delays in language development and/or motor coordination, attention and memory deficits, and low self-esteem. The most common companion of a learning disorder is attention deficit disorder. Research suggests that individuals with learning disorders are more likely to display antisocial behavior, although they also seem to have above-average IQs.

Learning disorders include Reading Disorder, Mathematics Disorder, and Disorder of Written Expression. Research has shown that boys are more likely to develop Reading Disorder than girls. Although learning disorders are typically diagnosed during childhood or adolescence, they do not go away without treatment, and indeed may become more severe with time. Children who have a reading disorder are far more likely than others to display antisocial behavior as an adult. At present, many researchers believe that reading disorders derive from problems with phonological processing. Proposed causes of learning disorders include:

- Incomplete dominance and other hemispheric abnormalities
- Cerebellar-vestibular dysfunction
- Exposure to toxins, like lead

Communication disorders

A number of disorders are lumped together under the heading of communication disorders:

- Expressive language disorder
- Mixed receptive-expressive language disorder
- Phonological disorder
- Stuttering

Stuttering typically begins between the ages of 2 and 7, and is more common in males than females. Research shows stuttering can be controlled through the removal of psychological stress in the home. Children who are constantly told not to stutter tend to stutter all the more. Many patients find success through controlled and regular breathing exercises, accompanied by positive encouragement. In most cases, though, the individual will spontaneously stop stuttering before the age of 16.

Developmental disorders

Autism

Autism is a pervasive developmental disorder because it entails a severe and pervasive impairment in communication and social interaction. Certain stereotyped behaviors are unique to autism, however. In order to diagnose autism, there must be at least six classic symptoms from three categories, with at least two symptoms from the first category and one from each of the second two categories. These symptoms must have had an onset before the age of three.

The first category is qualitative impairment in social interaction, which includes:

- Absence of developmentally appropriate peer relationships
- Lack of social or emotional reciprocity
- Marked impairment in nonverbal behavior

A child must display at least one symptom from the second category of autism, in order to be diagnosed with autism. Qualitative impairment in communication includes:

- Delay or lack of development in spoken language
- Marked impairment in the ability to initiate or sustain conversation
- Stereotyped or repetitive use of language or idiosyncratic language
- Lack of developmentally appropriate play

The third category of autism symptoms is restricted, repetitive, and stereotyped

- 42 -

behavior, interests, and activities. These include:

- Preoccupation with one or more stereotyped and restricted patterns of interest
- Inflexible adherence to nonfunctional routines or rituals
- Stereotyped and repetitive motor mannerisms
- Persistent preoccupation with the parts of objects

Some very noticeable, specific behavior patterns characteristic of autism are:

- Lack of eye contact and disinterest in the presence of others
- Infants who rarely reach out to a caregiver
- Hand-flapping
- Rocking
- Spinning
- Echolalia, imitating and repeating the words of others
- Obsessive interest in a very narrow subject, like astronomy or basketball scores
- Heavy emphasis on routine and consistency, and violent reactions to changes in their normal environment

One half of autistics remain mute for their entire lives. The speech that does develop may be abnormal. The majority of autistics have an IQ in the mentally retarded range. Asperger's syndrome autistics have good speech and normal IQ, but odd behavior.

Autism is frequently first suspected when an infant does not respond to his or her caregiver in an age-appropriate manner. Autistic babies are not interested in cuddling, do not smile, and do not respond to a familiar voice. Autistic babies are often misdiagnosed as profoundly deaf. Unfortunately, even a

small degree of improvement in autism takes a great deal of work. Only one-third of autistic children will achieve some independence as adults. Those autistics who have developed the ability to communicate verbally by age 5 or 6, and have an IQ over 70, have the best chance for future independence.

There are a few structural abnormalities in the brain that have been linked to autism. These include a reduced cerebellum and enlarged ventricles. Research has also suggested that there is a link between autism and abnormal levels of norepinephrine, serotonin, and dopamine. The support for a genetic etiology of autism has been increased by studies indicating that siblings of autistic children are much more likely to be autistic themselves. As for treatment, the most successful interventions focus on teaching autistic individuals the practical skills they will need to survive independently. Therapy should also include development of social skills and the reduction of undesirable behavior. Autistic individuals who reach a moderate level of functioning can be given direct vocational training.

Rett's disorder

Rett's Disorder is a pervasive developmental disorder that afflicts females and occurs after about five months of normal child development. Symptoms of Rett's Disorder are:

- Psychomotor retardation
- Head growth deceleration
- Loss of purposeful hand skills and/or stereotyped hand wringing
- Impaired, uncoordinated walking
- Loss of interest in the social environment
- Severely impaired language development

Childhood Disintegrative Disorder

Childhood Disintegrative Disorder has a distinct pattern of developmental regression in at least two areas of functioning after at least two years of normal development. These areas of functioning may include motor skills, play, social skill, and adaptive behavior.

Asperger's syndrome

Asperger's syndrome is characterized by a severe impairment in social interactions and a limited repertoire of behaviors, interests, and activities. Individuals with Asperger's syndrome will not display any other significant delays in language, self-help skills, cognitive development, or curiosity about the environment. Children with Asperger's syndrome have at least average intelligence, but their cognitive ability is asymmetrically skewed. They perform above average on verbal items, but have poor performance. They are extremely sensitive to touch, sounds, sights, and tastes, and have strong clothing preferences. The excellent verbal skill of Asperger's patients means many of them escape diagnosis until a much later age. Often, individuals with Asperger's are considered to be simply recalcitrant.

ADHD

Attention-deficit/hyperactivity disorder, commonly known as ADHD, can be diagnosed only if an individual displays at least six symptoms of inattention or hyperactivity-impulsivity. Their onset must be before the age of 7, and they must have persisted for at least 6 months.

Symptoms of inattention include:
- Difficulty sustaining tasks or play activities
- Not listening when addressed directly
- Failing to finish schoolwork or chores

- Being easily distracted by extraneous stimuli
- Forgetfulness

Symptoms of hyperactivity-impulsivity include:
- Frequent fidgeting or squirming in a seat
- Running or climbing in inappropriate situations
- Difficulty in playing quietly
- Excessive talking
- Interrupting
- Intruding on others

There are three subtypes of ADHD:
- Predominantly Inattentive Type is diagnosed when an individual has six or more symptoms of inattention and fewer than six symptoms of hyperactivity-impulsivity.
- Predominantly Hyperactive-Impulsive Type is diagnosed when there are six or more symptoms of hyperactivity-impulsivity and fewer than six of inattention.
- Combined Type is diagnosed when there are six or more symptoms of both hyperactivity-impulsivity and inattention.

ADHD is 4—9 times more likely to occur in boys than in girls, although the gender split is about half and half for Predominantly Inattentive Type. The rates of ADHD among adults appear to be about equal for both males and females.

Even though they are found to have average or above-average intelligence, children with ADHD typically score lower than average on IQ tests. Almost every child with ADHD will have some trouble in school, with about a quarter having major problems in reading. Also, social adjustment can be difficult for children with ADHD. Various reports give the

- 44 -

codiagnosis of Conduct Disorder with ADHD occurring 30—90% of the time. Other common co-diagnoses include Oppositional Defiant Disorder, Anxiety Disorder, and Major Depression. About half of all children who are diagnosed with ADHD are also suffering from some other Learning Disorder.

The behavior of children with ADHD is likely to remain consistent until early adolescence, when they may experience diminished overactivity, but continue to suffer from attention and concentration problems. ADHD adolescents are much more likely to participate in antisocial behaviors and to abuse drugs. More than half of all children who are diagnosed with ADHD will continue to suffer from it as adults. These adults are more susceptible to divorce, work-related trouble, accidents, depression, substance abuse, and antisocial behavior. Children with ADHD who are codiagnosed with Conduct Disorder or ADHD are especially likely to have these problems later in life.

Support for the contention that ADHD is a genetic disorder is that slightly higher rates of the disorder occur among biological relatives than among the general population, and there are higher rates among identical twins, rather than fraternal twins. ADHD is associated with structural abnormalities in the brain, like subnormal activity in the frontal cortex and basal ganglia, and a relatively small caudate nucleus, globus pallidus, and prefrontal cortex. Symptoms of ADHD vary widely, depending on the individual's environment. Repetitive or boring environments encourage symptoms, as do those in which the individual is given no chance to interact. One theory of ADHD asserts that it is the result of an inability to distinguish between important and unimportant stimuli in the environment.

Somewhat counterintuitively, central nervous system stimulants like methylphenidate (Ritalin) and amphetamine (Dexedrine) control the symptoms of ADHD. Side effects include headaches, gastrointestinal upset, anorexia, sleep difficulty, anxiety, depression, blood sugar and blood pressure increase, tics, and seizures. Research has consistently shown that pharmacotherapy works best when it is combined with psychosocial intervention. Many teachers have used the basic elements of classroom management to control the symptoms of ADHD. This involves laying out clear guidelines and contingencies for behavior, so that students do not have to speculate on what will happen in class or what they should be doing. Therapy that tries to increase the child's ability to self-regulate behavior has been shown to be less successful. It is always helpful when parents are involved in the treatment program.

Conduct Disorder

Individuals with Conduct Disorder persistently violate either the rights of others or age-appropriate rules. They have little remorse about their behavior, and in ambiguous situations, they are likely to interpret the behavior of other people as hostile or threatening. Individuals are diagnosed with Conduct Disorder when they display three of these four symptoms over the course of a year:
- Aggression to people or animals
- Destruction of property
- Deceitfulness or theft
- Serious violations of rules

Childhood-onset Type is a subset of Conduct Disorder in which the onset of symptoms is before age 10; if the onset is after age 10, the subset is Adolescent-onset Type.

According to Moffitt, there are two basic types of Conduct Disorder:
- Life-course-persistent type begins early in life and gets progressively

worse over time. This kind of Conduct Disorder may be a result of neurological impairments, a difficult temperament, or adverse circumstances.

- Adolescence-limited type is usually the result of a temporary disparity between the individual's biological maturity and freedom. Individuals with this form of Conduct Disorder may commit antisocial acts with friends. It is quite common for individuals with adolescence-limited Conduct Disorder to display antisocial behavior persistently in one area of life and not at all in others.

Research suggests that Conduct Disorder interventions are most successful when they are administered to preadolescents and include the immediate family members. Some therapists have developed programs of parent therapy to help adults manage the antisocial behavior of their children, as this has been demonstrated to have good success. Most programs advise rewarding good behavior and consistently punishing bad behavior. Oppositional Defiant Disorder is similar to Conduct Disorder and is characterized by:

- Patterns of negative or hostile behavior towards authority figures
- Frequent outbreaks of temper and rages
- Deliberately annoying people
- Blaming others
- Spite and vindictiveness

Separation anxiety disorder

Separation anxiety disorder is characterized by age-inappropriate and excessive anxiety that occurs when an individual is separated or threatened with separation from his or her home or family unit. In order to be diagnosed with separation anxiety disorder, the child must exhibit symptoms for at least four weeks and onset must be before the age of 18. Individuals with separation anxiety disorder will manifest some of the following symptoms:

- Excessive distress when separated from home or attachment figures
- Persistent fear of being alone
- Frequent physical complaints during separation

Children with separation anxiety tend to be from loving, stable homes; many manifest the disorder after suffering some personal loss.

Many children who suffer from Separation Anxiety Disorder will refuse to go to school and may claim physical ailments to avoid having to leave the home. In some cases, the child will actually develop a headache or stomachache as a result of anxiety about separation from the home or from an individual to whom they are attached. The refusal to go to school may begin as early as 5 or as late as 12. If the separation anxiety occurs after the age of 10, however, it is quite possibly the result of depression or some more severe disorder. There are various treatment plans for separation anxiety disorder, all of which recommend that the child immediately resume going to school on a normal schedule.

Reactive attachment disorder

Reactive attachment disorder of infancy or early childhood is characterized by a markedly disturbed or developmentally-inappropriate social relatedness in most settings. This condition typically begins before the age of five. In order to definitively diagnose this disorder, there must be evidence of pathogenic care, which may include neglect or a constant change of caregivers that made it difficult for the child to form normal attachments. There are two basic subsets of reactive attachment disorder:

- The Inhibited Type has a hard time initiating and responding to most social interactions. He or she may display a pattern of inhibited, guarded, or ambivalent behaviors.
- The Disinhibited Type has no trouble forming attachments, but does so with any person without any discrimination at all.

Behavioral pediatrics

Behavioral pediatrics, otherwise known as pediatric psychology, has become a more popular field because research revealed that many psychological disorders originate in childhood. For the most part, a pediatric psychologist should be open with the child about his or her condition. Children may need some psychological help if they are to undergo any major medical procedures. Psychologists must relay any information related to the mental or medical condition in language the child can understand. Multicomponent cognitive-behavioral interventions, in which the child is given information about his or her condition and armed with some coping strategies, are especially helpful.

Children who need to be hospitalized for a significant period of time are especially at risk of developing psychological problems, in large part because they have been separated from their families. Children and adolescents are generally less compliant with medical regimens. This may be because of poor communication, parent-child problems, or a general lack of skill. For adolescents, peer pressure and the desire for social acceptance may motivate noncompliance with potentially embarrassing medical programs. Children with serious medical conditions are more likely to have trouble adjusting to school. Problems may be caused by the illness itself, by the frequent absences it necessitates, or by

the social stigma of illness. Some treatments, like chemotherapy, are associated with deficits in neurocognitive functioning and greater risk of learning disabilities.

Other disorders

Feeding and eating disorders

There are a few common conditions grouped under the heading of feeding and eating disorders of infancy and early childhood. Among these are pica, rumination disorder, and feeding disorder of infancy or early childhood. Pica is the persistent consumption of non-food objects, like paint, paper, or feces. In order to be diagnosed, the symptoms must persist for at least a month without the child losing an interest in regular food. Also, the behavior must be independent and not a part of any culturally acceptable process. Pica is most often manifested between the ages of 12—24 months. Pica has been observed in developmentally disabled children, pregnant women, and anemics.

Tourette's syndrome and tic disorders

Tourette's syndrome is a neurological disorder characterized by at least one vocal tic and multiple motor tics that appear simultaneously or at different times, and appears before the age of 18. Tics are defined in the DSM as "sudden, rapid, recurrent, nonrhythmic, stereotyped motor movements or vocalizations that feel irresistible yet can be suppressed for varying lengths of time." Individuals with Tourette's Disorder are likely to have obsessions and compulsions, high levels of hyperactivity, impulsivity, and distractibility.

Chronic motor (vocal) and transient tic disorder patients exhibit:
- Blinking
- Grimacing

- Echokinesis (imitating the movements of another person)
- Grunting
- Barking
- Echolalia (imitating the sounds of another person)
- Coprolalia (repeating obscene words)
- Palilalia (repeating one's own words)

Most successful treatments for Tourette's syndrome include pharmacotherapy. The antipsychotics haloperidol (Haldol) and pimozide (Orap) are successful in relieving the symptoms of Tourette's syndrome because they inhibit the flow of dopamine in the brain; their success has led many scientists to speculate that Tourette's Disorder is caused by an excess of dopamine. In some cases, psychostimulant drugs amplify the tics displayed by the individual. In these cases, a doctor may treat the hyperactivity and inattention of Tourette's with clonidine or desipramine. The former of these is a drug usually used to treat hypertension, while the latter is typically used as an antidepressant.

Enuresis
Enuresis is repeated urinating during the day or night into the bed or clothes at least twice a week for three or more months. Most of the time this urination is involuntary. Enuresis is diagnosed only when the individual has reached an age at which continence can be reasonably expected (five is typical), and he or she does not have some other medical condition that could be to blame, like a urinary tract infection. Enuresis is treated with a night alarm, which makes a loud noise when the child urinates while sleeping. This is effective about 80% of the time, especially when it is combined with techniques like behavioral reversal and overcorrection. Desmopressin acetate (DDAVP) nasal spray, imipramine,

and oxybutynin chloride (Ditropan) may help control symptoms.

Mental disorders due to a general medical condition

The DSM-IV divides mental disorders into three categories:
- Disorders due to a general medical condition, like AIDS or syphilis
- Substance-related disorders
- Primary mental disorders

All disorders due to a general medical condition must be a direct physiological consequence of the medical condition. All of the conditions in this category share the following diagnostic criteria:
- Evidence from the history
- Physical exam and/or laboratory findings that prove the condition is the result of a general medical condition
- The disturbance is not better explained by a substance-related or primary mental disorder
- The disturbance does not only occur during an episode of delirium

Dementia

Individuals who suffer from dementia are likely to manifest a few cognitive deficits, most notably memory impairment, aphasia, apraxia, agnosia, and/or impaired executive functioning. Depending on the etiology of the dementia, these deficits may get progressively worse or may be stable. Demented individuals often have both anterograde and retrograde amnesia, meaning that they find it difficult both to learn new information and to recall previously learned information. There may be a decrease in language skill, specifically manifested in an inability to recall the names of people or things.

- 48 -

Individuals may also have a hard time performing routine motor programs, and may be unable to recognize familiar people and places. Abstract thinking, planning, and initiating complex behaviors are difficult for demented individuals.

Some of the cognitive symptoms of major depressive disorder are very similar to those of dementia. Indeed, this kind of depression is frequently referred to as pseudodementia. One difference is that the cognitive deficits typical of dementia will get progressively worse, and the individual is unlikely to admit that he or she has impaired cognition. Pseudodementia, on the other hand, typically has a very rapid onset and usually causes the individual to become concerned about his or her own health. There are also differences in the quality of memory impairment in these two conditions: Demented individuals have deficits in both recall and recognition memory, while individuals who are depressed only have deficits in recall memory.

Dementia due to Alzheimer's

Over half of all cases of dementia are caused by Alzheimer's disease. Alzheimer's begins slowly and may take a long time to become noticeable. Researchers have outlined three stages in dementia of the Alzheimer's Type:

- Stage 1 usually comprises the first one to three years of the condition. The patient suffers from mild anterograde amnesia, especially for declarative memories. He or she is likely to have diminished visuospatial skill, which often manifests itself in wandering aimlessly. Also common to this stage are indifference; irritability; sadness, and anomia.

- Stage 2 can stretch between the second and tenth years of the illness. The patient suffers increasing retrograde amnesia; restlessness, delusions, aphasia, acalculia, ideomotor apraxia (the inability to translate an idea into movement), and a generally flat mood.
- In Stage 3 dementia of the Alzheimer's type, the patient suffers severely impaired intellectual functioning; apathy; limb rigidity; and urinary and fecal incontinence. This last stage usually occurs between the eighth and twelfth years of the condition.

Alzheimer's disease is quite difficult to diagnose directly, so it is usually only diagnosed once all the other possible causes of dementia have been eliminated. A brain biopsy that indicates extensive neuron loss, amyloid plaques, and neurofibrillary tangles can give solid evidence of Alzheimer's disease. Individuals who develop Alzheimer's disease usually only live about ten years after onset. The disease is more common in females than males, and is more likely to occur after the age of 65.

Particular kinds of Alzheimer's disease have been linked with specific genetic abnormalities. For instance, early-onset familial Alzheimer's victims often have abnormalities on chromosome 21, while individuals whose onset is later are likely to have irregularities on chromosome 19. Victims of Alzheimer's disease have also been shown to have significant aluminum deposits in brain tissues, a malfunctioning immune system, and a low level of acetylcholine. Some of the drugs used to treat Alzheimer's increase the cholinergic activity in the brain. These drugs, which include the trade names Cognex and Aricept, can temporarily reverse cognitive impairment, though these improvements are not sustained when the drugs are removed.

Though Alzheimer's disease is a degenerative condition with no known cure, there are a number of different treatments that can provide help to those who suffer from the disease:

- Group therapy that focuses on orienting the individual in reality and encourages him or her to reminisce about past experiences
- Antidepressants, antipsychotics, and other pharmacotherapy
- Behavioral techniques to fight the agitation associated with Alzheimer's
- Environmental manipulation to improve memory and cognitive function
- Involving the patient's family in interventions

Vascular dementia
In order to be diagnosed with vascular dementia, the patient must have cognitive impairment and either focal neurological signs or laboratory evidence of cerebrovascular disease. Vascular dementia has varying symptoms, depending on where the brain damage lies. Focal neurological signs may include exaggerated reflexes, weaknesses in the extremities, and abnormalities in gait. Symptoms gradually increase in severity. Risk factors for vascular dementia are hypertension, diabetes, tobacco smoking, and atrial fibrillation. In some cases, an individual may be able to recover from vascular dementia. Stroke victims, for instance, will notice a great deal of improvement in the first six months after the cerebrovascular accident. Most of this improvement will be in their physical, rather than cognitive, symptoms.

Dementia due to HIV
AIDS patients develop a particular form of dementia. In its early stages, the Human Immunodeficiency Virus causes dementia that appears as forgetfulness, impaired attention, and generally decelerated mental processes. The dementia progresses to include poor concentration, apathy, social withdrawal, loss of initiative, tremor, clumsiness, trouble with problem-solving, and saccadic eye movements. One of the ways that dementia due to HIV is distinguished is by motor slowness, the lack of aphasia, and more severe forms of depression and anxiety. It shares these features with dementia due to Parkinson's and Huntington's diseases.

Dementia due to Parkinson's disease
The following symptoms are commonly associated with dementia due to Parkinson's disease:

- Bradykinesia (general slowness of movement)
- Resting tremor
- Stoic and unmoving facial expression
- Loss of coordination and/or balance
- Involuntary pill-rolling movement of the thumb and forefinger
- Acathisia (violent restlessness)

Most Parkinson's victims will suffer from depression at some point during their illness, and between 20—60% will develop dementia. Research indicates that Parkinson's victims have a deficiency of dopamine-producing cells and the presence of Lewy bodies in their substantia nigra. Many doctors now believe that there is some environmental cause for Parkinson's, though the etiology is not yet clear. The medication L-dopa (Dopar, Larodopa) alleviates the symptoms of Parkinson's by increasing the amount of dopamine in the brain.

Dementia due to Huntington's disease
Huntington's disease patients suffer degeneration of the GABA-producing cells in their substantia nigra, basal ganglia,

and cortex. This inherited disease typically appears between the ages of 30 and 40. The affective symptoms of Huntington's disease include irritability, depression, and/or apathy. After a while, patients display cognitive symptoms as well, including forgetfulness and dementia. Later, motor symptoms emerge, including fidgeting, clumsiness, athetosis (slow, writhing movements), and chorea (involuntary quick jerks). Because the affective symptoms appear in advance of the cognitive and motor symptoms, many Huntington's victims are misdiagnosed with depression. Individuals in the early stages of Huntington's are at risk for suicide, as they are aware of their impending deterioration, and will have the loss of impulse control associated with the disease.

Delirium

Delirium, like dementia, is characterized by a clinically significant deficit in cognition or memory as compared to previous functioning. In order for delirium to be diagnosed, the individual must have disturbances in consciousness and either a change in personality or the development of perceptual abnormalities. These changes in cognition may appear as losses of memory, disorientation in space and time, and impaired language. The perceptual abnormalities associated with delirium include hallucinations and illusions. Delirium usually develops over a few hours or days, and may vary in intensity over the course of the days and weeks. If the cause of the delirium is alleviated, it may disappear for an extended period of time.

Five groups of people are at high risk for delirium:
- Elderly people
- Those who have a diminished cerebral reserve due to dementia, stroke, or some other medical condition
- Post cardiotomy patients
- Burn patients
- Drug-dependent people who are in withdrawal

Delirium can also be caused by:
- Systemic infections
- Metabolic disorders
- Fluid and electrolyte imbalances
- Postoperative states
- Head trauma

The treatment for delirium usually aims at curing the underlying cause of the disorder and reducing the agitated behavior. Antipsychotic drugs can be good for reducing agitation, delusions, and hallucinations, while providing a calm environment can decrease the appearance of agitation.

Amnestic disorder

Individuals suffering from an amnestic disorder will have either an inability to recall previously learned information, an inability to learn new information, or a combination of the two. The diagnosis of amnestic disorder can be made only when the memory impairment can be directly linked to another medical condition, when the memory impairment does not occur during delirium or dementia, and there has been a significant decline in previous functioning. A similar condition, known as dissociative amnesia, is characterized by the inability to remember events that happened during a specific period of time, usually a time in which there was some trauma.

Substance dependence and abuse

An individual may be diagnosed with substance dependence if he or she persists in using a controlled substance despite the presence of three or more significant substance-related problems over a year. These significant problems include:

- Increased tolerance for the substance, meaning that more must be consumed in order to achieve the desired effect
- Withdrawal effects when use of the drug is suspended, or continued use to avoid withdrawal effects
- Frequently taking more of the substance than was intended
- Desire to control or cut down substance use, but attempts failed
- Large amounts of time spent obtaining, using, or recovering from the substance
- Cessation of important social, occupational, or recreational activities because of substance use
- Continued use of the substance despite persistent or recurring psychological or physical problems caused by use

A craving for the substance is usually present in the individual, but is not required for diagnosis.

Treatments for substance dependence include:

- Aversion therapy techniques like covert sensitization or Antabuse (disulfiram) for alcoholism
- Multicomponent interventions involving social skills training, stress management, moderation training, and contingency management
- Learning strategies for self-control
- 12-step peer group treatment programs like AA or NarcAnon
- Rapid Opiate Detoxification (ROD or Waismann Method) with general anesthesia

- Cold turkey withdrawal in detox facilities

While addiction is not a specific diagnosis made within the DSM-IV, it is frequently invoked to describe a person who is compelled to consume a substance and suffers from withdrawal symptoms when the drug is not consumed.

While many individuals are able to temporarily abstain from a substance on which they were formerly dependent, few of them will be able to avoid relapse. The researchers Marlatt and Gordon described substance dependence as a habitual behavior that has been overlearned. When an individual relapses into substance abuse behavior, he or she develops an abstinence violation effect that is manifested as self-blame, shame, and an increased susceptibility to relapse. Marlatt and Gordon took their theory of relapse psychology and created a relapse prevention program that attempts to frame relapse as a mistake with specific and controllable causes. This program tries to give individuals the knowledge and skills to avoid potentially tempting situations.

Nicotine dependence
Because of the major health risks associated with smoking, there have been numerous attempts to devise successful programs for smoking cessation. Unfortunately, nicotine addiction is very difficult to break; one study indicated that only 2.5% of all those who tried to quit were successful. This is especially tragic considering that the health risks associated with smoking are almost entirely negated after five years of cessation. At present, research suggests that the most successful programs for smoking cessation include nicotine replacement therapy (patches and gum); a multicomponent behavioral therapy including skills training, relapse

prevention, stimulus control, and/or rapid smoking; and support and assistance from a clinician.

Substance abuse
Substance abuse is a set of maladaptive behaviors associated with substance use. In order to be diagnosed with substance abuse, an individual must display at least one of the following symptoms during a year-long period:

- Recurrent substance use that results in a failure to fulfill major role obligations at home, school, or work
- Repeated use of a substance in situations in which use is known to be physically hazardous
- Recurrent substance-related legal problems
- Continued use despite having persistent or recurrent social or interpersonal problems that are caused or exacerbated by the substance

Substance-induced disorders
To diagnose substance abuse correctly, find a clear connection relating the patient's symptoms to the substance. There are a number of different ways to ascertain substance abuse:

- Direct physical evidence
- Time of substance use and subsequent onset of symptoms
- Cessation of symptoms after a period of abstinence
- Presence of symptoms not associated with any other mental disorder
- Direct empirical evidence of a relationship between the substance and the observed symptoms

The most common substances of abuse are nicotine, caffeine, alcohol, marijuana, amphetamines, phencyclidine, opiates, cocaine, sedative-hypnotics, anabolic steroids, hallucinogens, inhalants, and laxatives. Look for these substances first.

Alcohol intoxication and withdrawal
Symptoms of alcohol intoxication include:

- Maladaptive behavior and psychological changes
- Slurred speech
- Poor coordination
- Unsteady gait
- Nystagmus (uncontrolled eye movements)
- Impaired attention and memory
- Stupor or coma

Maladaptive behaviors and psychological changes associated with alcohol intoxication include: Inappropriate sexual or aggressive behaviors, impaired judgment, and emotional liability. Symptoms of alcohol withdrawal are:

- Autonomic hyperactivity (diaphoresis and tachycardia)
- Hand tremors
- Insomnia
- Nausea and vomiting
- Transient illusions or hallucinations
- Anxiety
- Psychomotor agitation
- Tonic/clonic seizures if use was heavy or prolonged

Symptoms associated with alcohol withdrawal delirium are:

- Disturbances in consciousness and other cognitive functions
- Autonomic hyperactivity
- Vivid hallucinations
- Delusions
- Agitation following periods of prolonged or heavy use

Alcohol-induced sleep disorders may be caused by either intoxication or withdrawal, and usually manifest as insomnia. Intoxicative sleep disorder entails a period of drowsiness followed by excessive wakefulness, restlessness, and vivid, anxious dreams. Withdrawal sleep disorder manifests as a severe disruption in sleep continuity, accompanied by vivid dreams.

Korsakoff syndrome
Alcohol-induced persisting amnestic disorder, otherwise known as Korsakoff syndrome, is characterized by retrograde and anterograde amnesia, and confabulation. Confabulation occurs when an individual unconsciously attempts to compensate for memory loss by making up memories. It is associated with damage to the frontal lobe and basal forebrain. Korsakoff syndrome is due to a thiamine deficiency; the condition is often preceded by Wernicke's syndrome, which is characterized by ataxia, abnormal eye movements, and confusion. In Korsakoff syndrome, the anterograde amnesia is more severe, especially for declarative memories. The retrograde amnesia seems to affect recent long-term memories more than those formed long ago.

Amphetamine and cocaine intoxication and withdrawal
Characteristics of amphetamine and cocaine intoxication are:
- Maladaptive behavioral and psychological changes, including euphoria, hyperactivity, grandiosity, confusion, anger, paranoid ideation, and auditory hallucinations
- Tachycardia
- Hypertension or hypotension
- Dilated pupils
- Perspiration or chills
- Nausea or vomiting
- Weight loss
- Psychomotor agitation
- Muscular weakness
- Confusion
- Seizures

Symptoms of amphetamine and cocaine withdrawal are:
- Dysphoric mood
- Fatigue
- Vivid and unpleasant dreams
- Insomnia or hypersomnia
- Increased appetite
- Psychomotor agitation or retardation
- Intense depression after prolonged or heavy use

Schizophrenia

In order to be diagnosed with schizophrenia, an individual must have a continuous disturbance of more than six months that includes one or more of the following active-phase symptoms:
- Delusions
- Hallucinations
- Disorganized sleep
- Severely disorganized or catatonic behavior
- Negative symptoms

Also, the afflicted individual must be suffering impairment in his or her performance at home, work, interpersonal life, or self-care. Schizophrenia is a psychotic disorder. Psychotic disorders are those that feature one or more of the following:
- Delusions
- Hallucinations
- Disorganized speech or thought
- Disorganized or catatonic behavior

The symptoms of schizophrenia may be positive, negative, or disorganized. Positive symptoms are delusions and hallucinations. Delusions are false beliefs that are held despite clear evidence to the contrary. The delusions suffered by a schizophrenic usually fall into one of three categories:

- Persecutory, in which the person believes that someone or something is out to get him or her
- Referential, in which the person believes that messages in the public domain (like song lyrics or newspaper articles) are specifically directed at him or her
- Bizarre, in which the person imagines that something impossible has happened

The most common sensory mode for hallucinations is sound, specifically the audition of voices.

For many psychologists, the tell-tale characteristic of schizophrenia is disorganized speech. Disorganized speech manifests as:
- Incoherence
- Free associations that make little sense
- Random responses to direct questions

Disorganized behavior manifests as:
- Shabby or unkempt appearance
- Inappropriate sexual behavior
- Unpredictable agitation
- Catatonia and decreased motor activity

Negative symptoms of schizophrenia are:
- Restricted range of emotions
- Reduced body language
- Lack of facial expression
- Lack of coherent thoughts
- Inability to make conversation
- Avolition (the inability to set goals or to work in a rational, programmatic manner)

The Paranoid type schizophrenic is preoccupied with one or more delusions and has frequent auditory hallucinations. Otherwise, cognition and affect are relatively normal. Delusions usually have a similar theme, often grandiose or persecutory, and the hallucinations are frequently tied into the content of the delusions. The Paranoid Type schizophrenic is most likely to have a family member with a similar condition, and has the best prognosis for the future. The Disorganized Type schizophrenic displays disorganized speech, disorganized behavior, and either a flat or an inappropriate affect. Any delusions or hallucinations suffered by this type will be fragmentary and unrelated in content.

The Catatonic Type schizophrenic has symptoms that include at least two of the following:
- Motoric immobility
- Excessive motor activity
- Extreme negativism or mutism
- Peculiarities in voluntary movement
- Echolalia or echopraxia

The Residual Type schizophrenic has in the past displayed prominent delusions, hallucinations, and disorganized behavior, but does not currently display these negative symptoms. Residual Type schizophrenics may continue to display some positive symptoms, like eccentric speech or beliefs. Undifferentiated schizophrenia is diagnosed when the patient does not have symptoms placing him or her clearly within one of the other categories.

Rather than distinguishing cases of schizophrenia by the predominant symptoms, some psychologists use the two-type model proposed by Crow in 1985:
- Type I schizophrenics display mostly positive symptoms; there is usually good premorbid functioning and the patient should respond well to antipsychotic medication. Type I schizophrenia

is believed to be due to neurotransmitter abnormalities.

- Type II schizophrenics more commonly manifest negative symptoms. Individuals with Type II schizophrenia typically have poor premorbid adjustment and will not respond well to traditional antipsychotic medications. Type II schizophrenia usually results from abnormalities in brain structure.

Features commonly associated with schizophrenia are:
- Inappropriate affect
- Anhedonia (loss of pleasure)
- Dysphoric mood
- Abnormalities in motor behavior
- Somatic complaints

One of the more troublesome aspects of schizophrenia is that the afflicted individual rarely has any insight into his or her own condition, and so is unlikely to comply with treatment. Schizophrenics often develop substance dependencies, especially to nicotine. Though many people believe that schizophrenics are more likely to be violent or aggressive than individuals in the general population, there is no statistical information to support this assertion. The onset of schizophrenia is typically between the ages of 18—25 for males, and 25—35 for females. Males are slightly more likely to develop the disorder.

Individuals typically develop schizophrenia as a chronic condition, with very little chance of full remission. Positive symptoms of schizophrenia tend to decrease in later life, though the negative symptoms may remain. The following factors bode well for prognosis:
- Good premorbid adjustment
- Acute and late onset

- Female gender
- Presence of a precipitating event
- Brief duration of active-phase symptoms
- Insight into the illness
- Family history of mood disorder
- No family history of schizophrenia

Differential diagnoses for schizophrenia include mood disorder with psychotic features, schizoaffective disorder, and the effects of prolonged and large-scale use of amphetamines or cocaine.

Both twin and adoption studies have suggested that there is a genetic component to the etiology of schizophrenia; the rates of instance (concordance) among first-degree biological relatives of schizophrenics are greater than among the general population. Structural abnormalities in the brain linked to schizophrenia are enlarged ventricles and diminished hippocampus, amygdala, and globus pallidus. Functional abnormalities in the brain linked to schizophrenia are hyperfrontality and diminished activity in the prefrontal cortex. An abnormally large number of the schizophrenics in the Northern Hemisphere were born in the late winter or early spring. There is speculation that this may be because of a link between prenatal exposure to influenza and schizophrenia.

For many years, the professional consensus was that schizophrenia was caused by either an excess of the neurotransmitter dopamine or oversensitive dopamine receptors. The dopamine hypothesis was supported by the fact that antipsychotic medications that block dopamine receptors had some success in treating schizophrenia, and by the fact that dopamine-elevating amphetamines amplified the frequency of delusions. The dopamine hypothesis has been somewhat undermined, however, by research that found elevated levels of norepinephrine and serotonin, as well as low levels of GABA and glutamate in schizophrenics. Some studies have shown that clozapine and other atypical antipsychotics are effective in treating schizophrenia, even though they block serotonin rather than dopamine receptors.

Treatment for schizophrenia begins with the administration of antipsychotic medication. Antipsychotics are very effective at diminishing the positive symptoms of schizophrenia, though their results vary from person to person. Antipsychotics have strong side effects, however, including tardive dyskinesia. Medication is more effective when it is taken in combination with psychosocial intervention. Many schizophrenics are prone to relapse if they receive a great deal of criticism from family members, so it may be a good idea to initiate family therapy in which the level of expressed emotion in the family is discussed. Recovering schizophrenics also benefit from social skills training and help with employment.

Schizophreniform disorder and brief psychotic disorder

An individual may be diagnosed with schizophreniform disorder if he or she has displayed symptoms consistent with schizophrenia for one to six months. It is not necessary for social or occupational functioning to have been impaired for this diagnosis to be made. The majority of those who receive a schizophreniform diagnosis eventually receive a diagnosis of schizophrenia or schizoaffective disorder. An individual may be diagnosed with brief psychotic disorder if he or she has delusions, hallucinations, disorganized speech and/ or severely disorganized or catatonic behavior. These characteristics must be present for at least one day, but less than one month.

Brief psychotic disorder typically follows an overwhelming stressor.

Delusional disorder

An individual receives a diagnosis of delusional disorder if he or she has one or more nonbizarre delusions that last one month or more. A nonbizarre delusion is one that could have happened; often these delusions are persecutory in nature. Psychosocial functioning is not otherwise limited, so any adverse consequences that befall the individual are directly attributable to the delusion. Common subtypes of delusions outlined in the DSM-IV are:

- Erotomanic (in which the individual believes that another person is in love with him or her)
- Grandiose (in which the individual believes that he or she has great but as yet unrecognized talent, or has a privileged relationship with a prominent person) Jealous (in which the person believes a romantic partner to be unfaithful)
- Somatic (in which the delusion somehow involves bodily functions or sensations)

Major depressive episodes

The two major symptoms of a major depressive episode are a depressed mood and/or a loss of interest in activities that formerly brought pleasure. This condition must persist for at least two weeks for the event to be classified as a major depressive episode. In order to make this diagnosis, the symptoms must cause significant distress or impairment. At least five of the following symptoms must be present:

- Depressed mood most of the time
- Diminished interest or pleasure in all activities

- Feelings of worthlessness or inappropriate guilt
- Psychomotor agitation or retardation
- Loss or increase in appetite and significant weight loss or gain
- Fatigue or loss of energy
- Insomnia or hypersomnia
- Reduced ability to concentrate
- Suicidal ideation

Manic episodes

A manic episode is a period of a week or longer in which the individual's mood is either abnormally elevated and expansive or irritable. These episodes are accompanied by at least three of the following symptoms:
- Increased goal-directed activity or psychomotor agitation
- Flight of ideas
- Decreased need for sleep
- Grandiosity
- Restlessness
- Distractibility
- Willingness to participate in pleasurable activities that have a high potential for danger

Also, in order for a manic episode to be diagnosed, an individual must either be significantly impaired in his or her occupational or social functioning, must require hospitalization to prevent harm to self or others, and/or must display psychotic behavior.

Hypomanic episodes and mixed episodes

A hypomanic episode is diagnosed as a distinct period of abnormally and persistently elevated, expansive, or irritable mood that lasts for at least four days and is accompanied by at least three of the symptoms associated with a manic episode. A hypomanic episode will be severe enough to be a clear departure from normal mood and functioning, but will not be severe enough to cause a marked impairment in functioning, or to require hospitalization. Often, there will not be any psychotic symptoms. A hypomanic episode is often marked by an increase in accomplishments, creativity, or efficiency. A mixed episode lasts for seven days and is characterized by rapidly alternating symptoms of manic and major depressive episodes. These disturbances are usually severe enough to cause marked impairment in social or occupational functioning, to require hospitalization, or to include psychotic symptoms.

Major depressive disorder

Major depressive disorder is diagnosed when an individual has one or more major depressive episodes without having a history of manic, hypomanic, or mixed episodes. There are a few different specifiers (categories of associated features) for major depressive disorder issued by the DSM-IV:
- Psychotic features
- Catatonic features
- Melancholic features
- Postpartum onset

Some studies estimate that 20% of women will have symptoms worthy of a diagnosis of major depressive disorder after giving birth. From the beginning of adolescence on, the rate of major depressive disorder is about twice as great for males as for females. Before adolescence, the rates are about the same. Most major depressive disorders occur in the mid-twenties.

Symptoms of major depressive disorder vary with age. For children, common symptoms are:
- Somatic complaints
- Irritability

- Social withdrawal

Male preadolescents often display aggressive and destructive behavior. When elderly individuals develop a major depressive disorder, it manifests as memory loss, distractibility, disorientation, and other cognitive problems. Many major depressive episodes are misdiagnosed as dementia. It is very common in non-Anglo cultures for the symptoms of depression to be described solely in terms of their somatic content. Latinos, for instance, frequently complain of jitteriness or headaches, while Asians commonly complain of tiredness or weakness.

The severity and duration of a major depressive episode varies from case to case, but symptoms usually last about six months before remission to full function. 20%—30% of patients have lingering symptoms for months or years. About 50% of patients experience more than one episode of major depression. Oftentimes, multiple episodes are precipitated by some severe psychological trauma. The catecholamine hypothesis suggests major depressive episodes are due to a deficiency of the neurotransmitter norepinephrine. The indolamine hypothesis proposes that depression is caused by inferior levels of serotonin.

Besides the catecholamine and indolamine hypotheses, there are a few other proposed ideas for the etiology of major depressive disorder. Some researchers speculate depression is caused by hormonal disturbances, like an increased level of cortisol. Cortisol is one of the stress hormones secreted by the adrenal cortex. Other researchers speculate there is a connection between depression and diminished new cell growth in certain regions of the brain, particularly the subgenual prefrontal cortex and hippocampus. The subgenual prefrontal cortex is the part of the brain associated with the formation of positive emotions. Many antidepressant drugs seem to stimulate new growth in the hippocampus.

Three major cognitive-behavioral etiologies have been offered for major depressive disorder:
- The learned helplessness model proposed by Seligman suggests afflicted individuals have been exposed to uncontrollable negative events in the past, and also have a tendency to attribute negative events to internal, stable, and global factors.
- Rehm's self-control model suggests depression occurs in individuals who obsess over negative outcomes, set extremely high standards for themselves, blame all of their problems on internal failures, and have low rates of self-reinforcement. coupled with high rates of self-punishment
- Beck's cognitive theory suggests depression is the result of negative and irrational thought and beliefs about the depressive cognitive triad (the self, the world, and the future).

The typical treatment program for major depressive disorder combines antidepressant drugs and psychotherapy. Three classes of antidepressant medication are commonly prescribed:
- Selective serotonin reuptake inhibitors (SSRIs) are prescribed for melancholic depressives; they have a lower incidence of serious adverse side effects than do tricyclics.
- Tricyclics (TCAs), are prescribed for classic depression, involving vegetative bodily symptoms, a

worsening of symptoms in the morning, acute onset, and short duration of moderate symptoms.

- Monoamine oxidase inhibitors are prescribed as a last resort for patients who have an unorthodox depression that includes phobias, panic attacks, increased appetite, hypersomnia, and a mood that worsens as the day goes on.

Electroconvulsive therapy and seasonal affective disorder

Electroconvulsive therapy (ECT) is not often employed at present. It has good results treating endogenous forms of depression that include delusions or suicidal ideation. ECT is only tried on patients who do not respond to antidepressant medication, because patients suffer temporary retrograde and anterograde amnesia after treatment. Amnesia can be mitigated by limiting the ECT to the right, nondominant hemisphere. Seasonal affective disorder (SAD) is a major depressive disorder that afflicts people in the Northern Hemisphere from October to April. Symptoms of SAD are hypersomnia, increased appetite, weight gain, and an increased desire for carbohydrates. Research suggests SAD is caused by circadian and seasonal increases in the level of melatonin production by the pineal gland from lack of sunlight. SAD patients are treated with phototherapy (exposure to full-spectrum white light for several hours each day), aerobic exercise, and SSRIs.

Dysthymic disorder

Dysthymic disorder is a chronically depressed mood for an extended period of time. For adults, the low mood must last most of each day for two years. For children and adolescents, the pervasive mood may be either depressed or irritable, and must last for a year. There cannot have been a two-month period in which there were no symptoms. Also, the depressive symptoms should not be severe enough to warrant a diagnosis of major depressive episode. 25%—50% of patients show sleep EEG abnormalities. Women are two to three times more likely to suffer dysthymic disorder than men. 75% of patients with dysthymic disorder develop major depressive disorder in five years. First degree relatives are likely to also suffer dysthymia or major depression. Treatment programs for dysthymic disorder usually include a combination of antidepressant drugs (especially fluoxetine) and either cognitive-behavioral therapy or interpersonal therapy.

Bipolar I and II disorders

Bipolar I disorders include the occurrence of one or more manic or mixed episodes, with or without a history of one or more major depressive episodes. The subtypes of Bipolar I disorder are:

- Single manic episode
- Most recent episode manic
- Most recent episode hypomanic
- Most recent episode mixed
- Most recent episode depressed

Bipolar II disorder is diagnosed when a person has had at least one major depressive episode and one hypomanic episode. Bipolar II is distinguished from Bipolar I by the fact that the individual has never had either a manic or a mixed episode. Males and females develop Bipolar I disorder equally, but Bipolar II is much more common for females. On average, the age of onset for the first manic episode is the early 20s.

Among all mental disorders, Bipolar I and II disorders are the most clearly linked to genetic factors. Identical twins are overwhelmingly more likely to develop the disease than are fraternal twins. Research suggests a traumatic event may precipitate the first manic episode, although later manic episodes do not need to be preceded by a stressful episode. The most effective treatment for Bipolar I and II is lithium. Lithium reduces manic symptoms and eliminates mood swings for more than 50% of bipolar patients. One major problem with lithium is that it works so well, many patients consider themselves cured and stop taking it, causing a relapse. Pharmacotherapy is most effective when combined with psychotherapy.

Bipolar patients who do not respond to lithium treatment are given anticonvulsants like carbamazepine or divalproex sodium. Anticonvulsants are also used in lieu of lithium for patients who have rapid cycling or dysphoric mania.

Cyclothymic disorder is another form of bipolar disorder, characterized by the occurrence of fluctuating hypomanic symptoms and numerous periods of depressive symptoms. The depressive symptoms must not be significant enough to warrant a diagnosis of major depressive episode, while the hypomanic symptoms will not warrant a diagnosis of manic episode. In order to receive a diagnosis of cyclothymic disorder, an individual must have symptoms that last at least two years if he or she is an adult, and one year if he or she is a child or adolescent.

Suicide

Suicide is the eighth leading cause of death for males in the United States, and sixteenth for females. Indicators that a person is at risk for a suicide attempt include:

- Previous suicide attempt in 60%—80% of cases
- Warning issued by the prospective suicide in 80% of cases
- The prospective suicide is age 24—44

Drug suicides are the most common (>70% annually). In order of preference, suicides use: Sedatives (especially benzodiazepines); antidepressants; opiates; prescription analgesics; and carbon monoxide from car exhaust. The most likely persona to commit a successful suicide is a male, Caucasian, 45—49 years of age. Women are more likely to be saved from an attempted suicide through treatment at an Emergency Department. The average age of those saved is 15—19. A sharp increase in suicides aged 10—19 may be due to the increased use of antidepressants, which now carry an FDA black box warning. 25% of suicide attempts by seniors over age 65 are successful.

Statistics indicate that four or five times as many males as females successfully commit suicide. However, females attempt suicide about three times as often as males. The reason for this disparity is that men tend to employ more violent means of self-destruction, including guns, hanging, and carbon monoxide poisoning. Among racial and ethnic groups, the suicide rate is highest among whites. The exception is American Indian and Alaskan Natives aged 15—34, for whom suicide is the second leading cause of death. As for marital status, the highest rates of suicide are among divorced, separated, or widowed people. The suicide rate for single people trails that of those groups, but it remains higher than the suicide rate for married people.

Research into suicide has indicated that hopelessness is the most common predictor of an inclination to self-destruction. It is a more accurate predictor even than the intensity of depressive symptoms. Self-assigned or society-assigned perfectionism has also been blamed for suicide. Many suicides are preceded by some traumatic life event, like the end of a romantic relationship or the death of a loved one. For adolescents, the most common precipitant of suicide is an argument with a parent or rejection by a boyfriend or girlfriend. Among adolescents, the common warning signs of suicide are talking about death, giving away possessions, and talking about a reunion with a deceased individual.

Most of those who commit suicide are suffering from some mental disorder, most commonly major depression and bipolar disorder. Suicide associated with depression is most likely to occur within three months after the symptoms of depression have begun to improve. The risk of suicide among adolescents with depression increases greatly if the adolescent also has conduct disorder, ADHD, or is a substance abuser, particularly of inhaled solvents. As for biological correlates, suicide victims have been found to have low levels of serotonin and 5HIAA (a serotonin metabolite). Individuals at risk for suicide need immediate psychological intervention and a 24-hour suicide watch.

Anxiety disorders

Anxiety disorders include the following:
- Panic disorder with or without agoraphobia
- Agoraphobia without a history of panic disorder
- Specific phobia
- Social phobia
- Obsessive-compulsive disorder
- Post-traumatic stress disorder
- Acute stress disorder
- Generalized anxiety disorder

The following symptoms are common to both anxiety and depression:
- Poor concentration and memory
- Irritability
- Fatigue
- Insomnia
- Feelings of hopelessness

Agoraphobia

Symptoms that distinguish anxiety disorders from Agoraphobia are the fears of being in a situation or place from which it could be difficult or embarrassing to escape, or of being in a place where help might not be available in the event of a panic attack. Agoraphobia usually manifests when the individual is outside of the home and alone, is in a crowd, or is traveling in a train or automobile. Individuals who suffer from agoraphobia will typically go to great lengths to avoid problematic situations, or they will only be able to enter certain situations with a companion and under heavy distress. One of the main problems with agoraphobia is that it causes the individual to severely limit the places they are willing to go. Patients become reclusive.

Panic disorder

An individual may be diagnosed with panic disorder if he or she suffers two or more unexpected panic attacks, and one of the attacks is followed by one month of either persistent concern regarding the possibility of another attack or a significant change in behavior related to the attack. Panic attacks are brief, defined periods of intense apprehension, fear, or terror. They develop quickly, and usually reach their greatest intensity after about ten minutes. Attacks must include at least four characteristic symptoms, which include:
- Palpitations or accelerated heart rate (tachycardia)

- Sweating
- Chest pain
- Nausea
- Dizziness
- Derealization
- Paresthesia (pins and needles or numbness)

The consensus of research is that 1% or 2% of the population will suffer panic disorder at some point during their lives. 30%—50% of these individuals will also suffer agoraphobia. Panic disorder has a higher rate of diagnostic comorbidity when it is accompanied by agoraphobia. Panic disorder is far more likely to occur in females than males, and females with a panic disorder have a 75% chance of also having agoraphobia. There is a great deal of variation in the age of onset, but the most frequent ages of occurrence are in adolescence and the mid-30s. Children can experience the physical symptoms of a panic attack, but are unlikely to be diagnosed with panic disorder because they do not have the wherewithal to associate their symptoms with catastrophic feelings.

The most effective treatment for panic attacks and agoraphobia appears to be controlled in vivo exposure with response prevention, known as flooding. Flooding is typically accompanied by cognitive therapy, relaxation, breathing training, and/or pharmacotherapy. Antidepressant medications are often prescribed to relieve the symptoms of panic disorder. If stand-alone drug treatment is used, the risk of relapse is very high. Differential diagnoses for panic disorder with or without agoraphobia include social phobia, and medical conditions like hyperthyroidism, hypoglycemia, cardiac arrhythmia, and mitral valve prolapse. Panic disorder can be distinguished from social phobia by the fact that attacks will sometimes occur while the individual is alone or sleeping.

Specific phobias

A specific phobia is a marked and persistent fear of a particular object or situation, other than those associated with social phobia or agoraphobia. When an individual with a phobia is exposed to the feared object or event, he or she will have a panic attack or some other anxiety response. Adults with a specific phobia should be able to recognize that their fear is irrational and excessive. The onset of a specific phobia is typically in childhood or in the mid-20s. According to the DSM-IV, there are five subtypes of specific phobia:
- Animal
- Natural environment
- Situational
- Blood-injection-injury
- Other

The blood-injection-injury subtype has different physical symptoms than the others. Individuals with blood-injection-injury phobia have a brief increase in heart rate and blood pressure, followed by a drop in both, often ending in a brief loss of consciousness. Other phobic reactions just entail the increase in heart rate and blood pressure, without loss of consciousness.

The two-factor theory proposed by Mower asserts that phobias are the result of avoidance conditioning, when an individual associates a neutral or controlled stimulus with an anxiety-causing, unconditioned stimulus. The phobic reinforces a strategy of avoidance because it prevents anxiety (even though the neutral stimulus was not to blame for the anxiety in the first place). Another theory for the etiology of phobias is offered by social learning theorists, who state that phobic behaviors are learned by watching avoidance strategies used by one's parents. As with panic disorder, in vivo exposure is considered the best treatment for a specific phobia.

- 63 -

Relaxation and breathing techniques are also helpful in dispelling fear and controlling physical response.

Social phobia
The characteristics of social phobia are a marked and persistent fear of social situations or situations in which the individual may be called upon to perform. Typically, the individual fears criticism and evaluation by others. The response to the feared situation is an immediate panic attack. Individuals with social phobia either avoid the feared situation or endure it with much distress. Adults should be able to recognize that their fear is excessive and irrational. As with other phobias, social phobia is best treated with exposure in combination with social skills and cognitive therapy. Antidepressants and the beta-blocker propanolol are helpful for treating social phobia.

Obsessive-compulsive disorder

An individual may be diagnosed with obsessive-compulsive disorder (OCD) if he or she has recurrent obsessions and/or compulsions that are severe enough to cause significant distress, to be time-consuming, or to interfere significantly with the individual's normal routine or relationships. Obsessions are persistent thoughts, impulses or images that the person experiences as senseless or intrusive, and that cause distress. Compulsions are repetitious and deliberate behaviors or mental acts that the person is driven to do either because of an obsession or according to rigid self-imposed rules. The aim of compulsions for the individual is to reduce distress or prevent some bad thing from happening. Often, though, the compulsion will have no logical connection to the feared event. In order to diagnose an adult with OCD, he or she must be aware at some point that his or her obsessions and compulsions are irrational and excessive.

OCD is equally likely to occur in adult males and adult females. The average age of onset is lower for males, so the rates of OCD among male children and adolescents are slightly higher than among females. Evidence suggests that OCD is caused by low levels of serotonin. Structurally, OCD seems to be linked to overactivity in the right caudate nucleus. The most effective treatment for OCD is exposure with response prevention in tandem with medication, usually either the tricyclic clomipramine or an SSRI. Therapies that provide help with stopping thought patterns seem to be especially successful in battling OCD. When drugs are used alone, there remains a high risk of relapse.

Post traumatic stress disorder

An individual may be diagnosed with post traumatic stress disorder (PTSD) if he or she develops symptoms after exposure to an extreme trauma. An extreme trauma entails: Witnessing the death or injury of another person; experiencing injury to self; or learning about the unexpected or violent death or injury of a family member or friend. The traumatic event must elicit a reaction of intense fear, helplessness, or horror. The characteristic symptoms of PTSD are:
- Persistent re-experiencing of the event
- Persistent avoidance of stimuli associated with the trauma
- Persistent symptoms of increased arousal (difficulty concentrating, staying awake, or falling asleep)

These symptoms must have been present for at least a month; symptoms may not begin until three or more months after the event.

The preferred treatment for PTSD is a comprehensive cognitive-behavioral approach that includes:

- Exposure
- Cognitive restructuring
- Anxiety management
- SSRIS to relieve symptoms of PTSD and comorbid conditions

Some psychologists criticize single-session psychological debriefings, because they believe one session amplifies the effects of a traumatic event. Another controversial therapy used to treat PTSD is eye movement desensitization and reprocessing; the positive benefits of this therapy may be more to do with the exposure that goes along with it than with the eye movements themselves.

Acute stress disorder

Acute stress disorder has symptoms similar to those of post traumatic stress disorder. Acute stress disorder is distinguished by symptoms that occur within four weeks of the traumatic event and last for between two days and four weeks. An individual is diagnosed with acute stress disorder when he or she has three or more dissociative symptoms, which include:
- Numbed senses
- Emotional detachment
- Derealization
- Dissociative amnesia

An individual with acute stress disorder persistently relives the traumatic event, to the point where he or she takes steps to avoid contact with stimuli that bring the event to mind, and experiences severe anxiety when reminiscing about the event.

Generalized anxiety disorder

Individuals may be diagnosed with generalized anxiety disorder (GAD) if they have excessive anxiety about multiple events or activities. This anxiety must

have existed for at least six months and must be difficult for the individual to control. The anxiety must be disproportionate to the feared event. Anxiety must include at least three of the following:
- Restlessness
- Difficulty swallowing (dysphagia)
- Feeling on edge (hypervigilance)
- Fatigue on exertion
- Difficulty concentrating
- Irritability
- Muscle tension
- Sleep disturbance

The treatment for GAD usually entails a multicomponent cognitive-behavioral therapy, occasionally accompanied by pharmacotherapy. SSRI antidepressants and the anxiolytic buspirone have both demonstrated success in diminishing the symptoms of GAD.

Somatization disorder

Somatization disorder (formerly hysteria) is a somatoform disorder, meaning that it suggests a medical condition but is not fully explainable by the medical condition, substance abuse, or other medical disorder. Individuals with somatoform disorder often describe their problems in dramatic, overstated, and ambiguous terms. Somatoform disorders cause clinically significant distress or impairment, and are not produced intentionally. A somatization disorder involves recurrent multiple somatic complaints beginning prior to age 30 and persisting for several years, for which medical attention has been sought, but no physical explanation has been found. In order to be classified as a somatization disorder, the complaints must include at least:
- Four pain symptoms
- Two gastrointestinal symptoms
- One sexual symptom and

- One pseudoneurological symptom

Conversion disorder

Conversion disorder is a somatoform disorder characterized by either loss of bodily functions or symptoms of a serious physical disease. The patient becomes blind, mute, or paralyzed in response to an acute stressor. Occasionally, patients develop hyperanesthesia, analgesia, tics, belching, vomiting, or coughing spells. These symptoms do not conform to physiological mechanisms, and testing reveals no underlying physical disease. The sensory loss, movement loss, or repetitive physical symptoms are not intentional. The patient is not malingering to avoid work, or factitiously trying for financial gain. The symptoms of a conversion disorder can often be removed with hypnosis or Amytal interview. Some researchers believe that simply suggesting to the patient that his or her symptoms will go away is the best way to relieve them. The patient can develop complications, like seizures, from disuse of body parts.

The etiology of conversion disorder is explained by the DSM in terms of two psychological mechanisms:
- A conversion disorder may be used for primary gain when the symptoms keep an internal conflict or need out of the consciousness.
- A conversion disorder is used for secondary gain when the symptoms help the individual avoid an unpleasant activity or obtain support from the environment.

In order to diagnose a conversion disorder, there must be evidence of involuntary psychological factors. Conversion disorder is occasionally confused with factitious disorder and malingering, both of which are voluntary.

Hypochondriasis and undifferentiated somatoform disorder

Individuals with hypochondriasis have an unrealistic preoccupation with a serious illness that is based on a misappraisal of bodily symptoms. This preoccupation remains despite an absence of medical evidence. Individuals with hypochondriasis likely know a great deal about their condition, and frequently go to a number of different doctors searching for a professional opinion that confirms their own. Individuals are diagnosed with undifferentiated somatoform disorder when they have one or more year-long physical complaints that cannot be fully explained by a medical condition or the presence of a substance. These symptoms cannot, however, meet the criteria for somatization disorder or another mental disorder.

Factitious disorder

An individual diagnosed with factitious disorder (FD) intentionally manifests physical or psychological symptoms to satisfy an intrapsychic need to fill the role of a sick person. The patient with factitious disorder presents the illness in an exaggerated manner and avoids interrogation that might expose the falsity. FD patients may undergo multiple surgeries and invasive medical procedures. FD patients often hide insurance claims and hospital discharge forms. A disturbing variation of FD is Munchausen's syndrome by proxy, in which a caregiver intentionally produces symptoms in another individual. Usually, a mother makes her young child ill.

Malingering is feigning physical symptoms to avoid something specific, like going to work, or to gain a specific reward. Consider malingering as a possibility when:

- A person obtains a medical evaluation for legal reasons or to apply for insurance compensation
- There is marked inconsistency between the patient's complaint and the objective findings, or if the patient does not cooperate with a diagnostic evaluation or prescribed treatment
- The patient has an antisocial personality disorder

Malingering contrasts with factitious disorder because in FD the patient does not feign physical symptoms for personal gain or to avoid an adverse event.

Dissociative disorders

Dissociative disorders are a disruption in consciousness, identity, memory, or perception of the environment that is not due to the effects of a substance or a general medical condition. Conditions included under the heading of dissociative disorders are:

- Dissociative amnesia
- Dissociative fugue
- Dissociative identity disorder
- Depersonalization disorder

Cultural influences can cause or amplify some of the symptoms of dissociative disorders, so take these into account when making a diagnosis. For instance, many religious ceremonies try to foster a dissociative psychological experience; individuals participating in such a ceremony may display symptoms of dissociative disorder without requiring treatment.

Dissociative amnesia

Individuals may be diagnosed with dissociative amnesia if they have more than one episode in which they are unable to remember important personal information, and this memory loss cannot be attributed to ordinary forgetfulness. The gaps in the individual's memory are likely to be related to a traumatic event. The DSM distinguishes five patterns of dissociative amnesia:

- Localized, in which the patient is unable to remember all events around a defined period
- Selective, in which the patient cannot recall some events pertaining to a circumscribed period
- Generalized, in which memory loss spans the patient's entire life
- Continuous, in which the patient is unable to remember events subsequent to a specific time and through to the present
- Systematized, in which the patient has no recall of a certain category of information

Dissociative fugue and depersonalization disorder

A dissociative fugue is an abrupt, unexpected, purposeful flight from home, or another stressful location, coupled with an inability to remember the past. The patient is unable to remember his or her identity and assumes a new identity. Fugues are psychological protection against extreme stressors like bankruptcy, divorce, separation, suicidal or homicidal ideation, and rejection. Fugues happen in wars, natural disasters, and severe accidents. Fugues affect 2 in every 1,000 Americans. There will be no recollection of events that occur during the fugue. Individuals in a fugue state may seem normal to strangers. Depersonalization disorder is diagnosed when an individual has one or more episodes in which he or she feels detached from his or her own mental processes or body. In order to be diagnosed, this condition must be intense

- 67 -

enough to cause significant distress or functional impairment.

Sexual dysfunctions

Sexual dysfunctions are categorized as lifelong or acquired, and generalized or situational, depending on their cause. Generalized dysfunctions occur with every sexual partner in all circumstances. Situational dysfunctions only occur under certain circumstances. The cause may be psychological, physical, or both. Many clinical guides refer to sexual dysfunctions as either primary or secondary. Primary dysfunctions are those that have always existed. Secondary dysfunctions are those that developed after a history of normal functioning.

Examples:
- Dyspareunia is any genital pain associated with sexual intercourse.
- Vaginismus is involuntary spasms in the pubococcygeus muscle in the outer third of the vagina, which make it difficult to have sexual intercourse.

Any patient with sexual dysfunction should be given a medical evaluation for diabetes, pelvic scars, kidney disease, hypertension, and drug interactions. Use sleep studies to determine if an impotent male gets an erection at night, and determine whether the cause of impotence is physical or psychological. Psychological impotence can be treated with cognitive-behavioral therapy. Sex therapy is most helpful in treating vaginismus and premature ejaculation. Sensate focus is used to reduce performance anxiety and increase sexual excitement. Kegel exercises, which strengthen the pubococcygeus muscle, can improve sexual pleasure. As for pharmacotherapy, Viagra is helpful in attaining and maintaining erections, and Rogaine is helpful for female orgasm.

Male erectile and orgasmic disorders
A sexual dysfunction is any condition in which the sexual response cycle is disturbed or there is pain during sexual intercourse, and this causes distress or interpersonal difficulty. There are five major sexual dysfunctions. Male erectile disorder is the inability to attain or maintain an erection. This condition is linked to diabetes, liver and kidney disease, multiple sclerosis, and the use of antipsychotic, antidepressant, and hypertensive drugs. Orgasmic disorders are any delay or absence of orgasm after the normal sexual excitement phase. Premature ejaculation is orgasm that occurs with a minimum of stimulation and before the person desires it. Premature ejaculation may be in part due to deficiencies in serotonin.

Paraphilias
Paraphilias are intense, recurrent sexual urges or behaviors involving either nonhuman objects, nonconsenting partners (including children), or the suffering or humiliation of oneself or one's partner. Common paraphilias include:
- Fetishism
- Transvestism
- Pedophilia
- Exhibitionism
- Voyeurism
- Sexual masochism
- Sexual sadism
- Frotteurism (rubbing against a nonconsenting person)

The most common treatment for paraphilia was in vivo aversion therapy, but now it is more common for treatment to include covert sensitization, in which the imagination is given aversion therapy. The medication Depo-Provera has been found to relieve paraphiliac symptoms for

- 68 -

many men, although this relief ceases as soon as the man stops taking the drug.

Gender identity disorder

Gender identity disorder is identification with the opposite gender and discomfort with one's own gender identity. Children with gender identity disorder may declare their desire to join the other sex, and may wear clothes associated with the opposite sex. Adolescents and adults will want to alter both their primary and secondary sex characteristics, and may attempt to pass for a member of the opposite sex in public. Though males with gender identity disorder may be attracted to anyone, females are likely to be solely homosexual. The onset of gender identity disorder is typically in childhood, between the ages of 2 and 4. Most of those who experience these symptoms as children will be homosexual as adults. Gender identity disorder may be confused with transvestic fetishism or simple nonconformity.

Sleep disorders

Sleep disorders may be either dyssomnias or parasomnias, depending on whether they are disturbances in the amount or quality of sleep or behavioral/physiological abnormalities during sleep.
Dyssomnias include:
- Primary insomnia
- Primary hypersomnia
- Narcolepsy (extreme daytime sleepiness accompanied by cataplexy [loss of muscle tone] and hypnagogic hallucinations)
- Breathing-related sleep disorder
- Circadian rhythm sleep disorder

Parasomnias include:
- Nightmare disorder
- Sleep terror disorder, which usually afflicts young children, marked by violent arousal soon after falling asleep, difficulty waking, and no memory of the event in the morning
- Sleepwalking disorder

Anorexia nervosa

The characteristics of anorexia nervosa are:
- Refusal to maintain a healthy weight
- Fear of gaining weight
- Significant disturbance in the perception of one's own weight
- Amenorrhea in females

A general standard used to determine the minimum healthy body weight is that it should be at least 85% of the norm for the individual's height and weight. Restricting type anorexics lose weight through fasting, dieting, and excessive exercise. Binging/purging types do so by eating a great deal and then either vomiting it or inducing immediate defecation with laxatives. Anorexics are preoccupied with food. The physical symptoms of starvation are constipation, cold intolerance, lethargy, and bradycardia. The physical problems associated with purging are anemia, impaired renal function, cardiac abnormalities, dental problems, and osteoporosis.

The vast majority of anorexics are female, and the onset of anorexia is usually in mid-to-late adolescence. Onset may be associated with a stressful life event. Some studies associated anorexia with middle and upper class families that have a tendency towards competition and success. Anorexic girls are likely to be introverted, nonassertive, and conscientious. Their mothers are likely to also be very concerned about food intake and weight. The immediate goal of any treatment program is to help the patient

- 69 -

gain weight. Sometimes this requires hospitalization. Cognitive therapy is also often employed to correct the individual's misconceptions about healthy weight and nutrition.

Bulimia nervosa

The characteristics of bulimia nervosa are:
- Recurrent episodes of binge eating in which the individual feels out of control
- Unhealthy behavior aimed at compensating for these binges (vomiting, taking laxatives, extreme exercise)
- A harsh conception of self that is largely based on weight

Binge eating and compensatory behavior must have occurred at least twice a month for three months in order for the diagnosis to be made. Binges are often caused by interpersonal stress and may entail a staggering caloric intake. The medical complications associated with bulimia are fluid and electrolyte disturbances, metabolic alkalosis, metabolic acidosis, dental problems, and menstrual abnormalities.

As with anorexia, the vast majority of bulimics are female. The onset is typically in late adolescence or early adulthood, and may follow a period of dieting. There are indications of a genetic etiology for bulimia. Also, there are links between bulimia and low levels of the endogenous opioid beta-endorphin, as well as low levels of serotonin and norepinephrine. The main point of any treatment for bulimia is encouraging the individual to get control of eating, and modifying unhealthy beliefs about body shape and nutrition. Treatment often involves cognitive-behavioral techniques like self-monitoring, stimulus control, cognitive restructuring, problem-solving, and self-distraction. Some antidepressants, like imipramine, have been effective at reducing instances of binging and purging.

Adjustment disorders

Adjustment disorders appear as maladaptive reactions to one or more identifiable psychosocial stressors. In order to make the diagnosis, the onset of symptoms must be within three months of the stressor, and the condition must cause impairments in social, occupational, or academic performance. Adjustment disorder is seldom diagnosed unless symptoms remit within six months after the termination of the stressor or its consequences, though the diagnosis can also be made over longer periods if the stressor is chronic or has enduring consequences. Adjustment disorders are given the following classifications based on the prevailing symptoms:
- Depressed mood
- Anxiety
- Mixed anxiety and depressed mood
- Disturbance of conduct or mixed disturbance of emotions and conduct

Personality disorders

Personality disorders occur when an individual has developed personality traits so maladaptive and entrenched that they cause personal distress or interfere significantly with functioning. The DSM lists five traits involved in personality disorders:
- Neuroticism
- Extraversion/introversion
- Openness to experience
- Agreeableness/antagonism
- Conscientiousness

Paranoid personality disorder
Paranoid personality disorder is a pervasive pattern of distrust and

suspiciousness that involves believing the actions and thoughts of other people to be directed antagonistically against oneself. In order to make the diagnosis, the individual must have at least four of the following symptoms:

- Suspects that others are somehow harming him or her
- Doubts the trustworthiness of others
- Reluctant to confide in others
- Suspicious without justification about the fidelity of one's partner

Schizoid personality disorder

Schizoid personality disorder is a pervasive lack of interest in relationships with others, as well as a limited range of emotional expression in contacts with others. For a diagnosis of schizoid personality disorder, at least four of these symptoms must be present:

- Avoidance of or displeasure in close relationships
- Always chooses solitude
- Little interest in sexual relationships
- Takes pleasure in few activities
- Indifference to praise or criticism
- Emotional coldness or detachment

Schizotypal personality disorder

Schizotypal personality disorder is pervasive social deficits and oddities of cognition, perception, and behavior. A diagnosis of schizotypal personality disorder requires four of the following:

- Ideas of reference
- Odd beliefs
- Magical thinking
- Bodily illusions
- Suspiciousness
- Social anxiety
- Inappropriate or constricted affect
- Peculiarities in behavior or appearance

Antisocial personality disorder

Antisocial personality disorder is classified in the DSM as a Cluster B personality disorder, meaning that it has to do with dramatic, emotional, or erratic behaviors. It is a general lack of concern for the rights and feelings of others. In order to receive a diagnosis of antisocial personality disorder, the individual must bee at least 18 and have had a history of conduct disorder before age 15. In addition, the individual must have shown at least three of the following symptoms before the age of 15:

- Failure to conform to social laws and norms
- Deceitfulness
- Impulsivity
- Reckless disregard for the safety of self and others
- Consistent irresponsibility
- Lack of remorse

Antisocial personality disorder may also include an inflated opinion of self, superficial charm, and a lack of empathy for others.

Borderline personality disorder

Borderline personality disorder is a pervasive pattern of instability in social relationships, self-image, and affect, coupled with marked impulsivity. A diagnosis of borderline personality disorder requires five of the following symptoms:

- Frantic efforts to avoid being abandoned
- A pattern of unstable and intense personal relationships, in which there is alternation between idealization and devaluation
- Instability of self-image
- Potentially self-destructive impulsivity in at least two areas
- Recurrent suicide threats or gestures
- Affective instability

- Chronic feelings of emptiness

The changes in self-identity may manifest as shifts in career goals and sexual identity; impulsivity may manifest as unsafe sex, reckless driving practices, and substance abuse.

Borderline personality disorder is most common in people between the ages of 19 and 34. Most individuals see substantial improvement over a period of 15 years. Impulsive symptoms are the first to recede. Dialectical behavior therapy (DBT) is often used to treat borderline personality disorder; it combines cognitive-behavioral therapy with the assumption of Rogers that the patient must accept his or her problem before any progress can be made. There are three basic strategies associated with dialectical behavior therapy:
- Group skills training
- Individual outpatient therapy
- Telephone consultations

Regular DBT has reduced the number of suicides and violent acts committed by individuals with borderline personality disorder.

Histrionic personality disorder
Histrionic personality disorder is excessive emotionality and attention-seeking behavior. Five symptoms from the following list must be present for a diagnosis:
- Annoyance or discomfort when not receiving attention
- Inappropriate sexual provocation
- Rapidly shifting and shallow emotions
- Vague and impressionistic speech
- Exaggerated expression of emotion
- Easily influenced by others
- Misapprehension of relationships as more intimate than they are

Narcissistic personality disorder
Narcissistic personality disorder is grandiose behavior along with a lack of empathy and a need for admiration. The individual must exhibit five of these symptoms for diagnosis:
- Grandiose sense of self-importance
- Fantasies of own power and beauty
- Belief in personal uniqueness
- Need for excessive admiration
- Sense of entitlement
- Exploitation of others
- Lack of empathy

Avoidant personality disorder
According to the DSM, avoidant personality disorder is a cluster C personality, meaning it involves feelings of anxiety or fearfulness. It is a pervasive pattern of social inhibition, feelings of inadequacy, and hypersensitivity to negative evaluation. A person with avoidant personality disorder exhibits at least four of these symptoms:
- Avoiding work or school activities that involve interpersonal contact
- Unwillingness to associate with any person who may withhold approval
- Preoccupation with concerns about being criticized or rejected
- Conception of self as socially inept, inferior, or unappealing to others
- General reluctance to take personal risks or engage in dangerous behavior

Dependent personality disorder
Dependent personality disorder is excessive reliance on others. A diagnosis of dependent personality disorder requires five of these symptoms:
- Difficulty making decision without advice

- 72 -

- Need for others to assume responsibility for one's actions
- Fear of disagreeing with others
- Difficulty self-initiating projects
- Feelings of helplessness or discomfort when alone
- Separate abnormal behavior in this vein from behavior that is culturally acceptable to the individual, or normal for a child

Obsessive-compulsive personality disorder

Obsessive-compulsive personality disorder is a persistent preoccupation with organization and mental/interpersonal control. Four of these symptoms are required for the diagnosis of obsessive-compulsive personality disorder:

- Preoccupation with rules and details
- Perfectionism that interferes with progress
- Excessive devotion to work
- Counterproductive rigidity about beliefs and morality
- Inability to throw away old objects
- Reluctance to delegate authority to others

Psychological assessment terminology

A standardized test is one in which the questions and potential responses from all tests can be compared with one another. Every aspect of the test must remain consistent. A behavioral assessment assumes that an individual can only be evaluated in relation to his or her environment. Behavioral assessments must include a stimulus, organism, response, and consequences (SORC). A dynamic assessment involves systematic deviation from the standardized test for the purpose of determining whether the individual

benefits from aid. This includes the process called "testing the limits," in which an examinee is provided with a sequence of extra clues. Domain-referenced testing breaks evaluation into specific domains of ability, for instance, reading or math ability.

Actuarial and clinical predictions

Actuarial (statistical) predictions are those based on empirically-validated data; they may incorporate regressive or multiple regressive equations. Clinical predictions are based on the intuition and experience of the observing clinician.

Assessing children

In order to obtain a useful interview from a child, the clinician must establish a good rapport and maintain the cooperation of the child. Establish rapport by:

- Using descriptive statements to encourage the child (e.g., "You're doing well.")
- Using reflective statements that encourage the child to think about what he or she has said (e.g., "You sound very angry about that.")
- Praising the child specifically for those things that contribute to a good interview
- Avoiding criticism

Some clinicians use anatomically correct dolls to help children discuss issues of sexual function and abuse.

Culturally-diverse populations

Guidelines psychologists should remember when assessing members of culturally-diverse populations are:

- Clarify the purpose of the evaluation for the examinee
- Be sensitive to any test material that unfairly discriminates against individuals of a particular culture

- Use an alternate method of assessment that is more appropriate to the individual, if necessary
- Before beginning an assessment, familiarize yourself with the norms and values of the examinee's culture
- Recognize that your job is to establish a good rapport with the examinee, and call a replacement psychologist if you cannot establish rapport

Intelligence

There are a few different ways of looking at intelligence. Spearman proposed the existence of a general intelligence factor (g) and any number of specific intelligence factors (s) unique to a task. Horn and Cattell adjusted this model by dividing g into two categories: Crystallized intelligence (Gc), the knowledge and skills acquired through education and experience; and fluid intelligence (Gf), the ability to solve new problems. Sternberg asserted that successful intelligence is composed of analytical, practical, and creative elements, and argued that standardized tests focus almost exclusively on analytical elements. Gardner proposed eight different kinds of intelligence: Linguistic, musical, logical-mathematical, spatial, bodily-kinesthetic, interpersonal, intrapersonal, and naturalistic.

Research has shown that individuals with a genetic similarity have similar levels of intelligence. Heritability estimates for intelligence range from about .6 to .8, meaning that 32%—64% of the variability in intelligence comes from genetic factors. Other research has sought to describe the link between environment and intelligence. One environmental factor that has been consistently linked to performance on

intelligence tests is socioeconomic status. The Flynn effect is the gradual increase in IQ test scores that occurs in industrialized nations. The Flynn effect does not seem to involve genetic factors, as it is a change of 3—6 IQ points over just one or two generations.

Once an individual enters school, his or her IQ scores will remain relatively stable through the rest of development. Most research suggests that intelligence continues to increase until about the age of 60, or until the period just before death. The Seattle Longitudinal Study was conducted by Schaie et al. at seven year intervals from 1956 to 2005. The study concluded "that there is no uniform pattern of age-related changes across all intellectual abilities, and that studies of an overall index of intellectual ability (IQ) therefore do not suffice to monitor age changes and age differences in intellectual functioning for either individuals or groups." Subsequent research in this line indicates perceptual speed is the only area in which the elderly experience significant decline. Research conducted by Horn indicated that while crystallized intelligence will continue to increase throughout life, fluid intelligence will peak in adolescence and decline thereafter. Decline in fluid intelligence has been linked to diminished processing speed, stemming from reductions in working memory.

Research suggests that females are better on certain tests of verbal ability, while males generally perform better on some tests of spatial and quantitative ability. Males are more likely to be at the extreme ends of score distribution for every type of intelligence. As for racial differences, whites outperform African-Americans on the Stanford-Binet, Wechsler, and other IQ tests by about one standard deviation, though this margin has diminished over the past few decades. Many researchers argue that whites perform better on these

- 74 -

tests because the tests were constructed from a white perspective. Critics cite two kinds of test bias: Slope bias, in which a predictor is more accurate for one group than for another; and intercept bias, in which a predictor consistently over-predicts or under-predicts performance for a particular group.

Stanford-Binet intelligence scales
The Stanford-Binet intelligence scales (SB5) measure cognitive ability, assist in psychoeducational evaluation, diagnose developmental disabilities, and perform various assessments for individuals 2 to 85+. The SB5 test measures five categories of intelligence:
- Fluid reasoning
- Knowledge
- Quantitative reasoning
- Visual-spatial processing
- Working memory

SB5 measures each of these domains through both verbal and nonverbal activities. Subtests indicate which components of the SB5 are appropriate for the examinee. These subtest scores are combined to give four kinds of composite score:
- Factor index
- Domain
- Abbreviated battery
- Full-scale IQ

The standardization sample of the SB5 was stratified to match the 2000 US census in terms of socioeconomic status, geographic region, and race.

WAIS-III
The third edition of the Wechsler Adult Intelligence Scale (WAIS-III) is used to measure the intellectual ability of late-adolescents and adults. Wechsler considered intelligence to be a global ability made up of a number of interrelated functions. This interrelationship between the various

types of intelligence is described in the current test in terms of four tiers:
- Full-scale IQ
- Verbal and performance IQ
- Factor indices
- Subtest scores

There are 7 verbal subtests on the WAIS-III:
- Vocabulary
- Information
- Digit span (the ability to remember a series of numbers both forwards and backwards)
- Arithmetic
- Comprehension
- Similarities
- Letter-number sequencing (a good test of short-term memory and attention)

There are 7 performance subtests on the WAIS-III:
- Picture-completion
- Picture arrangement
- Block design
- Digit symbol-coding (a good measure of visual-motor coordination and processing speed)
- Matrix reasoning
- Object assembly
- Symbol search

The administration of the test begins with picture completion and then a series of alternating verbal and nonverbal subtests. The only exception to this is that the digit span and information subtests are administered together. Some tests will be timed, while others will be allowed to go on until the examinee has finished. The raw scores for each subtest are converted into scaled scores with a standard conversion table. In the subtests, the mean score is 10 and the standard deviation is 3. For the full-scale, performance and verbal IQs and factor indices, the mean is 100 and the standard deviation is 15.

Level I of the WAIS-III is the full-scale IQ, which is a global estimate of the subject's mental ability. This score should be interpreted with a 90—95% confidence interval. Use caution if there is a large discrepancy between verbal and performance IQs, factor index scores, or subtest scores. Level II pertains to the verbal and performance IQs and to the factor indices. If the verbal-performance (V-P) discrepancy is greater than 12, then it is considered statistically significant. There are a number of reasons why an individual might have a large V-P discrepancy or large discrepancies in factor scores, including ADHD, Alzheimer's disease, a high professional attainment in one area, or poor-visual motor integration.

Level III of the WAIS-III pertains to subtest variability. This section of the test issues a profile analysis, which compares each subtest score to the mean full-scale, verbal, or performance score in order to evaluate the strengths and weaknesses of the candidate. Level IV pertains to intrasubtest variability. If performance is sporadic, the individual may have been missing items on purpose or may have diffuse brain damage. Level V of the WAIS-III pertains to qualitative analysis, in which the subject's responses are evaluated for clues to his or her personality or cognitive functioning.

Individuals who take the WAIS-III more than once typically do better the second time, as a result of so-called practice effects. The WAIS-III was standardized by race, age, sex, and socioeconomic status in accordance with the 1995 US census.

WISC-IV and WPPSI-III
The WISC-IV is a variation of the WAIS-III made especially for children between the

ages of 6 and 17. WISC-IV is closely based on neurocognitive models of information processing, and measures:
- Fluid intelligence
- Crystallized intelligence
- Visual processing
- Short-term memory
- Processing speed
- Quantitative knowledge

It gives scores through four indexes:
- Verbal comprehension
- Perceptual reasoning
- Working memory
- Processing speed

Use highly asymmetrical scores on the subtests to diagnose autism, ADHD, and other learning disorders. The WPPSI-I is made for children between the ages of 2.5 and 7.25. For children that are either 2 or 3 years old, the test can measure verbal comprehension, and perceptual organization; for older children these can be measured with processing speed.

Kaufman tests
The Kaufman tests include the Kaufman Assessment Battery for Children (KABC-II) and the Kaufman Brief Intelligence Test (KBIT-II). The KABC-II measures cognitive ability in children between the ages of 3 and 18. It provides scores on five scales:
- Simultaneous
- Sequential
- Planning
- Learning
- Knowledge

Minimize verbal instructions and responses on these tests to make them fair for all cultures.

Cognitive Assessment System
The Cognitive Assessment System (CAS) is based on the PASS (planning, attention, simultaneous processing, and sequential processing) model of intelligence, and is

appropriate for children between the ages of 5 and 18.

Slosson tests
The Slosson tests were designed to be fast ways of estimating intelligence in order to identify children at risk of educational failure.

Infant and preschool tests
Tests administered to children aged 2 or younger are good at screening for developmental delays and disabilities, but have poor predictive validity. The Denver II screens for developmental delays by observing a child's performance in four developmental domains:

- Personal-social
- Fine motor adaptive
- Language
- Gross motor

If a child fails an item that 90% of younger children pass, he or she is scored as having a developmental delay.

The Bayley Scales of Infant Development (BSID-II) assess the development of children 1 to 42 months on mental, motor, and behavior rating scales. The Fagan Test of Intelligence tries to gauge the information processing speed of an infant, in order to predict childhood IQ. It does this by introducing novel stimuli and observing the reaction time of the child.

Physical disabilities
The Americans with Disabilities Act of 1990 declares that any test administered to a disabled job applicant or employee should reflect only the person's ability on the test, and not his or her disability. Employers are also required to make reasonable accommodations for disabled employees. The Columbia Mental Maturity Scale (CMMS) is a test of general reasoning ability that does not require fine motor skills or verbal responses. It is useful for assessing students with cerebral palsy, brain damage, mental

retardation, and speech impediments. The Peabody Picture Vocabulary Test measures receptive vocabulary without requiring verbal responses. The Haptic Intelligence Scale uses tactile stimuli, so it is good for assessing blind and partially-sighted individuals. The Hiskey-Nebraska Test of Learning Aptitude contains twelve nonverbal subtests which can be administered verbally or in pantomime; it is good for assessing children with hearing impairments.

Culture-fair tests
In order to minimize the advantages of white, middle-class examinees, there has been a movement to develop culture-fair tests. At present, there is no research to suggest that culture-fair tests are any better at predicting academic achievement or job performance. The Leiter International Performance Scale (Leiter-R) is a culture-fair assessment of cognitive abilities for people between the ages of 2 and 21. Since it does not require verbal instructions, it can also be useful for examinees with language problems or hearing impairments. The test measures visualization, reasoning, memory, and attention. Raven's Progressive Matrices is a nonverbal measure of general intelligence; it strives to avoid rewarding specific education or cultural learning.

Group intelligence tests
Many different organizations, from schools to the armed forces, administer group intelligence tests. The Kuhlman-Anderson Test is for children in grades K—12; it measures verbal and quantitative intelligence. This test is unique in that it relies less on language than do other individual and group tests. The Woodcock Johnson III consists of a test of cognitive abilities and a test of achievement; the latter of which measures oral language and academic achievement. The Wonderlic Personnel Test takes about 12 minutes to fill out

with paper and pencil; it purports to measure the mental ability of adults. The Wonderlic is a good predictor of performance, but some critics maintain that it unfairly discriminates against some cultural groups in certain jobs.

Academic ability testing
Ability tests measure current status and predict future academic achievement. Curriculum-based measurement is any form of assessment that focuses on the student's ability to perform the work of the school curriculum. Usually, a teacher will set a minimum standard for performance and provide remedial attention for any student who performs below this level. Performance-based assessment evaluates students on their execution of a task or creation of a product. It is meant to be egalitarian and culture-fair. The Scholastic Achievement Test (SAT) measures verbal and mathematical reasoning skills; it is used to predict the college success of high school students. Studies show that the SAT is more effective as a predictor when it is combined with grade-point average. The Graduate Record Exam (GRE) measures general scholastic abilities and may be taken in lieu of a normal secondary course of study.

Multiple aptitude test batteries and special batteries
Multiple aptitude test batteries measure ability in a number of different areas; one of their weakness is that they often lack adequate differential validity, meaning that the various parts of the test do not have different validities for different categories. Differential aptitude tests (DAT) identify job-related abilities and are used for career counseling and employee selection. The general aptitude test battery (GATB) was developed by the US Employment Service for vocational counseling and job placement. There are other tests used to measure special

aptitudes. Psychomotor tests are used to assess speed, coordination, and general movement responses. These typically have low validity coefficients because they are highly specific and susceptible to practice effects. Mechanical aptitude tests are used to assess dexterity, perceptual and spatial skills, and mechanical reasoning. The different skills that fall within this category are relatively independent.

Structured personality tests
A structured (as opposed to projective) personality test measures emotional, social, and personal traits and behaviors through a series of multiple-choice questions or other unambiguous stimuli. There are four common strategies for structured personality tests:

- Logical content method bases its questions on deductive logic and a systematic theory of personality
- Theoretical method measures the prevalence of the personality structures identified by a particular theory of personality
- Empirical criterion keying has questions that are administered to different criterion groups; there are items that distinguish between the groups in the test
- Factor analysis tests administer a large number of items to a large group of examinees, and then analyze their answers for any correlations

MMPI-2
The Minnesota Multiphasic Personality Inventory-2 (MMPI-2) was originally developed to diagnose psychiatric patients. The attitude of the examinee towards the test is indicated by his or her scores on four validity scales:

- A lie (L) scale, which measures the degree to which the examinee lies in order to make him or herself look better or worse

- A frequency (F) scale, which indicates whether an examinee is rushing through or stalling during the exam
- A correction (K) scale, which measures the degree to which the person corrects his or her answers after they are given, which could indicate uncertainty or untruthfulness
- A cannot say (?) Scale, which measures the degree of trouble the examinee has in answering questions

The MMPI-2 takes raw scores and converts them into T-scores with a mean of 50 and a standard deviation of 10. If a person scores above a 65, it is considered to be clinically significant. The most common use of the MMPI-2 is as an assessment of personality and behavior through profile analysis. Most of the time, the code is simply the two highest scores on the various subtests. The validity scales are then used to ensure that the profile is the result of an honest attempt at the test. The standardization sample approximated the 1980 US census in age, gender, race, and social class. One criticism of the standardization sample of the MMPI-2 is that it has a disproportionate number of college graduates.

EPPS, 16 PF, NEO-PI-R
The Edwards Personal Preference Schedule, based on the personality theory of Murray, contains 225 items that present an either-or choice to the examinee. This test strives to prevent examinees from responding in ways that they know are socially desirable. The test provides ipsative scores, meaning that the strengths of the candidate are given comparative, rather than absolute, value. The Sixteen Personality Factor Questionnaire is a factor analysis-based exam that identifies 16 primary personality traits and 5 secondary traits. The NEO-Personality Inventory attempts to gauge an individual's level of the Big Five personality traits (extraversion, agreeableness, conscientiousness, neuroticism, and openness to experience). These traits are then broken down into facets, for example, neuroticism contains anxiety and depression.

The Rorschach Inkblot and TAT projective personality tests
Projective personality tests assume that unstructured and ambiguous stimuli can elicit meaningful responses from individuals, particularly about personality and underlying conflicts. Projective tests are typically open-ended and therefore less susceptible to faking. The most famous projective test is the Rorschach Inkblot Test, in which a person is presented with ten cards containing bilaterally symmetrical inkblots and asked to free associate on the design. Scoring the Rorschach is very complex, but relies on the following dimensions of the individual's response:
- Location (as in where the subject sees whatever he or she describes)
- Determinants (why the subjects saw what they saw)
- Form quality (resemblance of the response to the inkblot)
- Content
- Frequency of occurrence

The Rorschach may provide interesting results, but its use in clinical work is dubious. Another projective test is the Thematic Apperception Test (TAT), in which the examinee is asked to make up a story based on a random presentation of picture cards.

Neuropsychological assessments

The Halstead-Reitan Neuropsychological Battery (H-R) is a group of tests that are effective at differentiating between normal people and those with brain damage. The clinician has control over which exams to administer, though he or she is likely to assess sensorimotor, perceptual, and language functioning. A score higher than 0.60 indicates brain pathology. The Luria-Nebraska Neuropsychological Battery (LNNB) contains 11 subtests that assess areas like rhythm, visual function, and writing. The examinee is given a score between 0 and 2, with 0 indicating normal unction and 2 indicating brain damage. The Bender Visual-Motor Gestalt Test is a brief examination that involves responding to 16 stimulus cards containing geometric figures, which the examinee must either copy or recall.

The Benton Visual Retention Test (BVRT) assesses visual memory, spatial perception, and visual-motor skills in order to diagnose brain damage. The subject is asked to reproduce from memory the geometric patterns on a series of ten cards. The Beery Developmental Test of Visual-Motor Integration (Beery-VMI) assesses visual-motor skills in children; like the BRVT, it involves the reproduction of geometric shapes. The Wisconsin Card Sorting Test is a screening test that assesses the ability to form abstract concepts and shift cognitive strategies; the subject is required to sort a group cards in an order that is not disclosed to him or her. The Stroop Color-Word Association Test is a measure of cognitive flexibility; it tests an individual's ability to suppress a habitual reaction to stimulus. The Mini Mental State Exam measures the cognitive functioning of older adults, specifically their orientation, registration, attention and calculation, recall, language, and visual construction.

Specific Issues

Gerontology

Aging

The elderly are becoming a large part of our population because advancements in health care increase our longevity. Mental health problems among the elderly are also on the rise. Some of these mental health problems can be attributed to developmental issues. The elderly must adjust to having grandchildren, retirement, loss of activity levels, and the death of a loved one. The normal aging process is distinct from pathological aging that occurs from illness and disease. The distinction can readily be seen in the gradual progression of life transitions over long periods of time, as opposed to sudden, catastrophic illness. The elderly person may have a deficit in the form of a physical impairment, emotional deficiency, social issue, or financial inability to sustain a cherished lifestyle.

Life transitions

Typically, the elderly seek to cope with whatever problem comes their way without the benefit of mental health care. In 1991, Butler and Lewis developed a definition for loss in relation to the elderly. Elderly can experience a range of emotions whenever loss or death occurs. Examples of loss could be loss of friends, loss of significant others or spouse, a loss of social roles within the community, a loss of work or career, a loss of prestigious role, a loss of income, a loss of physical vigor, or a loss of health. Some may experience personality changes or changes in sexual appetites. Elderly people may have a situational crisis that put a strain on their resources. The resiliency of this population is evident by the large number of seniors who live independently with only a little support. Only 4%—5% are institutionalized, and 10%—15% receive homecare.

Commonalities and disparities between the elderly and the young

Age-related disease or illness can cause an elderly person to experience a variety of physical impairments. Factors in this issue are ethnicity, minority status, and socioeconomic status. A person who is incapacitated may experience mental health complications. The combination of these two problems can cause a state of clinical pathology to occur. The counselor may find that the deviations from normal make it difficult to provide a differential diagnosis. Erikson's life span developmental theory indicates that the elderly must achieve a sense of integrity at this stage of life or fall into despair. Butler theorized that the elderly find a sense of integrity by verbalizing stories about life events. The stories predominantly seek to give them meaning and purpose through a life well-lived. If a person cannot do this, the result may be a depressive state of being.

Mental health disorders experienced by the elderly

The elderly were believed to have a high degree of untreated mental health problems, but the studies of Gatz and Smyer in 1992 reviewed the data and determined that this was not true. In fact, only one third of the elderly population requires mental health services at all. Many older members of the population that do receive mental health services were previously diagnosed with severe depression, bipolar disorders, and affective disorders. The most significant problems experienced by the elderly are anxiety, severe cognitive impairment, and mood disorders. Anxiety is the most prevalent of these problems. These numbers may be skewed by the fact that the elderly may not be seeking help when needed. Sadly, suicide rates are higher in this population than in any other population. The older a person gets, the higher the rate of suicide. Anxiety and depression cause much suffering in the elderly.

In 1996, 11.4% of the elderly population suffered from an anxiety disorder. Younger persons suffer at a higher rate. Depression may be underreported because of its complexity. Some elderly suffer with severe cognitive impairments attributable to organic brain disorders. Organic brain disorders include Alzheimer's disease and dementia senilis. Most who suffer an organic brain disorder are also afflicted by depression and psychosis. Drug and alcohol abuse are often reported inaccurately because it is difficult to differentiate substance abuse from dementia and other health problems. Many of the elderly also experience sleep disorders and insomnia.

Suicide

Suicide rates are higher among the elderly than in any other population. 20% of those who commit suicide do so within 24 hours of a doctor's visit. A surprising 41% have been to the doctor in the same week. Another 75% have been to the doctor during the same month. Lethality (the drug amount that causes death) is decreased in the elderly because they have reduced kidney and liver functions, and cannot excrete drug overdoses as easily as younger people. One out of four seniors who attempts suicide succeeds. For the rest of Americans, one out of 20 is successful at suicide. The disparity suggests a lack of appropriate and timely suicide interventions for seniors. Outreach and case finding is called for to meet the

mental health care needs of the elderly. Persons who are homebound have difficulty getting appropriate mental health care. Physicians are their primary care givers, and may not recognize suicidal signs as quickly as mental health providers.

Issues associated with mental health care of the elderly

There are a number of factors that prevent the elderly from receiving mental health services. Part of the problem lies in the strong values which guide the elderly to solve their own problems. Other seniors feel they should keep quiet about private issues. Still others feel a negative connotation from past stigmas attached to those who needed mental health care. Baby boomers approaching old age have been bombarded with literature on psychology and healthy lifestyles. Therefore, the baby boomer generation may take on a healthier attitude about receiving the appropriate mental health care for their needs. A limited number of counselors are trained in geriatric care. Providers for the elderly have difficulties working with payment policies and insurance companies. In addition, seeing the client's aging problems may cause unpleasant personal issues about aging to surface for the counselor.

Bias may prevent student counselors from specializing in gerontology because they:
- Are disturbed by thoughts of their own impending death or the deaths of their own parents
- View treatment of a dying population as a waste of time when there is already a shortage of therapists
- Consider the elderly as noncompliant and unwilling to change their behaviors

- Buy into the belief that the elderly population is filled with physically sick, impoverished, antagonistic, resentful, pathetic, miserable and lonesome people who will have a poor treatment outcome

There is no doubt the elderly can benefit from having access to appropriate mental health services. These services are cost effective if the gerontological mental health counselor receives the proper training.

Multicultural counseling

Multicultural counseling movement

In recent years, the African-American population has grown and many moved to suburban areas and more lucrative socioeconomic positions. The Latino population has also grown and may outnumber the African-American population in the next few years. This anticipated growth will elevate the Latino population to the largest minority group in America. Native Americans are the smallest minority group in America. However, this small group has had a lucrative experience in the operation of reservation-based casinos and other service-oriented businesses. The Native American population has made economic gains from construction and retail. The counselor needs to be aware and cognizant of the diverse mental health needs of the minority groups in America. Competence in these areas include: Self-awareness about one's own prejudices and cultural backgrounds; knowledge about diverse populations; and skills in treating diverse populations.

Multicultural educational course improvement

Multicultural educational courses can be improved with a broader scope on diverse populations. America has a diverse populace of African-Americans, Latinos, Asians, and Native American groups. The Asian population should be revamped to include those of Middle Eastern descent. Currently, multicultural programs only look at the cultures of Japan, China, and Korea. The world is becoming one of mixed culture. The counselor should be apprised of issues that might arise in multiracial or multiethnic families. Educational courses include: Religious factors, spiritual factors, gender factors, sexual orientation, disability issues, socioeconomic statures, age factors, and immigrant issues. The multicultural element may be introduced across the curriculum in all areas of study. Counselor educators can promote multicultural competencies in educational courses. These competencies will influence the care the minority client receives, by ensuring that the counselor is skilled in consultation, outreach, and advocacy.

The United States of America has a populace derived from a variety of different countries and cultures. The Association of Multicultural Counseling and Development publishes a guide to the culture, ethnicity, and race of individual groups of people served by mental health providers. The foundation for the publication was laid by civil rights groups of the 1950's—1960s, renowned for their social justice reforms that addressed racial problems, discrimination issues, subtle biases, and segregation in schools and public places. Multicultural counseling promotes cultural competence as an ongoing training effort for counselors working in other disciplines. Cultural awareness outlines are used during multicultural counseling. Multicultural counselors must receive appropriate training and preparation that includes preventive care.

In 1990, Don C. Locke defined these four elements of the ever-changing role of multicultural counseling: (1) Multicultural counseling is aware of the cultural background, values, and world view of the client and the therapist; (2) multicultural counseling makes note of socialization aspects in regard to race, ethnicity, and culture of the client; (3) multicultural counseling makes every effort to see the individual within the group of people that he or she belongs; (4) multicultural counseling does not label the person as deficient, but acknowledges that there can be a difference between the person as an individual and his or her group. The differences in a person may need to be addressed to help the person come to terms with his or her own self-identity. The individual is also encouraged to value the racial or ethnic group of which he or she is a member.

Cultural competence

The linear tool used to help a counselor gain cultural competence is the Multicultural Awareness Continuum. The counselor cannot expect to achieve mastery, as the continuum is designed to be on-going and revisited throughout the career of the counselor. Progression allows the counselor to go on to the next level, but if the counselor is confronted by a deficiency in his or her awareness when treating a culturally diverse person, then the counselor returns to the previous level for insight into that aspect of the culture. Levels include: (a) Self awareness; (b) awareness of one's cultural groupings; (c) awareness of racism, sexism, and poverty in relation to cultural problems; (d) awareness of

individual differences; (e) awareness of other groups of people and cultures; (f) awareness of diversity; and (g) skills and techniques related to the multicultural counselor.

Multicultural Awareness Continuum

A high level of self-awareness is essential for the counselor to understand why he or she feels a certain way, and to identify biases in his or her own thinking. It is imperative for a counselor to understand how he or she interacts with others. Likewise, the counselor needs to examine his or her beliefs, attitudes, opinions, and values. A multicultural counselor must spend time in introspection to determine areas in which he or she may have cultural biases. The next level has to do with an awareness of one's own culture. Certain cultures may place values upon a person's name, its origin and cultural significance. Other cultures may place values upon birth order. Some cultures have naming ceremonies for infants. Language and its use can also play a significant part in the values placed upon a person through his or her culture.

The third level on the Multicultural Awareness Continuum is awareness of racism, sexism, and poverty bias. Counselors discover this awareness by looking closely at their own personal belief system. Sexism and racism are an entrenched part of cultural beliefs. Some counselors and clients may not have biases against token minority individuals whom they know personally, but may think of smaller cultures folded into the American melting pot as subtly inferior. Poverty touches everyone to some extent. Either you have experienced poverty directly, or have simply seen shocking evidence of its existence. The MHC must determine his or her own bias before helping others gain insights into a cultural belief system.

The MHC may choose to use a systems approach in exploring differences between personal prejudices, which determine how an individual acts, and organizational prejudices, which determine how an organization or institution acts. For example, discrepancies in behavior result when:

- The worker's personal beliefs conflict with official policies in the workplace
- The congregation's beliefs do not follow the church's official policy
- The electorate does not agree with government policy on sexism, racism, and poverty

Therefore, the MHC must determine what beliefs and attitudes are promoted by those organizations in which the MHC is a member. An MHC may wish to apply a systems approach to his or her place of employment to find out if there are institutional prejudices present within.

The MHC must not generalize any culture too much. Over- generalization leads to misconceptions founded on observations of only a few members of a culture. To avoid misconceptions, treat your client first and foremost as an individual with his or her own set of unique needs, and then as a member of his or her specific culture. Understand that the individual has to function both as a member of his or her own culture, and in American society at large. Avoid projecting your cultural beliefs on your client. Once you are aware of individual differences, then move on to the next level, illustrating an awareness of other cultures.

Level of awareness

Culture
Your awareness of other cultures begins with your client's language.   As a multicultural counselor, you do not need to learn a foreign language in its entirety,

but just certain words that have significant meanings. Your multicultural clients in the U.S. will predominantly be: African American; Native American Indians; Hispanics, Latinos or Chicanos; and Asian Americans. In 1980, Hofstede researched 40 countries to determine identifiable differentiations in their various cultures. He determined the following characteristics are the most identifiable:

- Power distance
- Uncertainty avoidance
- Masculinity/femininity
- Individualism/collectivism

In 1961, Kluckhorn and Strodtbect determined the following characteristics are the most identifiable:

- Time
- View of human nature
- Importance of relationships
- Human activity
- View of the supernatural

Use either Hofstede's or Kluckhorn's work for further study.

Diversity
Awareness of diversity begins with a grasp of just how erroneous the idea is that America's cultures have joined to become one super-culture. There are marked differences in the cultures of African Americans; White Anglo-Saxon Protestants; Native American Indians; Hispanics, Latinos or Chicanos; Asian Americans; and various religious groups and sexual orientations within races. In melting pot theory, the differences in these cultures went undervalued and unrecognized. Immigrants and the poor were encouraged to buy into the values, beliefs, and attitudes of mainstream America. Melting pot theory is being replaced by mosaic theory, and the terms "salad bowl" or "rainbow coalition". The salad bowl idea suggests a mix of ingredients that are best when the flavors

are allowed to stand out and compliment each other.

Counseling skills and techniques

The prerequisite for beginning the multicultural process is the counselor's general competence in counseling. The counselor is required to complete each level of study successfully, and satisfy internship requirements, to achieve general competency. The counselor should be thoroughly educated in counseling theories, standards, and applications. The historical significance of the theory must be understood in context of the time period in which the theory was framed. The theorist's own cultural belief system should be noted, in conjunction with the theory he or she developed. By studying the theory in context, the counselor can better understand how to maintain the integrity of the theory when applying it to cultural groups. A counselor should perform within his or her own cultural sub-group before attempting to perform those same duties with clients of other cultural groups. There is no replacement for basic counseling skills.

Framework for cultural awareness

The framework for cultural understanding is based on the diverse cultural backgrounds that exist between a client and counselor. Personal experiences shape the counselor's and the client's world view and impact behaviors of both. Areas in which different points of view surface are: Historical perspectives; social perspectives; economical perspectives; and political perspectives. Likewise, socialization and life experiences change the client's and counselor's world views and behaviors. Counseling sessions are impacted by differences between the counselor and the client because they can cause lack of empathy and understanding in the client/counselor relationship. Prejudices and biases are detrimental to the counselor/client relationship. If you wish to be a counselor, expect to have your own belief system scrutinized, and to establish an operations framework where you identify commonalities first to achieve empathy and understanding.

Belief systems

Some of the most common misconceptions held in relation to different cultures are as follows:

- The propensity for certain cultures to have color blindness
- The belief that every problem is a result of discrimination practices enforced on a specific ethnic or racial group
- The Great White Father Syndrome

The danger of projecting a specific trait onto a whole group lies in a misconception about the client and leads to pathological labels that can be discriminatory. Contrarily, these misconceptions can produce guilt in the counselor who is trying to make up for the client's feeling of oppression. The Great White Father Syndrome is a term coined by Vontress in 1971 to refer to the portrayal of the counselor as a figure of omnipotence or one that is all powerful. These misconceptions can get in the way of the counseling session.

Content of framework

The content of the framework for multicultural counseling is communicative, collaborative, open to alteration or exchange, and open to quality improvement according to the client's needs. Consider your client's existing issues and incorporate up-to-date research that impacts these issues. Some core structures are needed to provide consistency of care. The essentials are:

- Communication styles that involve an exchange of ideas and information
- Beliefs, opinions, and attitudes about psychological problems or issues
- Strategies or devised plans of actions for handling and solving problems
- Counseling expectations of conduct and performance levels
- Racial identity development (the way someone absorbs cultural behavior and societal thinking from birth)
- The way you see people, events, and happenings in relation to your world view

Following this framework will help you meet the needs of your client.

Communication

Communication incorporates a wide range of verbal and non-verbal patterns. The counselor must be aware of the different view points and perspectives from which two races or cultures approach the communication process. For example, a study was conducted involving black and white college students, which asked each population to make comments about the other. The African Americans used these descriptors for communication efforts made by the white students: Insistent and demanding; manipulative and scheming; organized and structured; rude and disrespectful; and critical and disparaging. The Caucasians used the following descriptors for communication efforts made by the black students: Loud-mouthed; exhibited a showy or vulgar display designed to impress people; a readiness to attack or do harm to others; active; and a tendency to make excessively proud comments.

The two groups held perceptions that need to be remediated before fruitful interactions can be made with members of the opposite group.

These results are taken from a study conducted by Srebalus and Brown: Typically, American Indians and Asian Americans regard self-control, soft-spoken voices, and uninterrupted speech as acceptable. They can handle well pauses that other cultures find awkward. Their speech uses less direct methods than other cultures. A firm handshake grasp is not acceptable to them; use a softer handshake, instead. Smiles and nods are not forms of communication that achieve the desired results. Some Asian Americans may offer a nod or two to indicate that they have an interest in something being said. Direct eye contact is not usually the norm, except for African Americans and European Americans. Many cultures like to keep a distance of about 3 feet or more from each other, except for Hispanics and Arabs, who usually can tolerate closer spaces.

Trust

Some cultures have specific viewpoints regarding how a personal problem must be dealt with in the scope of the family structure. African Americans and Asian cultures have firm beliefs that the person should solve the problem with the help of family members. However, to seek help outside of the family is unthinkable. This may be a roadblock that stops counselors from being trusted, especially when the counselor belongs to a dominant culture or may be perceived as one who does not understand the person's cultural background. This initial distrustful perception needs to be changed. The counselor must communicate genuineness, empathy and understanding of the client's needs, and build trust within the relationship. Trust is built when the driving force behind the client's expectations and conduct is seen as one that supports a therapeutic and beneficial relationship.

Shared views

In 2001, Gelso and Fretz exhibited a series of dimensions to describe the differences they found between ethnic groups and Caucasian groups within American society. Gelso and Fretz described five areas:

- Family relationships, and how the person perceived himself in relation to family
- Value of self over value of family
- Value of individual success or value of combined success of the family
- Importance of the past versus importance of the present or future
- Concepts regarding focus of control over one's life choices and events

In each of these five areas, the counselor must be able to understand and identify exactly what viewpoint the client holds. Out of this understanding, the counselor can provide explanations regarding the nature of the client's stress that will initiate a more trusted, shared view.

Client identification

The first step of client identification is determining through a series of questions if collateral social relations exist. These questions will help the counselor to avoid a stance that may seem racist or biased towards individualism. The client should be the one to determine who is involved in his or her choice. It is not up to the counselor to make this determination. Adhere to verbal and nonverbal communications in accordance with cultural expectations. These

communications mean different things to different cultures: Eye contact; interpersonal space; handshakes; facial expressions; verbal expressions that involve self-disclosure; loudness; rapid speech; interruptions of others' speech; pauses; and direct communications. Avoid elevated levels of self-disclosure. Avoid probing questions that might be perceived as rude.

Training

Since concepts of globalization are ever-widening, it is imperative that a counselor maintains constant vigilance to keep cultural competency. Assume your training and education will be a life-long venture. Your preparation methods should involve an all-inclusive educational program that takes into account the client's developmental capacities and a wide range of psychological theories and content available in colleges and institutions. The AMHCA stresses the importance of the counselor exploring his or her own cultural, ethnic, racial, and religious identity as the groundwork for this training. The counselor puts the client's needs first. To abide by AMHCA's code of ethics regarding diversity, the counselor must refer a client whenever an irresolvable conflict arises in the areas of culture, ethnicity, race, or religion.

Curricular guidelines

In 2001, the Standards of the Council for the Accreditation of Counseling and Related Educational Programs (CACREP) established a collection of rules in 8 core topics. These 8 core topics include:

- Professional Identity
- Social and Cultural Diversity
- Human Growth & Development
- Career Development
- Helping Relationships
- Group Work

- 88 -

- Assessment
- Research and Program Evaluation

Pre-service mental health counselors who desire to specialize in multicultural counseling are encouraged to apply to programs that support a multicultural sensitivity and which address these 8 core topics of study. However, some multicultural training programs only marginally address these characteristics. Most common counselor education training program offer a solitary multicultural counseling course of study. Others use an integration approach which offers multicultural aspects in all classes. Still others offer more specialized or focused multicultural counseling curricula. The serious student should look for a multifaceted program of study.

Primary prevention and systems approach

The multicultural mental health counselor uses his or her progressive insights and creativity to produce a positive result in helping clients. Different systems are incorporated within this task. Social justice and equity issues are a part of the lifestyle of the counselor. The counselor is willing to take preventive actions to make a difference for the client. The counselor worked hard to gain cultural awareness and understanding by learning through experience, study, and training to acquire needed skills. A systems approach makes note of the following parameters:
- The client and existing issues
- Societal surroundings attributed to the existing issues
- The way that the person relates to issues within his or her surroundings

The counselor makes an initial assessment to determine the client's overall mental health status and how that is impacted by the issues at hand.

Social justice

Social justice is equated with problematic issues in racial conflicts, sexism, and sexual preferences. Discrimination and prejudice negatively impact quality of life for both individuals and groups. Changing discriminatory practices and prejudicial viewpoints is preventive mental health. Domestic violence, sexual attacks, child abuse, discriminatory educational and suspension practices, discriminatory employment and promotion procedures, culturally insensitive managers and contemporaries are just some possible areas where social justice should be applied. The counselor instructs the client in coping or empowerment skills that assist the client to overcome the detrimental effects of the social injustice experience. The multicultural counselor works to change organizational, institutional, and societal thought patterns and actions of social injustice which have an adverse impact on a client's mental health status and general feeling of well-being.

Prevention

Prevention is any practice that eliminates client suffering from psychological, emotional, and social distress. The Surgeon General reports one out of five Americans has a mental disorder but only a small portion seek out mental health services. The Culture, Race, and Ethnicity Supplement of the U. S. Department of Health and Human Services reports persons of diverse ethnic and racial backgrounds are highly unlikely to access needed mental health services. Statistics would improve if multicultural counseling was available in areas not currently serviced. Ideally, at-risk groups should receive preventive care through schools, employers, social policy, vocational programs, and women and infant medical facilities. Communities can promote preventive care models through advocacy, outreach, psychoeducational interventions, and self-help groups.

Career Counselor

Career counseling from post WWI to 2004

After World War I, the works of Frank Parson were incorporated into career counseling efforts. Interest inventories, such as those created by E. K. Strong in 1927, became more popular. In 1932, G. Frederick Kuder created his own version of interest inventories. In 1962, many counselors adopted the popular Myers-Briggs Type Inventory. In 1972, John Holland developed a theory that led to the establishment of the Self Directed Search, the Harrington-O'Shea Career Decision-Making System, and the Interest Finder. In 1990, Donald Super expanded the narrow ideas found in interest inventories by adding a values-based approach and an examination of personality types. The Strong Interest Inventory was revised in 1994 and 2004. Hence, modern and comprehensive career counseling should include: Personality types, values, and interests of the client.

Career development

The changes in career development for the mental health counselor have been impacted by the increase in home-based workers. Employers want team players who can work independently, think critically, solve problems, and effectively communicate ideas and solutions. Workers may change jobs multiple times throughout the course of their careers. Theories have been established regarding employment and career development that report work holds significance in a person's life because it reflects self-worth.

Workers have a strong desire to reach a position of self-fulfillment in their careers. Work can create a sense of autonomy and personal independence. Work can give a person financial security and feelings of success in life. Counselors need to develop a broader view of the role of career development counselors, given recent changes in the work force.

The career development counselor in the modern world has a realistic viewpoint of today's working environments and its workers. The career development counselor will be needed throughout the individual's life span. No longer is the career development counselor confined to a one-time event in a younger person's life at the end of high school. Career counseling should include mental health counseling. A person's career can impact choice of social life, marriage partner, vacation plans, neighbors, and retirement goals. Occupational information must also have a technological aspect, as technology expands into all areas and all subjects. Changes in the job market can cause employment stability issues, relocation issues, financial losses, and other changes in lifestyle. Some workers are disappointed when their labor does not produce the desired results. These workers find child care, elderly parents' care, health coverage, transportation, and living expenses to be higher than incomes earned.

Values-based approach

One reason for including values in a career counseling discussion is as part of the self-evaluation process. Goal-directed behavior is stimulated by values. Values are an incentive. Therefore, the client gains satisfaction when he or she reaches a value-based goal. When the client does not reach a value-based goal successfully, disappointment and dejection are the likely outcome. Value-based goals can be well defined or based on a crystallized priority ranking. Three types of values are: Cultural, work, and life values. Cultural values are further divided into social relations, time, and relationship to nature, activity, and self-control. Social relations are further divided into individualism, collateralism, and hierarchy. (Collateralism's motto is: "Over and above one's basic needs, to each one according to one's needs, and from each one proportionate to one's collateral.") The values-based approach attempts to define motivating factors to develop a holistic lifestyle plan for the client.

Social relations

Social relations are derived from cultural values. Social relations are divided into individualism, collateralism, and hierarchy. Persons who prioritize individualism place a high level of importance on making independent decisions. Persons who prioritize collateralism place a high level of importance on making decisions that reflect positively on their peers or family members. Persons who prioritize hierarchy place a high level of importance on making a decision that will be approved of by the leader of their peer group or family. This is the alpha male in the patriarchal family and the alpha female in the matriarchal family. Understanding factors that affect a client's career decision may change your delivery of career counseling to include a member of your client's social relations group.

Self-control and time

Self-control is derived from cultural values, and is defined as the client's control over his or her thought patterns, emotions, and actions. Your client may have some reservations, especially if the client is of Asian American or American

Indian descent. Do not alienate your reserved client by asking questions that are too personal. European Americans, African Americans, and Hispanics are not as reserved. Time perspectives are cultural values separated into future, past-future, present, and circular. Future perspective clients are unconcerned with past events. Past-future perspective clients use past events as background to learn from while developing future plans. Present perspective clients are not worried about the future and live only in the now. Circular perspective clients see time as part of nature and are unconcerned with time schedules.

Time values are cultural values separated into future, past-future, present, and circular. Future perspectives are unconcerned with past events. Past-future perspectives use past events as learning tools for developing future plans. Present perspectives are not worried about the future and live only in the now. Circular perspectives see time as part of nature and are unconcerned with time schedules. Many Western Europeans share a future time perspective and rely on calendars and clocks to develop plans for their futures. Asian Americans and Hispanics usually have a past-future perspective. American Indians normally have a circular time perspective. Impoverished youths often have a present time perspective. Problems occur when future time perspective employers hire workers with circular time or present time perspectives, who do not understand stringent emphasis on deadlines, timeliness, and punctuality.

Activity

Activity value is derived from cultural values, and is the client's response to a dilemma that necessitates an action of some kind. In Western European cultures, the response is to do something to alleviate the problem, which is termed a doing activity. Persons who hold this stance may act for personal gain. Hispanics respond by waiting to see what happens next, which is termed a being activity. Native Americans respond with a being-in-becoming activity, which is deliberating in a controlled manner before commencing action in a calm and regulated manner. Activity values define how the client may respond to a work problem. Therefore, a career counselor must determine the client's activity value to find a good job fit.

Nature and life values

Typically, persons with a strong belief in the controlling power of nature also hold fatalistic viewpoints. Fatalistic viewpoints find problem solving is a useless task. Asian Americans and European Americans hold that people have controlling power over nature and their environments, and believe that there is every reason to problem solve. The Eurasian attitude is that the solution is a task that can have positive results because humans are in authority over nature.
Life values are classified into two groups, work and leisure. Three scales can be used to determine a client's work satisfaction. These three scales are the Values Scale, the Minnesota Importance Questionnaire, and the Life Values Inventory. Values and relationships involved in each are measured to determine levels of satisfaction felt by the client.

Work values

Twenty work values were defined under the Values Scale (VS) published by Super and Nevill in 1986. These include: Ability utilization; achievement/advancement; prestige; economic security; autonomy; working conditions; authority; economic rewards; aesthetics/creativity; physical activity; social interaction; variety; social relations; altruism; cultural identity; physical prowess; and lifestyle.

Needs

In 1975, Weiss, Dawis, and Lofquist presented a list of needs that can be combined with the Values Scale to help determine a client's work values. There are 20 values listed under the MIQ or Minnesota Importance Questionnaire, including: Ability utilization; achievement; social status; security; independence; working conditions; authority; aesthetics; activity; coworkers; variety; social service; responsibility; supervision-technical; supervision-human relationships; advancement; moral values; composing policies and practices; and risk. Clients expect fulfillment in these areas for work satisfaction.

Life Values Inventory

The Life Values Inventory (LVI) was created in 1996 by Crace and Brown. They categorized values under five life spectra: Work; leisure; spirituality; citizen; and relationships to significant others. Career planning cannot be made without regard to all spectra if the client is to reach fulfillment. Achievement contains social status, advancement, and authority. Belonging contains co-workers, social interaction, and working conditions. Concern for the environment contains altruism. Concern for others contains altruism and social service. Creativity contains aesthetics. Financial prosperity is categorized as compensation, economic rewards, security, and prestige. Humility, Objective Analysis, and Interdependence stand alone and are not further categorized. Health and activity is categorized as activity and physical prowess.

Independence contains autonomy, variety, cultural identity, and ability utilization. Responsibility contains supervision-technical, supervision-human relationships, and composing policies and practices. Privacy contains absence of co-workers. Spirituality contains moral values and altruism.

Priorities

The career counselor's role is one of facilitator who assists the client in coming to a decision on his or her occupational choices and in making other role choices. Collateral and hierarchical social values are of primary concern to some clients. Food and shelter are high priority for individuals who cannot find positions that meet their qualifications. Your client may be forced to take on a pot-boiler job to provide life's necessities. Consider working for necessities as a short-term solution only, and encourage your client to keep looking for a long-term solution. Geography, family obligations, and disabilities affect a person's ability to gain a desired position that is satisfying. When this happens, seek to help your client determine life roles that can bring satisfaction.

The career counselor makes note of the activity values observed by a client. Those clients who have a future or past-future perspective on time with a doing activity value should find the decision making process easy. Always consider third priorities. A client who has a very strong preference for either a collateral or hierarchical social value may have more difficulty deciding which career or life role to take on, as opposed to the client who prioritizes individualism. Use the fourth list of priorities to determine job satisfaction. Persons who value their individualism also find it important to gain direct feedback. Persons who have a collateral value thrive on indirect,

positive feedback from family and social groups.

The career counselor makes notes of job requirements as determined by the prospective supervisor, such as job related skills, aptitude for the work, interpersonal skills, and good work habits. Your client will be evaluated against the job requirements, so they should feature as a prominent part of your client's job assessment list. First, identify your client's values as distinct from interested family members' who attend your counseling session. Some families make known exactly what is required of the person making a career choice, and other families are less clear about the choice that should be made. This can make it difficult to define the expectations of the family or leader of the family.

Goal setting and assessment

Perform the stage of goal setting and assessment after your client states his or her expectations, desired outcomes, and motivation. Your client's goal:
- Does not need to be obtainable at this point
- May or may not confirm previous choice decisions
- May not meet your client's needs for life's necessities
- May not be compatible with your client's current relationships
- May require your client to change jobs
- May not meet the geographical criteria
- May not be the final product

However, if you follow the assessment regulations invented by Brown in 2002, your refinements will make your client's goal obtainable and fitting for his or her lifestyle plan.

Assessment

The first regulation requires you to assess your client for mental health problems that have not been previously identified and treated. Record problems already being treated in your client's profile. Persons with multiple disabilities may need a specialist in vocational assessment, so you may refer your client on to a specialist. Assess clients who do not have mental health issues according to their culture, work, and life values. Your goal in this assessment is to help your client reveal his or her core values and to sort out those values according to priorities. Educate your client about how his or her values influence motivation. Help your client to understand the process involved in goal setting and self-evaluation. Your client can expect to be apprised of life roles that do not directly involve an occupational choice, but may provide satisfaction and fulfillment in agreement with the client's life plan.

The end result of the assessment process will likely produce multiple employment options for your client. Use a balance sheet tool, developed by Janis and Mann in 1977, to help your client narrow down the options further. Originally, the tool was intended to help students select a college. However, you can adapt the balance sheet for career occupational choices. Instruct your client on how to check O*NET for up-to-date occupational data. Encourage your client to seek out professionals who are experienced in the field of interest and request information interviews. Clients must develop employment skills, a resume, job search skills, and job interview skills. The culmination is your review of the expected outcomes you discussed in the first session. Inform your client that he or she can return to you for further assistance.

The first part of the assessment data is rated on a ten-point scale known as the Educational Self-Efficacy Rating. The subjects rated in this section are: Math; chemistry; physics; foreign language; biology; history; arts/drawing; and music. The second part of this test is known as the Life Values Inventory Results. The results of this test are given a priority rating. The topics include: Responsibility; health and activity; concern for others; belonging; concern with the environment; achievement; loyalty to Family or Group; independence; creativity; privacy; financial prosperity; scientific understanding; humility; and spirituality. The LVI can help a person understand and explore the past and present choices made. The qualitative ratings found in the Life Values Inventory can give further insight into the life events and choices made based on the life values that the person holds most dear. Food, shelter, and safety must be a priority consideration.

Humor & Counseling

Role of humor

Humor can have some positive and negative impacts upon the counseling process. Humor has three separate categories: Incongruity, release, and superiority. Incongruity is depicted in humorous jokes, stories, or scenes that create one set of expectations for an outcome, which are altered in the punch line to produce a totally different outcome than first expected. Release is a humorous way to let off pent-up, negative emotions that have aggressive or sexual undertones. Sarcasm is a form of release. Sometimes, pent-up emotions are released after a physical event that was particularly stressful. Superiority is humor exercised at the expense of another, as in slapstick humor.

Correlates of humor

The correlates of humor are what make it work to produce an amusing result. There are three correlates of humor:

- The suddenness of the punch line, or surprising conclusion that gives the audience the opportunity to laugh at the unexpected twist.
- Optimal arousal derived from an appropriate level of intellectual, emotional, or physical stimulation, e.g., adults find it difficult to laugh at childish jokes that have ceased to be of interest.
- Play frame is setting up the joke or story to be non-threatening for the listener. Some jokes may be too intense for the individual's comfort level. Play frame involves cueing the listener through your facial expressions or vocal tones that you intend a time for play.

Definition of humor

The American Association of Therapeutic Humor defines therapeutic humor as an intervention. An intervention is an action that seeks to stop something from happening that may be undesirable. The intervention of therapeutic humor can be an expression of laughter that can stimulate playful discovery about a problem that the patient may be experiencing. Some therapeutic benefits are found in humorous expressions or in the appreciation of such expressions. Humor can help people deal with absurd, bizarre, or out of the ordinary life events in a healthy manner. This therapeutic result can lead to an increase in work performance. Likewise, humor can be used to reinforce learning. Another benefit can be found in improving the person's sense of well-being. Humor can help treat persons with an illness of some type. Bad health can be evidenced in emotional, cognitive, spiritual, social, or physical infirmities.

Physical symptoms

Physical effects that may be relieved from the use of humor are: Reduction of pain; an increased immune system response; improved mental functions; muscle exercise and relaxation; improved respiration; stimulated circulation; and decreased stress hormones. The three most beneficial areas are improved mental functions, muscle exercise and relaxation, and improved respiration. Humor increases levels of immunoglobin A, a disease-fighting antibody found in mucous membranes that repels attacks by viruses and bacteria. Blood pressure is lowered by laughter. In 1979, Norman Cousins, editor of the Saturday Review, developed a serious illness. He made a concerted effort to fill his days with humorous tapes, books, movies, and laughter. He was able to beat his illness. He credits this victory to the daily doses of humor that he sought out (and megadoses of Vitamin C).

Historical use of humor

In 1951, Carl Rogers promoted the therapeutic relationship that could be gained through bonding between the counselor and the client. Use humor to improve this bond, promote trust, make important interpersonal connections, and help your clients deal with subjects that make them anxious. Social interaction can increase dialogue. Studies indicate people are more likely to trust someone who is amusing over someone who appears sober-minded. Humor may indicate to the client that the counselor shares his or her world view. Freud said humor indicates the client and counselor have reached an agreement of some kind.

Psychotherapeutic benefits

Tensions, aggression and negative feelings can be released by humor. In 1942, Obrdlik studied a group of citizens who used humor to relieve the tensions of being in a town occupied by Nazi soldiers. In 1959, Coser studied patients using humor during their hospital confinements. In 1960, Frankl proposed exaggerating to make the patient laugh at absurd solutions to a problem. Expressive therapy was explored by Albert Ellis in 1977. In 1985, Murstein and Brust explored humor linking romantic couples. In 1994, Minden used humor to treat military veterans suffering with depression. Six sessions produced a reduction in their anxieties. In 2004, Berk declared humor helps the client to gain a new perspective on problems. Encourage your client to express his or her negative feelings. Explain that expression is much healthier than repression, which leads to physical health problems.

Possible harmful effects

In 1994, Brooks warned counselors to ensure that their relationships with clients are conducive before making humorous attempts. Do not make your client the butt of your humor, or ridicule your client. Do not fall back on humor to relieve your own inner tensions about a subject. The session is not for your benefit. Your client's needs are paramount. Avoid humor when you have any hint of negative feelings about your client. Do not allow your client to use humor as a defense mechanism to avoid painful topics. Only apply humor when a substantial time has passed after a crisis.

Domestic Violence, Terrorism, and Addictions

Domestic violence

Incidence

The U.S. Bureau of Justice reported in 2006 that the per capita rape rate fell by 85% since 1979, although other violent crimes are only down by 59%. However, rape, abuse, and incest are still perpetrated on men, women and children each year. Criminologists say the rates are underreported by 61%. Underreporting may be due to widespread use of date rape drugs like Rohypnol, Ketamine, GHB, MDMA, PMA, Ya Ba, alcohol, methamphetamines, PCP, scopolamine, LSD, benzodiazepines, OxyContin, burundanga, marijuana, heroin, and cocaine. More than 70,000 prisoners are raped or sexually abused each year (1:20). Nebraska reports the highest rate of staff-on-inmate abuse. Texas reports the highest rate of inmate-on-inmate abuse. In 2000 there were 89,500 cases of child sexual abuse reported, down from 150,000 cases in 1992. Domestic violence accounts for 11% of all violent incidents. In 2002, 22% of U.S. murders were committed by family members. 15% of U.S. prison inmates are incarcerated for violent crimes against family members. 67% of reported sexual assault victims are juveniles under 18.

Abusive behaviors of domestic violence

Abusive behaviors have a series of escalating degrees. The series begins with verbal abuse in the form of mocking comments, put-downs, name-calling, or abusive language. The next degree is emotional abuse in the form of rejecting, degrading, terrorizing, isolating, corrupting, financially exploiting, and denying emotional responsiveness. Physical abuse is next on the continuum, in the form of restraining, slapping, beating, biting, burning, striking with an object, strangulation, and the use of weapons with the intent of wounding or causing death. 31% of women are abused. Reported male abuse rates range widely from 4.8% to 28%, depending on the study.

Violence Against Women Act of 1994

President Bill Clinton signed the Violence Against Women Act of 1994, a law based on zero tolerance for violence. Zero tolerance means no reported abuse will be ignored; the perpetrator always faces stiff penalties. The Violence Against Women Act was not a productive deterrent from abuse because the stiff penalties caused women to withdraw from legal protection. Abused women feared:

- Police would take their children away from the violence
- Their husbands or significant others would retaliate after release from jail
- They would be unable to cope financially without their husband's or significant other's income to help support the family
- Taking on the fees charged by lawyers, bondsmen, and the courts

Women are frequent targets for abuse because they are:

- Often untrained in self-defense
- Usually small enough to wound and intimidate easily
- Socialized not to leave a relationship except under extreme duress

Staying in an abusive relationship

Women tend to stay in abusive relationships for many reasons, including:

- Watching their parents participate in similarly dysfunctional relationships makes violence seem normal
- If they leave, their children will have no traditional nurturer
- A social responsibility to keep up the façade of a happy home
- Early training from childhood that they are inferior and deserve abuse

Abuse screening tools have been implemented in doctors' and mental health providers' offices in an effort to identify abused women who do not spontaneously disclose. The woman is asked:

- Whether or not she has been physically struck over the last year
- About the safety of her present relationship
- About past relationships that may threaten her present safety

Problems associated with abuse

Abuse costs the American economy in excess of $4 billion dollars per year. This total captures:

- Care for physical injuries by medical practitioners
- Care for psychological injuries by mental health professionals
- Violence prevention campaigns for victims and perpetrators
- Police and judiciary costs
- Emergency housing
- Social Services costs

It does not include hidden costs from eroded social capital like:

- Increased morbidity from stress
- Lost pay from work absences
- Low productivity from worry at work and painful movement
- Lower earnings and savings

- Increased mortality from suicide through depression
- Poor school performance by traumatized children
- Increased mortality from murder

The victim can be either member of an intimate relationship. The children in violent homes are often neglected or abused. Victims of childhood abuse often become the perpetrators of violence in later life. Many suffer from poor self-esteem that undermines their job choices and social interactions.

Children of abuse

Physical and mental issues often develop in a child from an abusive home that follows him or her into adulthood. Some common behavior and social problems are: Deficient social skills; inadequate problem-solving skills; aggressiveness; delinquency; oppositional behaviors; attention deficit/hyperactivity disorder (ADHD); obsessive-compulsive disorders (OCD); suicidal tendencies; drug and alcohol abuse; social disengagement; denial; anxiety and depression; social withdrawal; avoidance of problems; excessive self-criticism. These social, behavioral, and intimacy problems are very prevalent and costly to our society, and degrade the quality of life for children.

Types of abusers

Male abusers were usually abused as children, or watched their mothers being abused, or saw abuse perpetrated by male friends (e.g., gang rapes as initiation rites for girls at skip parties). The male abuser often has a disproportionate sense of entitlement that he has the right to hurt others, especially females. The male abuser usually does not have a good opinion of women because that is the way he has been socialized. The male abuser

often justifies his behavior by stating he was drunk or high on drugs at the time of an attack. The abuser truly believes he has the right to hit a woman if she is unfaithful or withholding sex from him. One type of abuser may have Post Traumatic Stress Disorder (PTSD), a delayed reaction caused by trauma or witnessing an event that caused him a great deal of suffering. Other psychological problems common to abusers are depression, poor self-esteem, personality disorders, and psychopathy.

Male abusers may have been abandoned as children. Abandonment leads to a state of rage in the adult male. Be alert to three states of child abuse that commonly have detrimental effects on the future adult male:
- The father or an adult male authority figure inflicts physical abuse on a male child
- The father inflicts emotional abuse by rejecting and humiliating his son
- The mother does not form a maternal bond with her son

Anger is part of the attachment process. The attachment object may be the victim of the violence as the male abuser takes out his feelings of jealousy or rejection. The male's veneer of icy indifference conceals a strong emotional dependency on the significant other or wife.

Abusers of either sex have various unmet psychological needs or motivations. These types of abusers are common:
- A person who assaults his or her victims in the home setting and has a strong need to dominate relationships with his or her intimate partners.
- The abuser suffering from significant psychological issues, like antisocial personality disorder, who is a convicted

criminal or has past assault and battery charges (often dropped by intimidated victims).

- The person who works through a continuum of abusive behaviors, beginning with verbal and emotional abuses, which lead to throwing objects at the victim, intimidation, and an effort to dominate the relationship by withholding money or restraining movement and social access. Violence can escalate, followed by feelings of remorse. The pattern can become part of a never-ending cycle of behavior. Abuser #3 often victimizes seniors or the disabled.

Treatment

Your first step is to determine if abuse actually exists and to diagnose the type of abuser. Rule out addiction to drugs or alcohol. If the abuser is an addict, refer the abuser to a separate drug or alcohol intervention program, in conjunction with your treatment. Next, determine the severity of past abuses perpetrated on the abuser when he or she was a child. The abuse need not have been directed at the child. It is sufficient that he or she witnessed violence being perpetrated on other family members. Evaluate the abuser for borderline personality disorder and Post Traumatic Stress Disorder. Provide the abuser with anger management training in a group setting. Anger management involves discussions of dominant and controlling behaviors, and the development of personal responsibility. The abuser needs to control his own or her own behavior. Counsel the male abuser regarding the abuse that was perpetrated on him as a child. The male adult should understand that he was a victim himself, and is not to be blamed for the past abuse perpetrated upon him as a child. He is not the one that

caused others to hurt him. Bring to light his wrong assumptions. Try to develop his understanding of the root of his self-esteem issues. The male needs to develop a healthier self-view and learn thought patterns that lead to appropriate behavior. Encourage him to discuss and deal with internal conflicts and the internalized pain of his past. Use a motivational approach to help your male client gain a healthy perspective on his behavior. Base your approach on cognitive, emotional, and behavioral conflicts in your patient's life.

Treatment that involves discussing your client's abusive relationship with others may unearth feelings that are uncomfortable for both your client and you. (The terms "he" and "his" are used here because the abuser is statistically more likely to be male.) Your client may want to place blame for his actions on his wife or significant other. Help your client to understand the motivations behind his actions and his desire to lay the blame elsewhere. Understanding helps your client to establish a closer relationship with his wife. Do not force your client to take responsibility for his behavior, or criticize him, as your client will become defensive. Do not force a confrontation that could turn into an aggressive act. Confrontations increase the sense of humiliation your client is feeling. Humiliation will lead your client to express feelings of blame and anger. The anger management treatment group should consist of 6—8 male members.

Do not to try to counsel a couple in an abusive relationship, as this can lead to further abuse. Assess your clients individually, followed by group therapy. The small group of 6—8 members should be led either by a sole male counselor, or male and female co-counselors to help the clients see positive interaction between a male and female. The co-leader relationship must be evenly balanced in power and control of the group. The focus of the group is self-improvement. Each individual in the group examines his or her emotional responses that are reflected in angry behaviors. The emotions behind the anger are usually sadness, pain, rejection, and humiliation. Turn angry behavior to the appropriate expression of emotion. Discuss families and relationships. Relate childhood experiences to present attitudes and behaviors.

Anger management

Anger management group therapy can be accomplished in 20 weeks with one session per week. Here is a suggested outline for your discussion topics:

- Week 1: The group makes a participation agreement. Each individual shares his personal violence statement.
- Week 2: Clients learn to take a time-out from anger. Discuss other anger management principles. Give some stress management skill instructions.
- Week 3: Each client participates in a discussion on issues he faces in his daily life that he can or cannot control. Follow this discussion with another on conflict, emotions, and actions. Encourage clients to practice the use of "I" messages to communicate their feelings. Help your clients to gain insight into assertive requests and refusals.
- Week 4: Involve your clients in an examination of values and discuss the clients' reactions.
- Week 5: Discuss the continuum of abuse and the power wheel.
- Week 6: Discuss childhood experiences, especially the parental relationship that the

child witnessed, and parenting styles.
- Week 7: Discuss how abuse of the child is reflected in the life of the adult. The resulting conversation will deal with emotions that this discussion conjures up.
- Week 8: Clients discuss the difference between punishment and discipline.
- Week 9: Clients discuss praise and respect.
- Week 10: Discuss self-talk and its impact, and examine scripts.
- Week 11: Discuss the abuse cycle along with a conversation regarding communication.
- Week 12: Involves empathy, listening, and reflection.
- Week 13: Discuss assertiveness.
- Week 14: Summarize and consolidate the communication skills you taught in the first 13 weeks.
- Week 15: Review the power wheel and include a practice exercise.
- Week 16: Discuss intimacy.
- Week 17: Give empathy exercises.
- Week 18: Follow-up to the empathy exercises.
- Week 19: Outline a relapse prevention plan.
- Week 20: Summarize and reinforce what was learned in the previous 19 weeks. In your ending conversation, discuss ways to implement the relapse prevention plan in case a problem develops.

Terrorism

Impact on victims

Terrorism can lead victims to lose the safe assumptions they made about the world around them. Loss of assumption means the terror victim loses his trust in mankind's ability to perform good or charitable acts. The terror victim may question the significance and meaning of humanity's existence. Loss of assumption leads to a form of post traumatic stress disorder (PTSD) in terror victims. Terrorists typically use bombs, acts of violence, or intimidation. The psychological problem occurs when the victim is faced with the motivations and antisocial logic that cause the actions of the terrorist. A severe, violent terrorism event can cause temporary mental disturbance, like Stockholm syndrome, where the victims bond with their captors and defend them against police. Other terms for Stockholm syndrome are Bonding-to-the-Perpetrator and Trauma-Bonding, seen in domestic abuse where the battered spouse and children refuse to leave their abuser.

The terror victim loses assumption about the world by experiencing great fear and loss of his or her sense of personal invulnerability. The victim may lose sight of meaningful interpretations of mankind's position in the world. The victim may lose confidence in that which was previously within his or her control. The victim may be overwrought and afraid of future possible acts of terrorism. Fear invades the victim's daily life and routines, causing a state of incapacitating and irrational apprehension. The victim finds that his or her self-image has changed from confident to unsure, and is full of self-doubts.

Vicarious impact

Terrorism has a vicarious effect on those associated with the victim. Vicarious traumatization is experienced by members of a community that has been subject to bombings or deliberate acts of terrorism. The United States experienced vicarious trauma nation-wide after the fall of the World Trade Center on 9/11 and the Oklahoma City bombing of the Alfred Murrah Federal Building. Members of the media added to the vicarious trauma by broadcasting these events to the general public. The unintended effect of this exposure caused adults and children to suffer from post traumatic stress disorder. PTSD patients suffer depression, apprehension, and are more susceptible to alcohol or substance abuse.

Cognitive appraisal

The person who adopts a positive cognitive appraisal of the terrorist act develops coping styles to deal with the event. Those who take on a negative cognitive appraisal find they feel out of control of the situation and that there is nothing they can do to prevent future acts of terror from being directed against them. This feeling of helplessness is especially concentrated in members of the community who lived or worked near the disaster site. The negative individual may have sustained injuries as a result of the terrorists' actions, or lost people they knew and cared about, and is extremely likely to suffer from PTSD.

Stages experienced after a disaster

The survivors of a disaster go through a series of emotional and psychological stages. In the first stage, the survivor sees himself or herself as a hero and acts out these heroic thoughts by helping to save someone else or their property. These altruistic feelings of individual heroism are followed by a honeymoon period, in which the whole neighborhood joins together to work as one unit to save others. The honeymoon period is followed by the disillusionment stage, which comes as a result of the postponement of help from others. The person feels let down by others. The final stage involves the reconstruction period. The survivor no longer looks for help from others, but instead takes control and responsibility for his or her situation, and works to resolve the problem.

Recent terrorism on the American population

Recent events that changed the psychological world view of Americans:

- September 11, 2001: al-Qaeda attacks on the World Trade Center in N.Y.C., the Pentagon in Washington, D.C., and United Airlines Flight 93 over Shanksville, PA. 2,998 people were killed and more are dying from associated lung disease. Terror alert levels are broadcast from the newly-formed Homeland Security. Travelers to the U.S. from Canada now require passports.
- September—November 2001: Anthrax-contaminated mail killed 5 and injured 17. E-mail use increased. Workers began to use latex gloves and scrutinize packages.
- April 19, 1995: The Oklahoma bombing of the Murrah Federal Building by McVeigh and Nichols killed 168, wrecked 324 buildings, left hundreds homeless, and destroyed much property. Jersey barriers are now erected around federal buildings.

September 11, 2001
Some bereaved family members of 9/11 victims accepted monies from the September 11th Victim Compensation Fund. Some bereaved did not take compensation, because then they could not sue airlines and security companies over alleged negligence. The decision to accept or reject compensation caused division in the groups suffering from 9/11 losses. War veterans' families were angry

that they received only $7,750 for a dead soldier, whereas 9/11 victims' families got an average of $2 million each in compensation. Oklahoma City bombing victims' families were angry that they only got a two-year reprieve on their federal income taxes. Global assumption is how a person feels about his or her place in the world, including economics. Specific assumption is the relationship the mourner had with the deceased. Do not use the terms "recovery", "normal", or "closure" when talking to the mourner, as these words imply a state that cannot be regained. Help the mourner to develop coping skills. Facilitate sessions to help the mourner reinterpret assumptions and regain the meaning of life.

Role of mental health providers

Expect an act of terror or a natural disaster to increase demand on you to provide mental health services in the field. As a first responder, provide psychological first aid by letting victims know they have reached safety. Your secondary response should be one of direction by setting up triage. Give workers and bereaved priority care. Stabilize the survivors. Your third response should be one of connection. Rescue workers need to be connected to support systems that give them the psychoeducational support they need to complete the tasks at hand. Follow up with acute care treatment. Your final response is consultation or referral to other specialized service providers.

Three-phase framework

The three-phase framework consists of: The pre-attack phase; the acute event management phase; and the reconstruction phase. In the pre-attack phase, crisis intervention sites are set up and support services move in close proximity to the disaster site. The therapist gives pre-incident resiliency training to emergency response teams. In the acute event management phase, the mental health therapist provides continuing psychological support and encouragement to the emergency response teams and seeks to provide the victims and the community with factual information that is age-appropriate. In the reconstruction phase, the counselor instructs people on coping strategies and communication skills, reassures the victims and helps them feel safe by reconnecting them to their normal routines and schedules. Specifically, the counselor tries to help the victim adjust to a loss of assumption and change in world view.

Interventions

Help the victim to cope by re-establishing feelings of well-being, predictability, and stability. Let the victim see that social support is available and the counselors assigned are caring and kind. Next, help the victim grasp the meaning of the traumatic event, and adapt to changes in world view and loss of assumption. This can involve the development of an appreciation for life. The victim may find that his or her priorities have changed as a result of the trauma, and requires direction in order to formulate new priorities and positive expectations. Help the victim find outlets that can produce feelings of good will and help build confidence. Suggest the victim may help others to partake in the heroic actions of the community.

The mental health counselor must consider the local customs and values of the community. The spiritual beliefs of the victim may have been shaken by the trauma. Help the victim re-establish feelings of significance, belonging, and empowerment. Your psychological intervention should help the victim develop coping skills. The intervention should also address the victim's feelings of vulnerability and insecurity that result from the trauma. The victim may feel threatened and will need time to heal. Healing is accomplished through meaning management techniques. Help the victim understand the significance of his or her place in a world that has changed. Encourage the victim to adapt his or her interpretation of events. Appropriately applied healing interventions can help prevent PTSD, depression, or irrational fears from developing in the victim.

There are five phases of intervention: Pre-incident; impact; rescue; recovery; and return to life. The goals of the pre-incident phase include preparation, set-up, and improving coping skills by training first responders. The counselor works in partnership to shape policy and inform others. The counselor sets up and organizes structures that are capable of providing swift assistance. The goals of the impact phase include survival and communication techniques within 0—48 hours of the event. The survivor may be in denial at this point, or may display "fight-or-flight" reactions. The victim may appear unable to respond, as if frozen in an admission of defeat. The first responder's job is to rescue and protect the victim. The counselor seeks to provide four types of services to the victim and first responders:

- Basic needs
- Psychological first aid
- Assessment of the impact on the environment
- Technical assistance, consultation, and training opportunities

Impact stage

The counselor provides the victim and first responders with:

- Basic needs to help the victim in a physical way with food, shelter, and medical treatment

- 103 -

- Psychological first aid by reassuring the victim that he or she is safe and keeping the victim who is in shock from interfering with the efforts of the first responders
- An assessment of the impact on the environment, like harmful toxins, physical hazards, or dangerous people
- Technical assistance by reconnecting loved ones; establishing communications in the community; and reducing psychological arousal that makes people act out

The counselor uses keen observation to triage the victims with the most severe symptoms for priority treatment. The counselor keeps check on factors that may introduce further stress to the situation. The counselor also provides technical assistance, consultation, and training to the victims and the first responders to re-establish community structures. Families may require some grief counseling and training on how to cope with their feelings that are a result of the disaster. Organizations may need the counselor's help to connect the appropriate service to the caregivers, first responders, and leaders within the community. The counselor can improve the organization's ability to provide care to survivors.

Outreach and information stage
The rescue stage occurs within the first week of the disaster. This stage has adjustment goals. The survivor may be resilient or exhausted in this stage. The first responders are assisted by other helpers who seek to orient the survivors and provide secondary assistance. The counselor's role in the rescue stage is to perform a needs assessment to determine the status of the survivor and to ensure that his or her needs are being met. The

counselor establishes a recovery environment, where he or she can assess the needs of various groups and individuals. The counselor performs a walk-through to determine if everyone has gained the assistance that is needed, because some are unwilling or unable to seek out help on their own. A clinical assessment is performed in the triage stage. Survivors may be referred to other specialists, or hospitalized. High risk individuals are targeted for immediate treatment.

Rescue stage
In the outreach and information distribution stage, the counselor seeks to inform those in need of the services that are available. Information can be shared through Web sites, community structures, bulletin boards, runners, word of mouth, or fliers. The counselor works to re-establish social interaction. The survivor may need instruction in coping strategies, and the helpers need education about stress responses found in survivors, including triggers that can cause the victim to experience traumatic flashbacks. Helpers should be aware of risk factors, services that are available, and the difference between normal and abnormal functioning levels. The counselor also provides family and group support systems and spiritual support. The counselor fosters natural social supports and helps care for those suffering with bereavement. The counselor participates in debriefings as part of the rescue operations.

Recovery and return to life stages
The recovery stage extends from one to four weeks after the disaster. The recovery stage goals involve planning and appraisal. Survivors are grieving, and some have intrusive memories. Teach helpers to be sensitive in response to the survivors. Monitor the recovery process and the environment. Watch and listen to

traumatized survivors. Look for toxins or physical dangers that could be present at the site. Watch for potential threats that may become an issue. Examines and observe the services that are provided to the surviving community. The return to work stage occurs within two weeks to two years of the disaster, and its goal is regeneration. Try to reduce or alleviate psychological symptoms by offering psychotherapy to individuals, families, or groups. If your client's trauma is still not responding to psychotherapy, refer him or her to a psychiatrist for pharmacotherapy, and perhaps hospitalization.

Defusing and debriefing

The immediate post impact stage ranges from 24—48 hours after a traumatic event. This is the stage where mental health providers give psychological first aid to the victims to stabilize them. The Critical Incident Stress Management (CISM) system is designed to reduce negative psychological reactions to trauma. Disaster survivors and rescue workers are given the opportunity to discuss the trauma and its resulting conditions by defusing in one hour long conversations with a counselor. Support and encourage the participants to calm them. Debriefing is a two hour long meeting to provide information to the rescue workers about the survivors and how to best meet their needs. Psychoeducational debriefings are designed to provide assistance and direction to those suffering from post traumatic stress disorder (PTSD).

The communal debriefing is given to victims who have endured an experience that caused them to feel marked as socially unacceptable in some manner. Do not conduct a communal debriefing before giving pre- and post intervention assessments to the group members

individually. The victims have experienced an emotional shock, producing extreme, acute traumatic symptoms, like: Suicidal ideation; severe disassociations; and substance abuse. Survivors with any of these symptoms should be referred for specialized, higher level treatments as soon as they become available. Exclude victims who are acutely bereaved by the death of a loved one from psychological debriefing, because research indicates that debriefing is a leading contributor to PTSD in some survivors. The American Red Cross and the Federal Emergency Management Agency (FEMA) both employ debriefing practices as part of their standard intervention procedures.

Cognitive-behavioral intervention of later phase treatments

Cognitive-behavioral intervention (CBI) is for those victims who have shattered basic assumptions. Class size should be 8—10, and no more than 15. Deliver 15 lessons, two to three times per week, for 90 minutes each. Two instructors are required to address stress and anxiety in traumatized victims. Teach victims how to identify and modify disturbing thoughts, and how to independently employ relaxation techniques when anxious or stressful reactions are triggered. Some survivors should not use this technique, including: Children under 7 years old, because they do not have established self-talk; the bereaved; sex offenders (unless the entire group consists of sex offenders); violent offenders; diagnosed psychopaths, because CBI increases their recidivism; survivors who suffer from intense, intrusive fear or panic attacks; survivors with an IQ below 80; those who cannot engage in abstract reasoning; those adults who do not have at least a 5th grade education; and heart patients with uncontrolled arrhythmias. Survivors who disassociate should not perform deep relaxation strategies that could produce trance-like states. Instead, incorporate breathing exercises into their treatment therapy.

Exposure strategies of later phase treatments

Exposure strategies are part of the cognitive-behavioral intervention (CBI) for treating survivors of traumatic events. The survivor ire-exposes himself or herself to an imaginary traumatic place that resembles the initial trauma scene. Alternatively, the survivor may choose to revisit the actual trauma scene. Eye Movement Desensitization and Reprocessing (EMDR) is a treatment successfully used with Vietnam War veterans who suffer from post traumatic stress disorder (PTSD) from wartime assignments. EMDR joins two interventions, exposure strategies and cognitive-restructuring, into one procedure. Doctors Silver and Rogers support EMDR in their Humanitarian Assistance Program that helps victims around the world.

Bereavement, grief counseling, and grief therapy

Bereavement is the physical, psychological, social, and spiritual grief response of family members and close friends to a loved one's death. In 1991, William Worden distinguished grief counseling from grief therapy:

- Grief counseling facilitates the normal, uncomplicated response to death in a reasonable amount of time
- Grief therapy uses special techniques to end abnormal, complicated grief that is prolonged, or produces somatic symptoms or behavioral derangement, or is exaggerated

Worden said the counselor should attempt to change the bereaved's subjective experience and behavior, and provide symptomatic relief. Treat the bereaved in a private area. Conduct one hour sessions for individuals, and 90 minute sessions for groups. Sessions can be closed (registration is required, and the number of treatment sessions is limited), or open (no registration is required, and treatment sessions are ongoing). Get referrals from crisis intervention hotlines. Use "empty chair" Gestalt technique, art and music therapy, journaling, meditation, role playing, and reviewing photos or personal possessions of the dead to relieve grief.

Rituals and expressive strategies

Constructivist intervention is underpinned by the ideas that the loss of one human beings affects us all, and every human needs to express grief when they experience loss. Grievers may find meaning through allegorical reflections that allow them the opportunity to carefully consider the traumatic events that resulted in loss. Many people find comfort in formal rituals, like memorial services, which bring survivors together to act as a single entity. Community-wide memorial services help affected neighborhoods to reconstruct meaning and redefine their life roles for the future. Informal family rituals help the survivors to honor the loved one who died, privately. Verbal expression of grief is also therapeutic. Both local and national communities can be comforted and supplied with hope by watching or reading about the humanitarian efforts of rescuers and donors.

Terrorism's effect on children

Children who are subjected to trauma and terrorism are either not psychologically mature enough to cope with the event, or have not reached the developmental age to understand what has actually happened. Look for these signs and symptoms of trauma in children: Depression; anxiety; behavioral changes; aggression; dissociative responses; helplessness; generalized fear; heightened arousal; nightmares or sleep disturbances; acting out the trauma in a repetitive play scenario; school avoidance; preoccupation with danger and the parents' concerns and fears; rebelliousness; social withdrawal and attempts to distance themselves from others; recklessness and excessive risk-taking. Research was conducted on families living within a six mile radius of Ground Zero in New York after 9/11. This research indicated that children's stress levels are strongly correlated with their caretaker's stress levels.

The child has specific counseling needs after a traumatic event:
- Make conversations age-appropriate and talk to the child in a language that he or she understands well
- Present opportunities for the child to demonstrate tenderness and love for the surviving parent and continue to develop their relationship
- Ensure surroundings are safe and healthy to restore feelings of security and place in the world
- Plan opportunities for play and enjoyable activities to build his or her confidence
- Find a way for the child to contribute to the solutions of problems
- Tell the child the truth, but omit unnecessary details, because they may overwhelm the child
- Allow the child to express concerns about the traumatic event in ways that help him or her develop understanding

Do not provide cognitive-based interventions (CBI) to children under 7, because they do not develop self-talk until age 5 or 6, and have not yet mastered it. Do not minimize the danger that caused the trauma, or encourage the child to delve too deeply into negative emotions. Instead, help the child to develop a story that relates the factual events of what happened. Many young children are not equipped to express their emotions because they lack the correct vocabulary. Nonverbal communications help children who cannot accurately express their emotions. Repetitive play means the child is reliving the traumatic experience. Play therapy helps the child deal with anxiety over a traumatic event. Try re-enactments, role-plays, or art forms. If the child has obsessive thoughts, sleep disturbances or bedwetting, or behavioral problems for more than a few days after the traumatic incident, then refer the child to a psychiatrist for further assessment. The child may require drug therapy or more intensive psychotherapy.

Play therapy treatments
Play helps children communicate and understand traumatic events, even if they do not have good language skills. For example, child survivors of 9/11 re-enacted the crash using blocks and toy planes, and role-played firemen and other helpers in this scenario. Role-play allows the child to attach a deeper meaning to tragic events. Creative art therapists use an art form as a play therapy intervention. Art provides the child with a safe environment to explore feelings about the traumatic event. Play related to 9/11 depicted: Immediate death; disability from inhaled particles; victims' bodies that could not be recovered from the rubble of the twin towers; loss of privacy through media attention; disenfranchised grief, because certain deaths were trumpeted as heroic, while others went unacknowledged; botched

efforts to break the news to children who lost a parent; doubts over the memorial service, because victims' status depended on whether they were civilians or public service members; loss of control over the memorial service; and intrusive media presence at the memorial service.

Resources

Family Readiness Kit

The Family Readiness Kit is a tool that parents can use to prepare their families for emergency situations. This disaster plan was created by the American Academy of Pediatrics. The plan involves listing emergency contacts and other pertinent information. Children are taught to keep their identification and cards listing medical needs with them in an emergency. The family designates meeting points in case of a disaster. These meeting points include a destination nearby home, a family member's or trusted friend's home in another town, and the children's school plan and meeting location. Families who evacuate their homes shut off all utility, fuel, and water supplies, circumstances permitting. The family leaves a note stating their destination. Find The Family Readiness Kit at www.aap.org.

ARC and NASP resources

The American Red Cross (ARC) recommends that families create a four-step Family Disaster Plan before an impending natural disaster or if Homeland Security anticipates terrorism. ARC states making children part of disaster planning relieves their anxiety and feelings of helplessness during an actual event. ARC also offers a financial plan for emergency preparedness, explains how to stock an emergency supplies kit, and explains how to take care of pets in a disaster. Visit http://www.redcross.org/ for details.

The National Association of School Psychologists (NASP) has prepared a publication that adults can use with children subjected to terrorism. The leaflet, A National Tragedy, Helping Children Cope: Tips for Parents and Teachers is available at www.nasponline.org. A trusted adult uses it as a guideline to help the child regain feelings of safety and security, and to cope with the changes in his or her world, following a catastrophic event.

NCCEV, NACCT, and NMHA resources

The National Center for Children Exposed to Violence (NCCEV) is at Yale University's Child Studies Center. NCCEV publishes materials for mental health providers working with children who have been subjected to acts of terror or natural disasters. The center makes a strong distinction between how to respond to natural disasters versus how to respond to acts of terror. The publications can be found at www.nccev.org. The National Advisory Committee on Children and Terrorism (NACCT) suggests that early intervention is critical in helping a child develop resiliency after a traumatic event. NACCT's publications can be found at www.bt.cdc.gov. NACCT's material makes distinctions between age groups and cultural diversities for counselors. The National Mental Health Association (NMHA) also produces materials that can be found at www.nmha.org.

Certification

The American Red Cross (ARC) has developed a certification procedure to ensure that mental health providers are trained to be disaster responders. Mental health providers who wish to receive ARC-certified training can find it at www.redcross.org. The events of 9/11 caused some anxious moments and a great deal of unorganized response.

Many mental health providers were ill-prepared to meet the demands of the survivors. The providers needed to learn how to prioritize their self-care needs before helping others. The first rule of first aid is not to become a victim yourself.

Counselors who responded to the 9/11 crisis found out after the fact that they were ill-prepared to meet the needs of the survivors. This awareness resulted in a substantial increase in responders taking Red Cross DMHS training courses in 2002. 9/11 responders wanted to be adequately prepared for the next disaster and to prevent future problems in caring for survivors. Before seeking DMHS certification, the mental health provider must have these prerequisites:
- A relevant degree in counseling
- Work experience in the mental health field
- Licensure by applicable boards

After receiving their DMHS certification, counselors should become standing members of the DRHR nearest to their homes, and make prior arrangements with their employers allowing them to take necessary time off from work to assist in a disaster.

Issues faced by counselors

Vicarious traumatization and compassion fatigue

Disaster and terrorism counselors must prioritize and cover their own needs before helping others. Evaluate your own self-care areas. Ensure you do not become so caught up in the victim's suffering that you become a victim of vicarious traumatization. Do not allow yourself to reach a state of compassion fatigue. These two conditions are a direct result of a long term commitment to care. The counselor becomes so caught up in the pain that he or she witnesses in the survivors that prolonged stress leads to burnout. Burnout appears as: Sleep disturbances; backaches; fatigue; headaches; irritability; mental confusion; cynicism; depression; or intense vulnerability.

Secondary Traumatic Stress Disorder, countertransference, under-responsiveness, and over-responsiveness

Secondary Traumatic Stress Disorder (STSD) appears when a counselor ignores his or her physical and emotional symptoms of distress and burnout. Sometimes, countertransference reactions occur in mental health providers, making their reactions appear under-responsive or over-responsive. Under-responsive reactions indicate that the counselor has ceased to be affected by the pain and suffering of the survivor. Over-responsive reactions indicate that the counselor has lost the ability to remain emotionally detached from the survivor's pain. Either reaction is inappropriate and can lead to a serious problem for both the counselor and the survivor. Counselors should be able to access help for themselves from other mental health providers. Counselors require adequate rest, physical and mental breaks or vacations, relaxation and recreation, and social support systems. Use these strategies to help you maintain a balanced state.

American Red Cross response system

The American Red Cross founded a system in which organized volunteers respond to disasters systematically. The Red Cross first responds with the Disaster Assessment team (DA), who evaluate what is needed. The Mass Care team (MC) then provides food and medical supplies to the first responders and survivors. Disaster Response Human Resources (DRHR) includes Disaster Mental Health Services (DMHS), who provide psychological assistance to the survivors.

DMHS delivers an organized response, and assures quality control during a disaster. The Red Cross requires their mental health counselors obtain Red Cross licensed training. Psychologists, psychiatrists, social workers, marriage and family therapists, and psychiatric nurses are eligible to receive DMHS-certified training. There is no hierarchy that reflects external training. Doctors are not automatically given leadership positions. In fact, DMHS nurses can act as supervisors over doctors.

The professionals working in Red Cross' Disaster Mental Health Services (DMHS) provide psychological assistance to the survivors at the disaster site. Service given is in an interventional format. The client may be seeking food, medical care, or information. Confidentiality is difficult in this setting. The counselor either gives interventions to a small collection of survivors, or to a large group of people, such as family and friends awaiting casualty lists. The counselor may supply information to the media to reach a wide audience. Many interventions are a single point of contact where the counselor tries to keep survivors occupied or entertained, e.g., the counselor asks clients to help with clean up and issues cleaning supplies, or distributes reading material, coloring books and toys to children. Counselors assess survivors for sound mental health and stability during casual conversation and observation.

Addictions

History and scope

Over 50% of Americans drink alcohol as part of their daily routine. 10% of these routine drinkers will fall into addictive, habitual use. Marijuana is an illegal drug with which 25% of the population has had some experience. Statistics show that approximately 2% of the American

population is addicted to illegal drugs, despite the Harrison Narcotic Act of 1914, the first legislation to ban the use of illegal drugs. Emergency rooms have exponentially increased their caseloads of patients who are drug abusers that accidentally overdose, take poisonous drug substitutes, or try to commit suicide. ER caseloads of drug casualties have also increased, for example: Date-rape victims; drug mules whose swallowed condoms broke; drunk or impaired driving victims; and children who are accidentally poisoned by eating their parents' stash, or through toxins absorbed from grow-ops. Alcohol and drugs are linked to thefts and domestic violence. Children who watch intoxicated parents come to accept addiction, and may suffer similar problems later in life.

The first recorded use of cocaine in the U.S. was as tea in 1596 by the Spaniards. France exported cocaine-laced wine to the U.S. in 1863. Surgeons and psychiatrists touted cocaine as a cure-all and anesthetic in the 1880's. John Styth Pemberton patented Coca-Cola in 1892 as a commercial tonic for the elderly and debilitated. Many over-the-counter products contained cocaine until the Harrison Narcotic Act of 1914 limited it for medical use only. 1970's Controlled Substances Act also prohibited cocaine manufacturing, production, and distribution except for medical use as a Schedule II drug. Temperance and religious groups tried to stop the sale, manufacture, transportation and distribution of alcoholic drinks during Prohibition from 1920—1933 through the 18th Constitutional Amendment of 1919. Crime syndicates flourished. In 1933, the 21st Amendment was passed to cancel out the 18th Amendment. This was the only time in America's history that an amendment was rescinded.

In the 1960's, the U.S. turned to gateway drugs like marijuana, then hallucinogens, and then to hard core, addictive drugs. Society accepted the use of drugs first on college campuses, then in high schools, in the workplace, and the military. Vietnam War veterans returned with addictions to heroin. By the 1980's, cocaine use mushroomed to include much of middle class America. Texas and New York gave convicted criminals a life sentence for possession of marijuana. Hard core drugs like heroin are still popular. However, designer drugs like China White, Ecstasy, Cat, Aminorex, and gamma-Butyrolactone outstrip heroin now because they are very cheap to produce but can be sold at an astronomical profit, e.g., $500 of China White raw ingredients can translate into $2,000,000 in profits. The commonest drugs of abuse are: Alcohol; amphetamines; antipsychotics (phenothiazines); cocaine; codeine; heroin and derivatives (morphine, Dilaudid and methadone); hypnotics (meprobamate, methaqualone, ethchlorvynol, and chloral hydrate); PCP; pain relievers (acetaminophen and propoxyphene); sedatives (barbiturates and benzodiazepine); and THC. Narcotics were removed from most pharmacies because of robberies.

Familial addictions, detox problems, and relapse

Illegal and pharmaceutical drugs alike may be abused by your patients. Addicted parents have children who are addicts at birth. Often, parents share drugs with their children. Children who live in grow-ops or meth labs can be accidentally poisoned. It is not uncommon for a therapist to find drug problems affect an entire family because drugs are so cheap and readily available. Remember that letting a detox center patient suffer through opiate withdrawal syndrome "cold turkey" or via Rapid Opiate Detoxification (ROD or Waismann Method) can be lethal. Ensure your patients get Naltrexone after rapid detox to give addicts a time cushion to make lifestyle changes. They often resist ongoing treatment. 45% to 80% of patients relapse within six months because of psychological dependence. Some heroin addicts are on methadone withdrawal therapy for 10 years. Often, recovering addicts go on to abuse a different drug, like alcohol.

Stages of progression

Not everyone who has used drugs or alcohol has a problem with addiction. You must determine if your patient has a pathological addiction or just engages in experimental use. Grade your patient on the continuum of drug use, based on a five-stage progression. Stage 1 is the patient who is abstinent or involved in self-denial of use. Abstinence may allow for an occasional glass of wine. However, the person who chooses this route probably was heavily addicted to alcohol in the past, and completely abstains now to keep from falling back into old, addictive ways. Twelve step programs like AA and NarcAnon advocate complete abstinence. Self-help groups like these are complementary reinforcement for your formal therapy because meetings are held daily in most metropolitan areas, and peer pressure can prevent a relapse. Your therapeutic role in cases of past addictions is to help them stay "on the wagon" of abstinence. Even one drink can be detrimental to an alcoholic because it can trigger a drinking binge.

Stage 2 of progression on the continuum of drug use involves experimental use. Teens and young adults partake of a chemical to find out what it feels like. It is an expected rite of passage for many segments of our culture. Problems with experimentation include drunk driving and date rape. GHB is dissolved in alcohol at raves because it enhances the libido and lowers inhibitions. Victims enter a dream state and act drunk. They relax, sometimes to the point of unconsciousness, have problems seeing clearly, are confused, and have no recall of events or the passage of time while drugged. Stage 3 of the progression involves social use of drugs or alcohol. The test to determine if a person is a social user or addicted is whether or not the person can stop drug use. Social users do not get outside help without coercion from either a parent or an authority figure. Counseling involves an educational group to develop coping skills and relationship skills with peers.

Stage 4 of progression on the continuum of drug use involves abuse. Your patient's problem can be physiological or psychological in nature, or both. The addiction is detrimental to personal safety, family relationships, academic life, and work functions. Spousal and child abuse often coincide with drug abuse. Drunk driving and theft to support a habit are societal problems resulting from addictive behavior. Friends and associates are probably uncomfortable around the abuser by the time the addiction is visibly evident. At this point, the employer can insist the abuser get help on a professional level through Employee Assistance or public programs as a condition of continued employment. Abusers benefit from psychological counseling on a weekly basis and an intervention program to stop the alcohol or drug abuse. Antabuse (disulfiram), methadone, LAAM, buprenorphine, ibogaine, and naltrexone are useful adjuncts to counseling to wean the abuser off the drug. Intensive out-patient programs may be sufficient for recovery.

Stage 5 of progression involves chemical dependency or addictions that must be relieved. The addict experiences withdrawal symptoms when the drug or alcohol is not available for consumption. The addict builds up a tolerance to the drug to the point that more and more is needed just to keep from experiencing physical withdrawal. The high is harder and harder to reach. The addict is now at increased risk for unintentional overdose, because street drugs have inconsistent strengths. The addict is now on the verge of failing in marriage, academics, and work. The addict experiences serious medical issues like ventricular tachycardia and atrial fibrillation and more powerful drugs like Clonidine (Catapres patches or tablets) are used to prevent death. Permanent damage from Korsakoff's syndrome or Wernicke's encephalopathy may result from a poor diet lacking in vitamins. Long-term, in-patient rehabilitation programs are crucial in most cases. Intensive out-patient programs may be sufficient for the minority.

Models and Theories

Disease model
The disease model is accepted by self-help organizations such as Alcoholics Anonymous (AA). The disease model contends that alcoholism is chronic (an unremitting, gradual disease that becomes more severe over time) and requires treatment. Alcoholism likely has a genetic root. Persons predisposed to the disease of alcoholism have genetic markers for lowered levels of platelet MAO activity, serotonin function, prolactin, adenylate cyclase, and ALDH2. Other theorists believe alcoholism is a learned behavior, rather than genetic. Research in this area is inconclusive. In 1956, E. M. Jellinek endorsed the American Medical Association's adoption of alcoholism as a disease. He described alcoholism as an infirmity with four stages of progression: Pre-alcoholic;

prodromal; crucial; and chronic. Jellinek believed that alcoholics suffered from chemical dependencies that became relentless cravings for alcohol.

Psychoanalytic model
The psychoanalytic model states the use of alcohol or drugs is the way a person has chosen to cope with anxiety or unconscious conflicts within his or her mind. The psychoanalytic model is directly related to the work of Sigmund Freud, who used the term id to describe instinctual urgings. He believed id instincts are seen in the libido and in aggressive acts. The superego tries to control the instinctive urges of the id. This is where internal conflict develops and is displayed in the ego, which exhibits states of anxiety. Defense mechanisms take the form of denial, projection, or redirecting the unacceptable impulses. Conflicted people use drugs and alcohol to disguise emotions that are too painful to confront. Addiction is a form of self-medication.

Ego psychology and Object-Relations theory
Ego psychology encourages the addict to cope with the pain that caused the dysfunction. The Object-Relations theory holds that the alcoholic or drug addict is really trying to deal with negative feelings about botched relationships. The addict may experience: Depression; anxiety; anger and aggression; insularity; negativity, atypicality; and post traumatic stress disorder (PTSD). Often, the addict was the victim of child sexual abuse (CSA), or neglect, or physical abuse as a child. Memories of these abuses were suppressed as a survival mechanism, and festered untreated in the person's mind. The addict may also have residual physical damage, like improper development from malnutrition that leads to poor academic and intellectual functioning, and sequellae like

dyspareunia from scar tissue. The addict tries to assuage the pain with a chemical that lessens it for a while. Alcohol, legally prescribed drugs, toxic herbs, or street drugs are self-medication to decrease the pain by making it difficult to think clearly.

Conditioning
Classical conditioning theory was developed by Russian Ivan Pavlov in the 1890's. Pavlov's experiments were based on the reflexive reactions of dogs who had been conditioned to salivate (the conditioned response) at the sound of a bell (the conditioned stimulus) that meant they would be fed soon. Addicts have a conditioned response associated with circumstances where drugs or alcohol were used. The conditioned response can be psychological (craving the drug or alcohol), or physical (e.g., involuntary defecating in anticipation of a dose of heroin). The circumstance or environment is the conditioned stimulus. Operant conditioning was developed by American B.F. Skinner in the 1930's using rats and pigeons. It describes responses of the conditioned individual to negative or positive reinforcers. Negative reinforcers are the addict's withdrawal signs and symptoms. The positive reinforcer is relieving the withdrawal symptoms by taking the drug or alcohol. Addictive behaviors can be switched off by removing the reinforcers.

Social learning theory
In 1977, Albert Bandura developed his social learning theory to describe the relationship of a person to his or her environment. Bandura theorized that people learn from watching other people. He believed people self-regulate and manage their behaviors based on their established principles and inner values. Inner values are not influenced unduly by external rewards or retributions. An inner value that does not oppose drinking to excess contributes to a person's

alcoholic behavior. An inner value (standard) that opposes drinking to excess means the person has a restrictive view of drinking and will self-regulate by stopping before he or she is intoxicated. The person who experiences a distinct difference between values and behaviors finds it necessary to change one or the other. The person finds his values win out over the undesired behavior. This leads to a change of behavior that befits the person's set of values.

Developmental preventive model
The mental health counselor helps the client to handle life stresses by applying developed skills. The MHC also helps the client to evaluate his or her own character strengths. The MHC operates on a developmental preventive model. This positive approach model concentrates on the client's normalcy and the client's ability to obtain wellness. The MHC attempts to prevent relapses of the mental illness or disorder, and to keep new illness from developing. The MHC model recognizes that each person will go through certain crises in life. The way a person deals with the crises constitutes normal development. The developmental preventive model allows for a more natural way to view and accept needed mental health services.

Chemical dependency assessment and the clinical interview

A chemical abuse and dependency assessment is not a tox screen or brain scan alone. A tox screen is performed on blood, stomach contents, or urine to determine the amount of toxin in a person's body at the time of testing. Clients can defraud a urine drug screen by adding bleach, chromium VI, nitrites, or water to a urine specimen from a small vial hidden in the underwear or sock. Your client can dilute drug levels by drinking 120 ounces of liquid before the

test, or using colonics, diuretics, golden seal, and psyllium. Do not accuse your client of attempting internal dilution, as there may be a bona fide problem with ADH the doctor of record needs to investigate. Substitution is via a prosthetic belted under the client's clothes that delivers a clean, drug-free urine specimen into the collection container by a straw or through simulated, color-matched genitals connected to a reservoir. Simulated urine can also be substituted. Use 12 standard questions to conduct your clinical interview. Record your client's history and personal data. Question members of your client's social group. Construct a picture of your client from the data collected. Differentiate casual drug use from addiction. Create rapport with your client.

Here are the questions you should ask a client in a clinical interview:

- Question 1: Find out your client's motivation for getting a mental health referral.
- Question 2: Obtain historical background about the beginning and severity of your client's drug and alcohol use. Discuss changes or deterioration in your client's behavior from the alcohol and drug use.
- Question 3: Determine the longest length of time that your client has stayed sober. Delve into the reasons why this period of sobriety ended.
- Question 4: Ask about the intoxication level that your client reaches when drinking or drugging. Are there blackouts? Violent incidents? Is it harder to get a high now than when the client first started using drugs?
- Question 5: Find out the arrest record of your client. Pay particular attention to impaired driving (DUI) and domestic

violence charges resulting from chemical abuse.

- Question 6: Find out about military service where drug or alcohol use was part of the client's service time.
- Question 7: Discuss addictive cycles of abuse found in your client's family. Note psychological disorders in family members and dysfunctional family relationships.
- Question 8: Find out the psychiatric history of your client.
- Question 9: Ask your client about his or her educational and work experience, including any drug or alcohol activities at school or in the workplace.
- Question 10: Get the medical and substance use history of your client. Note chronic pain treated with OxyContin or other pain relievers, which subsequently led to addiction.
- Question 11: Ask about prior drug and alcohol abuse treatment programs in which your client participated. Is your client a recidivist? If so, you must use a different treatment technique.
- Question 12: Discuss drug and/or alcohol levels revealed by your client's latest tox screen.

The answers you glean in the clinical interview should correspond with other data collected from various sources. If there is a discrepancy, determine the truth of the situation.

MAST and DAST assessment tools

The Michigan Alcohol Screening Test (MAST), developed in 1971. The client must answer yes or no to 22 questions. Clients who score 0—2 have no alcohol problem. Clients who score 3—5 are early to middle problem drinkers. Clients who score 6 or more are problem drinkers. This test is accurate to the .05 level of confidence, according to the National Council on Alcoholism and Drug Dependence. Some research indicates that the 6-point cut-off for labeling an alcoholic should be raised to 10 points. The Drug Abuse Screening Test (DAST) is the non-alcoholic counterpart to the MAST. If either the MAST or DAST is positive for addiction, then use the Addiction Severity Index (ASI) to determine in what areas the drug use has been the most invasive. The areas assessed include: Medical; legal; family; social relations; employment; psychological; and psychiatric conditions. The ASI test is longer, covering 180 items.

DSM-IV-TR criteria

The Diagnostic and Statistical Manual (DSM-IV-TR) is published by the American Psychiatric Association. This book is in its fourth edition. One chapter is devoted to diagnosing substance abuse and determining dependency or addictive behaviors. One set of standards is furnished in the area of substance abuse. The person who qualifies as a substance abuser meets at least one of the following qualifying criteria: (1)The person has demonstrated an inability to fulfill a major role in his or her life over the past year; (2)The person has used the chemical to the point of causing a perilous situation to himself or others over the past year; (3)The person's use of the chemical has resulted in legal problems; (4)The person's on-going use of the chemical has caused relationship problems between him and members of his social group.

The DSM-IV-TR contains one set of rigid standards to determine substance dependency. The person who qualifies as substance dependent meets at least three of the following qualifying criteria:

(1)The person demonstrates a tolerance for the chemical; (2)The person demonstrates withdrawal symptoms when the drug is unavailable for use; (3)The person demonstrates a tendency to over-use the drug; (4)The person is unable to reduce or stop using the drug; (5)The person exerts time and effort in getting high on the chemical; (6)The person loses sight of other, more important relationships or commitments in his or her life; (7)The person cannot stop, even though there is an obvious physical or mental problem associated with its use.

Substance Abuse Subtle Screening Inventory

The Substance Abuse Subtle Screening Inventory (SASSI) was developed in 1988 to help disclose covert abusers. Typically, abusers hide their drug problems with lies, subterfuge, and defensive responses because they are:

- Unwilling to accept responsibility
- Unwilling to rake up bad feelings and pain
- Afraid of the consequences (incarceration or rehabilitation programs)
- Conflicted (have mixed feelings) about quitting use of the chemical

The counselor uses the SASSI to determine the truth, and produce profiles useful for treatment planning, and understand the client. It can be administered as a one-page, paper and pencil test; or a computerized test with automated scoring; or an audio tape test. SASSI takes 15 minutes to complete and 5 minutes to score. The adult version has an overall accuracy of 93%. The Adolescent SASSI-A2 has an overall accuracy of 94%. They both contain face-valid and subtle items, which do not tackle drug abuse in a directly apparent way.

Substance abuse treatments

Substance abusers do best when they abstain from drug and alcohol use entirely during their treatment programs. Relapses in the client's use interfere with treatment. Try not to conduct a session with an intoxicated client. Encourage your client to reschedule his or her session. Make travel arrangements to ensure your client does not operate a vehicle on the way home while in an intoxicated state. Encourage your client to stay out of old hangouts where alcohol or drugs were used, and to discard drug paraphernalia and t-shirts associated with drugs or alcohol because they can evoke a conditioned response. Teach your clients relaxation and imagery exercises to help them curb their urges and anxiety. Use operant conditioning to help your clients tone down euphoric memories. Clients need reminders of negative consequences like divorce, arrest, hangover, loss of income, or loss of health.

Alcoholics Anonymous

Alcoholics Anonymous is a 12-step self-help plan with many locations throughout the U.S. that encourages sobriety. Meetings are held in church halls, libraries, and clubs. AA should be offered along with appropriate counseling by a therapist, because the meetings are not considered psychological therapy. The benefit of an AA meeting to your client is as a reinforcement of the coping skills you teach and a peer group that is supportive. The group provides a same-sex sponsor to help your client see a good role model who has enjoyed a long period of sobriety. The alcoholic develops a more positive outlook of self and a sense of unity with the group, so feelings of isolation are removed. The client gains a sense of hope about his or her future, and comes to recognize that the substance use is out of control. Alcoholics are encouraged to seek God or a higher power of authority for outside help.

The alcoholic carries an AA relapse prevention card. Your client is given this card to help him or her find alternative activities that do not include drugs or alcohol. The card contains instructions to communicate his or her feelings to a trusted AA member, and phone numbers for the sponsor and the client's spouse, or parents. The card may also instruct your client in relaxation techniques or imagery to get through the cravings. Your client may find it beneficial to write down his or her feelings in a journal and bring it to your counseling sessions. Teach your client assertiveness techniques to stand up to his or her AA peers if they make inappropriate suggestions.

Strategies to prevent a relapse

Clients find it beneficial to get a reward when they have abstained from drugs or alcohol successfully, as a positive reinforcement. This strategy is known as a contingency management or contractual agreement. The reward should be one that the client wants, otherwise it will be an ineffective reward. Cognitive therapy is marked by replacing negative thought patterns with positive self-talk. Thought patterns that are automatically negative may trigger the client to relapse. When negative thought patterns happen, the client should replace them with a more functional action. Some techniques for reducing negative self-talk include free association, dream interpretation, and memory techniques. The client may rely on drugs to replace relationships. A new approach, called Motivational Enhancement Therapy, uses role playing to teach the client how to communicate goals and feelings.

Mental Health Providers

Work Settings and Private Practice

Professional counselors and mental health counselors

Professional counselor and mental health counselor are titles that gained popularity from 1980—1990. The mental health counselor's role was described in the AMHCA's 1981 manual. In 1984, the MHC's job description was listed in the Dictionary of Occupational Titles and the Occupational Outlook Handbook. This allowed the role of MHC to be added to the core provider list for mental health services. Previously, the list included: Psychiatrists, psychologists, psychiatric nurses, and clinical social workers. Today, the list has been expanded to include licensed professional counselors, family counselors, and marriage counselors.

Professional counselors help their clients adjust and function in their everyday surroundings. Environments consist of work, school, home, and neighborhood communities. Professional counselors help individual clients gain better awareness of personal growth and self development. The progression of this awareness is directed in care that helps the client cope with crises and issues in everyday life situations. The client is directed to develop appropriate coping methods. The client may also be referred for other health care services when the client has more complex needs or stresses that are not handled within the professional counselor's scope. The counselor educates the client in coping strategies for particular situations.

Professional Counselors provide similar services to those of the psychologist or social worker. However, the PC does provide a distinctive professional service in its own right. The professional nature of a PC is defined by six criteria:

- The first criterion defines objectives for the PC position
- The second criterion provides instruction on how to meet those defined objectives
- The third criterion requires training techniques to be applied to meet an individual's needs, and those techniques are part of a subset of intellectual procedures
- The fourth criterion mandates that intellectual procedures or techniques are founded within the principles of science, theology, and law, and these procedures cannot easily be applied by untrained personnel
- The fifth criterion requires membership in an organization
- The last criterion defines the ethical operation of the PC position as one that is service-oriented for the betterment of others

Self-awareness helps a counselor to provide foundational therapeutic benefits. The counselor comes with his or her own experiences that provide a good backdrop for relating to others. The counselor allows the client to explore his or her own thought patterns, wishes, wants, and goals in a session. The counselor may discuss his or her own comparative experiences in the session while giving the client feedback about an incident. This approach can be seen in the work of Carl Rogers, who believed in promoting an atmosphere of therapy that provided a sense of self-respect and honor for others. Roger's approach is contrary to the long-established, more analytical therapeutic method found in the works of Freud. Self-awareness is one attribute that put PCs in a distinctive class not commonly found in other counseling vocations.

Client crises

The life of a client is bound to be impacted by a crisis at one time or another. Most people experience a number of crises in the course of their lifetimes. A crisis can originate from the death of a loved one, a divorce, debilitating illness or injury, or other personal problems. However, the professional counselor (PC) is more concerned with how the client copes with the situation resulting in the crisis, rather than in the prevention of the crisis. The client who exhibits an inability to function in a crisis situation is considered temporarily dysfunctional, but this dysfunction is not considered sickness. The PC believes that the person can grow from the experience and may only need some temporary counseling to get over the hurdles of life. This growth is part of the person's normal self-development process.

Psychiatrist

Psychiatrists are medical doctors with four years of residency in psychiatry. Psychiatrists assess and prescribe treatment for more complex mental disorders, and provide expert consults for other mental health service providers. Psychiatrists are qualified to conduct psychotherapy and psychoanalysis, to order laboratory tests, to hospitalize patients, and prescribe all legal drugs. Psychologists conduct psychotherapy, cannot order lab tests, and most cannot prescribe drugs. Psychotherapy provides the client and family with a series of discussions involving treatment methods proven to be effective in resolving

behavioral problems. Psychoanalysis includes psychotherapy and medications for an extended time. Prescription drugs help correct chemical imbalances at the root of emotional problems. In cases where medication is ineffective, the psychiatrist provides an alternative treatment, like electroconvulsive therapy.

Clinical psychologists

Clinical psychologists work in these settings to assist a wide range of people: Physical rehabilitation departments; family or marriage counseling centers; independent practices; group practices; and hospitals. Clinical psychologists may be needed after a surgical procedure or other life-altering event, such as divorce, separation, death of a loved one, stroke, brain injury, paralysis, spinal cord injury, or debilitating illnesses. Clinical psychologists can specialize as: Health psychologists; geropsychologists; or neuropsychologists. Health psychologists help people gain and retain good health practices. Neuropsychologists help people understand brain injury from stroke or trauma. Geropsychologists work with the elderly to ameliorate the effects of age-related diseases. Only the state of New Mexico has laws that give clinical psychologists permission to prescribe medications.

Social workers

Demand for social workers increased when their roles expanded to providing care in the community. They are classified as Clinical or Licensed Clinical Social Workers. Educational requirements are stringent. Most social workers obtain a Master's degree in social work, with a specialization in psychiatry, as the minimum requirement for employment. Most social workers provide assistance to children and families in schools, homes, or within the community. Some social workers assist with support groups geared to teenage mothers, the elderly, at-risk students, and unemployed or untrained workers. Social workers can hold the titles of child welfare social worker, family service social worker, child protective social worker, occupational social worker, or gerontology social worker.

The Clinical or Licensed Clinical Social Worker can expect that a Master's degree in social work with a specialization in psychiatry will be needed for employment. However, not all social work requires a master's degree. Some positions have bachelor degree requirements. Social workers with a bachelor degree can expect to gain employment in agencies, institutions, hospitals, or certain positions within the community. The worker fulfills the duties required by the agency as well as assuming the role of a counselor. This additional responsibility can be linked to the expanding role of social workers within the community. There are even some social workers who have gone into private practice recently. For the most part, social workers provide support for clients by coordinating services that are available. The social worker also monitors the effectiveness of services that have been provided to the client.

Psychiatric nurses

Psychiatric nurses are the only mental health professionals besides psychiatrists who have experience in the medical field, along with mental health instruction and training. The psychiatric nurse works closely with individuals suffering from severe emotional problems. The psychiatrist holds the psychiatric nurse responsible for providing quality medical care and for the administration of prescribed medications. The psychiatrist may delegate some therapeutic

counseling and intervention program responsibilities to the psychiatric nurse. A psychiatric nurse can provide a patient with outpatient care that is easily accessible. Insurance accepts claims for these services because of the licensure and training requirements associated with this position. Usually, psychiatric nurses do not open independent private practices within a community.

Education settings

Elementary and secondary school positions
In the past, certified school counselors filled Guidance positions in both the elementary and secondary school systems. Over the past two decades, special programs were initiated to counter non-educational problems that students experience, such as drug and alcohol addictions and teenage pregnancy, which lead students to drop out. Individual counseling is usually conducted on a weekly basis to help students cope with problems they are having at home, school, or in their communities. Some students benefit from group therapy counseling sessions that present skills in socialization, behavior management, and problem solving in the context of their family situations.

Counselors may consult with educators, principals, administrators, guidance counselors, and other school staff to help a child deal with life roles. Some students require specialized interventions to alleviate a crisis situation. Crisis services may help a student who has become a behavior problem at school, or who is on the verge of committing suicide, or who is inflicting self-injury. Crisis situations cause the student's educational performance to deteriorate. Therefore, the school counselor has a responsibility to evaluate students' academic successes and failures. The counselor seeks to identify the career interests and aptitudes of at-risk students. The counselor assists in college selection and in the general social development of the student. In New Jersey, Licensed Professional Counselors (LPC's) are engaged for teen pregnancy preventions, employment, GED testing, individual and group counseling, support groups, and classroom education.

College setting positions

Counselors may seek employment with college students in individual or group counseling, on a consultation basis or as a liaison between the faculty and students. Students self-refer to the counselor. However, if a student is in significant need of ongoing care, the counselor refers the student to an outside agency for mental health care services. Cost-cutting has reduced college staffing, yet the need still exists to provide qualified counselors to cope with emergency situations and make the needed referrals. Career center counselors may prepare resumes, interest and aptitude assessments, job placement services, and career counseling services. Some counselors specialize in proactive drug and alcohol prevention programs.

Medical rehabilitation setting

Counselors may seek employment in a rehabilitation program. Rehabilitation counselors work to help a person gain skills to compensate for a disability. The effects of the disability may impair the person's personal, occupational, or social life, and psychological well being. The counselor must examine the strengths and weaknesses of the client to determine the course of treatment to be followed. The counselor works to collect personal information and data regarding training programs that will fit the individual's needs. Long range planning goals are established. The title of these counselors is Certified Rehabilitation Counselor (CRC). Most CRC's have a graduate

degree in rehabilitation counseling. Rehabilitation work is a growth area for counselors because of the increasing age of the population.

Hospice and grief counseling setting

Hospice centers opened in the 1970's. The professional counselor seeking a hospice care position can expect to deal with families experiencing a crisis situation of catastrophic illness and the impending death of a loved one. The PC helps the family through the end-of-life experience and grieving. Ideally, the family comes to terms with the situation prior to the death, and the patient gains insights and coping skills regarding death and dying. The PC helps the patient deal with living wills, financial concerns, family of origin issues, and other associated problems that may need to be handled. The goal of the PC is to help the patient and his or her family to experience caring in the dying process and to retain their dignity.

Elder care settings

The skills that a professional counselor needs in positions which serve the elderly are numerous. The PC receives training in: Cognitive and emotional assessments specifically geared to the aged; grief and bereavement counseling procedures; how to establish a good rapport with the elderly; looking at the patient holistically and noting any medical problems or medications that impact a patient's daily functioning; and laws that apply to treatment. The counselor listens to the concerns of family members involved in the patient's care. The counselor is aware of the services and facilities that would benefit the patient, and acts as a referral resource regarding lawyers, medical doctors, financial advisors, insurance specialists, and community support services.

Community mental health positions

Community mental health counselors can expect to have a variety of age groups in their treatment programs. One specialized area where the young and the old alike need treatment is domestic abuse. Community mental health counselors also work to provide assessment and treatment for patients with drug and alcohol addictions. Some community mental health counselors help families during child adoption interviews and the assessment process. Some counselors work in geriatric treatment centers with the elderly. Still others may only work in AIDS treatment and support service centers. Some families require conflict resolution and psychoeducational services. Still other counselors find work as employment counselors, helping others to find work by assessing clients' interests and aptitudes.

Criminal justice system

The number of professional counselors in the state-run criminal justice system has recently increased to alleviate some of the overpopulation found in prisons. The criminal justice counselor serves: Prison inmates; detainees; the accused on trial; recovering drug addicts and alcoholics. The job titles are: Probation officer; juvenile offender officer; and prison counselor. The entry requirement is a bachelor's degree including criminology, counseling, psychology, social work, family relations or theology, and a one-year internship. The counseling segregation trend replaces models that previously incarcerated all prisoners together, regardless of the nature of their crimes. Addiction centers are specifically designed to treat criminals with drug addictions who commit crimes to support their habits. Career criminals and sexual predators are now separated from young offenders. Criminal justice counselors have high-stress but rewarding jobs.

Business and industry

Employers hire professional counselors to help improve job performance through Employee Assistance programs. On-going counseling helps to: Alleviate job discontent; enhance coping skills for dealing with family problems; provide drug and alcohol addiction treatment; resolve work problems; and ameliorate retirement issues. Some counselors provide contract training and educational workshops and seminars addressing job satisfaction, work productivity, family and personal problems. The counselor may work as a consultant to directly support supervisors, managers, and employees, and refers them to outside resources when necessary. Some counselors work on-call to provide crises interventions on job sites, including: Catastrophic workplace accidents; deaths on the job; violence at work; sexual harassment; and layoffs or terminations of employees. Brief counseling is a cost-effective way to help employees cope with the transition process.

Coaching positions

Professional counselors may find employment as a personal coach. Coaching certification, insurance, and job restrictions vary from state to state. Generally, a coach provides a client with: Advice and coping strategies for specific issues; helps the client to focus on life goals; realizing potential; recognizing own value and self-worth. The coach can perform his or her duties in face-to-face interviews, online, or on the telephone, so the coach has more freedom than a licensed professional counselor. The coach may expect to find an increase in employment opportunities in the future.

Private practice

The private practitioner must be dedicated to the business at hand, whether it is run as a part-time or full-time operation, because the start-up time and effort is significant in both cases. Use this standard calculation to determine the number of hours you need to bill for: Multiply the hours you spend directly with your client by two. The additional office hours not in the company of your client you spend doing paperwork and preparing for treatment. For example, if you have 15 clients, each of whom is booked weekly for an hour-long session, then you will spend 30 hours a week working. 30 clients mean 60 hours a week of work time. Make a realistic commitment for life-work balance. Look at problems associated with charging fees for services in the mental health industry in perspective. If you are a counselor in private practice, find out which services are offered free in your community, and do not duplicate them. Survey the surrounding geographic areas to find out which mental health service models your colleagues there use. Assess how you will deliver mental health services to the consumer based on your comparative survey. Private practice has a multitude of service options for you to explore. Make practical decisions about the delivery model that you will use, because the model you choose has financial implications for your business. You must thoroughly understand the advantages and disadvantages of setting up and running a private practice, and understand how insurance companies work in regard to reimbursement for services delivered. Balance financial concerns with your sound ethical background.

Requirements
Have a set schedule that includes face-to-face therapy time with your clients,

research and preparation time, answering client phone calls and e-mails, coping with ethical issues, and handling everyday paperwork and operations. Plan ahead and budget for cancellations and payment problems that cause you financial losses. Do not overextend your resources, either in time or in financial considerations. Make referrals based on your confidence in your level of training and understanding of the client's needs. Evaluate what types of mental health services are delivered in your community. There are four types of services, which include: Counseling; consultation; supervision; and community involvement. Provide a flexible model to make your services more attractive to the community.

Counseling services offered
Counseling is the main source of income for the private practitioner. Evaluate potential needs to be addressed in the community you serve. Good contacts for you to make within your community include: Pastors; social workers; school counselors; medical personnel; helping agencies; and employers. Other private practitioners in nearby geographic areas, with whom you do not compete for clients, may provide you with additional insights into the business. Some counselors are generalists. Others specialize in: Individual or group counseling sessions; marriage or family counseling; children, teens, or elders; rehabilitation counseling; drug and alcohol abuse counseling. You may choose a variety of different deliveries to ensure a more lucrative practice.

The private practitioner engages in two kinds of consultation services: Unpaid and paid. Unpaid consultation involves communication between two professionals about the private practitioners' client. The counselor does not pay for or accept money for this exchange of information. Obtain a signed release of information consent form to protect your client's right to privacy. Your consultation relationship with other professionals can lead to additional referrals for your services. Offer paid consultations to schools, agencies, industries, hospitals, vocational programs, nursing homes, or community organizations. Your services can benefit those who cannot afford full-time counseling services. You may receive payment based on renewable contractual agreements made for a specific period of time.

Supervisory roles

The private practitioner performs supervisory roles to obtain additional credentials, or education credits required for licensing. When you provide clinical advice and supervision to other professionals in the field, you need keep your own skills up-to-date. The complexity of some patients' cases requires the counselor to seek advice from peer supervision groups. These groups meet periodically to converse about cases and to review procedures. Insurance carriers and HMO's often require private practitioners to have some supervision by a licensed psychologist or psychiatrist. The LPC, LCSW or LMFT receives payments based on the decisions of the overseeing psychologist or psychiatrist and the insurer. Not every private practitioner finds supervision acceptable, and many turn down work that necessitates this relationship with a supervisor.

Community involvement

Visibility within your community is good for your business. If you provide some free services to community groups, you create bonds and respectful relationships between yourself and the community members that could lead to paying referrals. Some organizations that may be in need of free services include: Parent Teacher Associations; diabetes and other illness support groups; and local church groups. Groups may require the services of a counselor to conduct seminars on bereavement, violence, or other social problems experienced in the community. All counselors should provide some community service as a demonstration of their ethics, but it can be especially difficult to fit volunteerism into a private practitioner's role.

Work settings and networking

The three work settings of the private practitioner are: Incorporated office groups; expense-sharing groups; and sole proprietorship. Incorporated office groups share the same workspace and the members are not personally liable for legal judgments against the corporation. Expense-sharing groups share resources and costs but not office space. Counselors can benefit from local, state, and national counseling group relationships. Group practice gives the counselor an outlet from the isolation and burnout associated with private practice. Sole proprietorship indicates a single person is in charge of the business, and is liable to pay business damages out of personal funds, if sued successfully. This business owner is not entirely alone, as he or she must continue to network with other mental health professionals. Make your work setting selection based on which type of work fits your life and occupational goals. Your choices will be influenced by the opportunities available in your geographic region, and limited by your type of training and licensing.

Incorporated office groups are mental health specialists who have signed on as legal partners with shares in a business. The specialists can include: Psychologists; psychiatrists; social workers; and professional counselors. Their salaries can be weekly, bi-weekly, or monthly

- 124 -

payments, based on: Time spent on the job; the status of the specialist in the business; and the initial investment of the professional as a partner. The legal arrangements include an exit plan for leaving the practice, relocation of the practice, and expected changes in the practice. Consult an attorney to help you thoroughly scrutinize and understand all aspects of the legal contract before making the commitment to become a partner. Your understanding may prevent you from making costly and illegal decisions.

Expense sharing groups consist of mental health specialists who have not signed on as legal partners in a corporation. Their contractual agreements should define their financial and business relationships and costs incurred by each person in the group. A clear understanding prevents future misunderstandings and legal entanglements. The specialists can include: Psychologists; psychiatrists; social workers; and professional counselors. Their salaries are paid in the same way that a sole proprietor is paid. The group fees pay for office expenses and any consulting fees charged by other professionals. However, the private practitioner does not share his or her counseling payments received from patients or other agencies for services rendered. The legal options for the private practitioner include remaining in the group, incorporating the group, or leaving to start his or her own private practice.

Group settings

Benefits associated with working in a group setting include having:
- Vacation and sick coverage by a trusted colleague (locum tenens)
- Quick access to consultation and referrals by other members
- Specialized services offered by other members

- Protection if a patient becomes violent or makes threats
- Centralized bookings, accounting, and filing, if you can afford a clerk
- Higher group practice rates negotiated with insurance companies under a single tax number
- Better equipment than you could afford alone

There are also risks involved in working with a group:
- If a group member is sued or has legal issues, the consequences impact the whole group
- Staff supervision, consultations, and office meetings detract from therapy time with your patients

Ask your attorney and accountant to address these possibilities in the initial business legal documents. Write a clear policies and procedures manual for your staff.

Business considerations

The first practical consideration for beginning a private practice is the type of office space you require. Your next consideration should be the length of time you plan to remain in private practice. You may rent space on a part-time basis from other mental health providers in your area. This provides you, as new professional counselor, with an already established location and recognized business address that may be more prestigious than you could afford alone. Sharing office equipment will minimize your start-up costs. However, if your financial resources permit, you may choose to purchase office space or a separate building. You may choose to open a home office if you have space and money for office furniture, a computer, phone and internet service, answering machine, fax, office supplies, liability insurance, and restroom facilities for clients and their families.

Practical issues associated with opening a private practice decrease the time you spend on your personal activities and with your paying patients. A home business opens your family to intrusions by insistent patients, undesirables, or criminals. Install a security system. Teach baby-sitters, family and staff how to use it. You may spend time making structural changes to satisfy your insurance company and accountant. Set up a record keeping system to last at least seven years from the last time you saw the patient. Avoid feeling shut off from the mental health network by establishing connections and maintaining contacts. Keep your equipment functional and ensure you learn new software that meets the growing needs of your office. You are legally required to record a referral number for patients who cannot reach you by phone in an emergency (usually the nearest hospital that offers 24-hour mental health services or your locum tenens). Instruct your answering service in all procedures to be followed during emergency situations, and how to contact your locum tenens while you are sick, on vacation, or attending training.

Liability insurance and attorneys
Liability insurance is a policy that provides protection against negligent acts and omissions, such as failure to remove ice from a walkway that results in a patient's accidental injury. Malpractice insurance provides protection against injurious conduct by the counselor when acting in his or her professional capacity, like misdiagnosis or incorrect treatment. Office equipment and the office space itself need separate policies. Most groups require a new partner to obtain these types of insurance before work begins. Attorney services are enlisted to protect the practitioner's business and financial investments. Hire an attorney who is knowledgeable about mental health legalities. Ask your attorney to explain your HIPAA duties (a law that protects the privacy of the client). Your attorney may hire counselors to consult in custody or abuse cases, which can bring in revenue for you.

Accounting
An accountant helps the professional counselor to set up and maintain accounting and billing systems for the business, to fill out Internal Revenue Service paperwork and file income taxes. An accountant offers good advice regarding sound financial investments, selecting a retirement plan, business goals and growth plans for the business. An accountant can help the counselor determine projected income for the following year. Projected income is vital for you to know how much time you should allocate to counseling services, consultation services, and other professional time use. The Internal Revenue Service will not consider your practice to be a viable business if it does not make an income within three years of operation.

Referral base
The practical needs of setting up your office cannot overshadow your need to establish a referral base. Your private practice will grow out of referrals from your community. Referrals can come from: Educational facilities; private and public organizations; churches; corporations; manufacturing firms; other mental health providers; hospitals; medical physicians; and rehabilitation programs. Professional counselors increase public awareness of their services by writing for publications. Enhance your public image by volunteering individual or group counseling, consultation services, support groups, workshops or seminars. School

- 126 -

personnel, medical professionals, and other community professionals seeking free services for an individual are good contacts to widen your referral base. A strong referral system is an investment in future revenue opportunities.

Goal setting

Goal setting involves a yearly evaluation. Set goals in these areas: Professional growth; financial growth; skills development and refinement; personal growth; and family interests. Gear professional growth goals to those that you can accomplish within one year's time. Determine how many cases or clients you will serve annually, and break that figure into monthly and weekly averages. Evaluate the types of clients you are willing to handle. The types include individuals, couples, families, and groups. Evaluate which skills you need to improve or gain to obtain these clients. Monitor your supervision to determine if you devoted enough time to this task.

Set goals for financial growth by the number of clients that you have the ability to serve. The number is limited by your opportunities, time constraints, and voluntary performance. Skill development requires you to make a financial and time investment in university courses or seminar training. Professional organizations within the mental health community may make demands for professional counselors to obtain increased training in specialized areas. Plan time for your family and personal life activities because your clients model their behavior of "wellness" after that of their counselor. The professional counselor must stay balanced in both professional and personal lives.

Insurance options

Mental health insurance coverage and payments options are complex. There are three kinds of insurance plans in which your client may be involved: Indemnity plans; Preferred Provider Organizations (PPO's); and Health Maintenance Organizations (HMO's). Indemnity plans reimburse the client directly after the client has paid you for a service. The client usually pays a deductible as a qualification before any additional reimbursements are paid by the insurance company. A PPO offers the client the ability to visit any caregiver within their network provider list at a low fee, but if the client goes to a caregiver not on the list, the client must pay more. The PPO establishes set fees that the counselor can charge the client. An HMO contracts with the provider for bulk discount care. You must get a referral from the client's general practitioner or other gatekeeper before commencing service. Outpatient mental health care is extremely limited at an HMO.

The Preferred Provider Organization (PPO) establishes what fees the counselor can charge the client. The client usually pays co-payments and deductibles to the provider, and the PPO pays the rest of the monies owed to the provider. The HMO is like a PPO, except that the primary care physician pre-certifies the need for mental health services in an HMO. Some Health Maintenance Organizations demand that the counselor submit a prescribed treatment plan as part of the pre-certification process. The provider sends the plan to the insurance company for pre-certification. The care and insurance coverage restricts the client to only going to an in-network provider for services. The HMO has a set fee for services. There usually is not a deductible with an HMO, but there is co-pay required. Normally, the premiums for an HMO are lower than other insurance plans.

Education, Training, and Credentials

Education

Changes in the mental health counseling profession

Mental health counselors have had an influx of clients in recent years. Part of the reason for this influx in clients can be found in the changes in attitudes and perceptions of other professionals. Human Resources departments recognize that mental health counselors can assist workers by providing short term counseling to address work performance issues. Psychiatrists recognize that mental health counselors provide a necessary component in treatment, along with medication. Managed care plans pushed for counseling treatments. Mothers Against Drunk Driving (MADD) worked toward increasing alcohol and drug programs. The Internet has provided counselors with different counseling formats. State licensure boards give clients reassurance about the treatment they will receive under the care of a licensed professional counselor.

The increase in both long and short term psychotherapies wrought a number of changes in the education system. Mental health counselors found that those responsible for their educational needs changed curricula and techniques to improve the quality of education. Education counselors added the following courses to their curricula: Multicultural counseling; brief therapy; and ethical issues. Counselors began learning about conflict resolution, community consultations, case management, and client advocacy. Counselors were taught sound business practices. Counselor education programs have been encouraged to seek accreditation

privileges from the Council for Accreditation of Counseling and Related Educational Programs (CACREP). The program objectives and curriculum follow approved standards with clinical instruction. Faculty and staff will meet prescribed CACREP standards regarding organizations and administrative structures. In addition, the college must be willing to undergo program evaluations set by CACREP standards.

Research

Cost has become an issue in the mental health care system. This issue has increased the need for counselors to be accountable in their work. Accountability is found in the documentation and data collection methods used by counselors. The National Institute of Mental Health (NIMH) issues funding grants to various research institutions. The research is performed on clients in the daily practice of mental health counselors. The research is concerned with gaining insight into the practicality of the counseling interventions applied in the daily life of the client. Therefore, it is necessary for research courses to be offered in college programs. Research courses may be used to instruct the student in standardized tests and evaluation, experimental research design, descriptive and inferential statistics, and the critique of research designs. Some students feel that research has little practicality in their daily work.

Counselor educators

Counselor educators can become bridge builders who create an understanding between mental health practitioners and those that do research. Educators seek to help their students see the rationale behind research. Likewise, the educator strives to help the research student to see the relevance of understanding sound counseling practices. One way that this is accomplished is to provide the counselor with an assignment that delves into the procedures used in cognitive therapy. The student counselor learns to appreciate research and its applications. The research student will find that an assignment in qualitative research provides ample opportunity to use counseling techniques. The current accountability movement makes it imperative for the counselor and the research student to share outcome data obtained in these areas. The practicing counselor will find that research is relevant to patient counseling and the techniques used.

Managed care programs

Mental health services are impacted by the need for cost- effective service deliveries. Managed care programs implement treatment plans that are supervised under case managers and review boards. Under the managed care programs, it is not uncommon for treatment plans to be restricted to a limited number of visits. Many counselors switched to fee-for-service contractual agreements. These agreements were made with medical facilities, agencies, and private businesses to reduce the cost of having a salaried counselor on staff. Counselors had to change their business plans to compete for government contracts and insurance reimbursements. This change provides the counselors with a more secure source of income for services rendered. In addition, the compromise in care became an issue for counselors in consideration of their ethical duties.

Managed care programs have strict guidelines for treatment plans. These guidelines are used to restrict and limit the number of visits that a counselor can prescribe for treatment. This guideline does not take into account any difficulties that may need to be addressed in establishing relationships between different cultures or races. The managed care program's reporting structure may compromise the confidentiality of the client. The counselor may need to review his own personal identity principles to alleviate the stress that results from these types of compromises. The counselor should receive instruction in therapeutic relationships, contextual care in the community or private practice, writing case notes, informed consent issues, treatment plan development, selection of counseling interventions, and applying ethical decisions.

Counselor educators have not been strong supporters of incorporating the managed care component into the curriculum. There have been some attempts to include the managed care component, but on the whole, the changes to the curriculum have not been enough. A stronger component that addresses these concerns in managed care restrictions is imperative soon:

- Minimum competencies
- Ethical standards
- Informed consent
- Confidentiality issues
- Reporting procedures
- Citing appropriate diagnosis
- How to terminate management when problems cannot be resolved

If managed care is incorporated into the curriculum, then the counselor will be better prepared to work in that setting.

Mental health counseling education programs should include these topics in relation to managed care treatment:

- Diagnosis and treatment of patients
- Treatment plans

- Methods of brief and goal directed counseling sessions
- Standards of practice for groups and families
- Pharmacological interventions that can be offered to the client.
- Networking and consultation skills
- Record keeping procedures
- Understanding evidence-based research
- Practicum placement in a managed care setting during their internship experience

Integrated care model

The integrated care model for treatment is increasing in mental health service delivery and is directed towards providing services to those in underserved populations. Integrated care is provided by the mental health counselor and the medical staff. The counselor is responsible for:
- Giving an appropriate assessment and diagnosis of the client's mental state
- Supplying psychoeducational services
- Offering brief-structured counseling sessions

Integrated care models require the counselor to accurately diagnose the mental health of the client. The counselor will need to be apprised of brief-structured counseling methods that utilize pharmacological interventions and individual and group approaches. The counselor should be able to follow specific guidelines in reporting procedures. The counselor should be able to write a grant application to compete for contractual agreements. The counselor should be able to network and collaborate with other service professionals.

Credentialing

Credentialing process

The credentialing process depends on the counselor's work setting and specialty. Generally, credentialing begins with the student obtaining a Master's degree of 48—60 semester hours in Psychology or Education. Some states still accept a bachelor's degree with additional post graduate courses in counseling, or for substance abuse and behavior counselors in certain settings, a high school diploma and certification. There are eight core areas of study: (1) Human growth and development; (2) relationships; (3) assessment; (4) social and cultural diversity; (5) career development; (6) group work; (7) program evaluation and research; and (8) professional identity. Student counselors complete a supervised clinical experience, usually 3,000 hours or 2 years, and obtain two letters of professional endorsement. Licensure differs state by state. The candidate must pass a state exam. Most licenses require annual continuing education credits for maintenance. The counselor agrees to follow certain standards and ethical codes. Some jobs require additional credentials, for example, a school counselor must have both a teaching certificate AND a counseling certificate, AND teaching experience.

Professional practice standards

The professional practice standards for counselors require significant command of mental health care theory and its application. Graduate students must be prepared to accept entry level positions to become proficient and competent in all skills. A standard set of criteria is used to assess whether or not the graduate student has reached the level of professional proficiency. The criteria include:

- Meeting accreditation requirements
- Following ethical practice standards* for the public good
- Achieving competencies required in entry level positions
- Satisfactory completion of all academic classes
- Satisfactory completion of a supervised clinical experience (usually 3,000 hours)
- Meeting all certification provisions, e.g., two professional endorsement letters

*Ethical standards apply to testing of humans and animals and refraining from sexual or other harmful relationships with clients. Ethical standards stipulate scrutiny and disciplinary actions for violators.

History behind the adoption of standards

In 1961, the American Personnel and Guidance Association (APGA) adopted the ethical standards of the mental health counseling profession. In 1964, the Association for Counselor Education and Supervision (ACES) provided training standards for secondary school counselors. In 1973, the Standards for Preparation of Counselors and other Personnel Services Specialists were embraced by the ACES association. In 1977, standards were agreed on that met master and doctoral degree requirements. The American Mental Health Counselors Association (AMHCA) wrote standards for mental health counseling programs. In 1995, the ethical standards went through a thorough process of revision. These new standards have been adopted by other groups that provide certification. AMHCA Standards are applied and enforced by the AMHCA Ethics Committee. The most stringent of these enforcements are found in the regulations that allocate expulsion from the association.

Accreditation

Accreditation is quality control for the programs that train mental health counselors. Most universities observe accreditation standards in each academic department. Not all private schools, colleges, and universities that offer counseling courses are accredited. You will probably not be able to obtain an internship to complete your practicum, or obtain a license if you did not attend an accredited school. Internship positions are usually found in hospitals, community mental health centers, clinics, and schools, so most of them require accreditation. The stakeholders involved in accreditation are: The pre-service programs; professional preparation programs; local agencies; state agencies; and federal agencies. Accreditation is founded on a set of standards that can either be tied to the professional standards, or to a general set of standards. The program and the standards must be defined in such a way that the accreditation is acceptable to future employers.

Licensure and professional certification requirements

Counselors receive state authorization to work as mental health practitioners either through licensure or professional certification. Licensure is the law in most of the country. Some states do not issue licenses; instead, they recognize professional certification as the practice credential, meaning the candidate obtained the National Certified Counselor designation through the National Board for Certified Counselors, Inc. National certification is voluntary. It is distinct from a state license and requires a separate exam and 100 hours of continuing education every 5 years. The Commission on Rehabilitation Counselor Certification is required for rehab counselors, and includes an exam every 5 years or 100 hours of education, an internship, and work experience in rehab if the counselor graduated with another specialization.

State licensing boards supervise mental health professionals in their work. State licensing boards set internship hours, supervisor qualifications, the amount of direct patient contact, and monitor ethics. For example, Arkansas requires a 2,000 hour internship with at least 500 hours of direct patient contact, whereas Idaho requires a 1,000 hour internship and has no definition of direct contact. When a board finds that a counselor acted unethically, then the state can suspend or revoke the counselor's license and apply penalties. Counselors who wish to renew their licenses may be required to complete continuing education credits and pay additional fees to the state board. If a counselor is discovered practicing without a legal license, then he or she can be charged and prosecuted. Each state posts its minimum education and work experience standards for statutory certification, and every counselor in the state must meet them. The counselor can use the civil law system to fight the state board's charges and to sue for monetary restitution.

In 1976, the Virginia Counselors Association passed licensure laws. This was the result of a lawsuit by an unlicensed, counselor. In 1979, Arkansas and Alabama passed licensure laws, also. By the end of 1985, more than 13 states had passed similar licensure laws. Currently, there are only two states that do not have these laws in place. Licensure laws give the public a sense of protection that there therapists are qualified professionals who have met the requirements of the state to hold those positions. All states mandate a written assessment and some even have oral assessments in place. The professional who gains a license is a Licensed Professional Counselor, Licensed Clinical Mental Health Counselor, or Certified Professional Counselor. Ethical violators are penalized by the legal system. Exemptions are given to those in private and public practice who counsel in related professional groups.

CACREP accreditation

ACES developed a manual for training counselors in the field of mental health in 1978. This manual was used in five regional workshops in 1979 for a pilot program. APGA and ACES began developing an accreditation program for mental health counselors. In 1981, the Council for the Accreditation of Counseling and Related Educational Programs (CACREP) was founded as an independent organization that could provide accreditation to the mental health counselor. By the year 2004, over 179 universities could boast of CACREP accredited educational programs in their schools. These universities have increased the number of master and doctoral level programs that they now offer. Many other universities are in pursuit of the CACREP accreditation for their programs. Many states mandate the necessity of the CACREP accreditation as a requirement for obtaining a license.

The CACREP standards provide sequencing and clinical experience that can make a solid foundation for the professional counselor's education. The standards help the counselor to develop a professional identity. The student learns about social and cultural diversity, human development and growth, career development, helping relationships, group work, assessment, research, and

Copyright © Mometrix Media. You have been licensed one copy of this document for personal use only. Any other reproduction or redistribution is strictly prohibited. All rights reserved.

program evaluation. The student receives clinical instruction and experience at a supervised practicum and internship opportunities, in addition to the theory. The number of clinical hours, the type of supervision, and supervisory credentials are included in the CACREP standards. Curriculum development can also be improved with contributions made by counseling practitioners.

Students who find they have difficulty meeting the prescribed CACREP standards are not alone. Many returning students have jobs and families that cut into the time they have for education. Cost can be an added problem. The students must meet prescribed practicum and internship hours required by the training programs in each state. However, some colleges find that meeting these standards for accreditation is not a possibility for their particular population of students. In addition, colleges are cutting budgets, which decreases faculty and increases class sizes. Larger class sizes can make it harder for a student who is already having problems with academic achievement because of family and work demands. Even when a college cannot attain accreditation, it can still adhere to CACREP standards for its program. The program standards provide sequencing and clinical experiences that can be a solid foundation for the professional counselor's educational pursuits.

Endorsement

In 1970, three structures were put into effect that applied to new endorsement regulations. The first structure involved the state psychology licensing boards' refusal of candidates for their tests. The boards were refusing counselors with doctorate degrees. This was a result of the national health insurance requirements for stricter professional standards. The boards did not feel that the candidates would meet the strict professional standards that the national health insurance required. There was a dwindling demand for Ph.D.'s. School budget cuts were a contributing factor in the dwindling demand. School counseling positions were hard to find. Therefore, the professional sought work in mental health centers, hospitals, and clinics. These new positions did not have credential options. Counselors were performing different functions in their work, and their roles were performed in the schools, in the community, and in social work settings.

History of professional certification

There is one generic certification available to mental health counselors, which remains suitable for a broad range of positions. There are five specialty certifications available on a national or international level. There are many minor types of certification in place. The Commission on Rehabilitation Counselor Certification or the CRCC was established in 1973. In 1976, the CRCC initiated its first national assessment. Currently, the CRCC boasts over 30,000 certifications and over 15,000 valid certification holders. The National Academy of Certified Clinical Mental Health Counselors was founded by AMHCA in 1979. The first 50 candidates had to provide a clinical work sample and pass the national assessment exam. Throughout the years, the exacting standards for this voluntary credential have kept the numbers of credentialed counselors low.

In 1982, the National Board of Certified Counselors or the NBCC was established under the APGA. This organization offered a generic counseling certificate to mental health counselors. In 1983, the NBCC gave the assessment to certify over

2,200 mental health counselors. In 1985, the National Counsel for the Credentialing of Career Counselors or the NCCC offered professional certification. However, this certification is no longer available. The NCCC does maintain the NCCC credential previously achieved by its candidates who passed the assessment given. In the latter part of the nineties, the National Academy of Certified Clinical Mental Health Counselors joined the National Board for Certified Counselors. The joint entity offers the National Certified School Counselor (NCSC) and the Master Addictions Counselor (MAC) certificates.

Dual certification and licensure

A license gives the holder the authority or right to work in a particular state. The license also provides a lawful description of the standards that are applied to the occupation. A counselor who violates these laws is subject to legal sanctions, such as suspension or revocation of a license. The violator may be subject to fines and imprisonment. Professional certification boards have more exacting standards that supersede the standards followed in the licensure process, because there is less political involvement in setting the standards. Licenses are required in most states. However, two states have not set this requirement yet.

AMHCA

In 1976, the American Mental Health Counselors Association (AMHCA) was established. In 1981, Florida law impacted the AMHCA's licensure interests. In 1980, AMHCA issued War Chest Grants to states desiring licensure legislation. Many of the AMHCA leaders transferred into prominent positions in the ACA at that time. Insurance companies began to recognize the MHC certification holders. AMHCA also began efforts in the political arena to move forward their credentialing agenda

program. This political movement gained momentum through AMHCA's National Legislative/Government Relations Committee. Their work directly impacted federal recognition, making it possible for CCMHC's and licensed professional counselors to become core providers in the Medicare system. This resulted in changes to the Social Security Act legislation. In 1984, Tricare expanded their recognition to allow CCMHC's to work as providers, provided they were supervised by MSWs, psychologists, or psychiatrists.

Role in the 21st century
The American Mental Health Counselors Association (AMHCA) increased its membership after the National Defense Education Act of 1958, which allocated funding for counselors in the school system in response to Sputnik legislation. The primary function of school counselors was to interest students in mathematics and science. The economic recession of the 1970's changed the counselors' educational direction. Counselors obtained their masters and doctorate degrees for clinical careers, partly due to the Community Mental Centers Act of 1968, which increased employment prospects for mental health professionals. The AMHCA became part of the American Personnel and Guidance Association in 1976, which later became the American Counseling Association. Mental health professionals can expect to take a 60-credit course program and two years of supervised working experience before obtaining their masters degree or licensure.

Licensure for mental health professionals
The American Mental Health Counselors Association (AMHCA) established the National Academy of Certified Clinical Mental Health Counselors under the National Board of Certified Counselors. The standards of the Council for

Accreditation of Counseling and Related Educational programs adopted in 1986 were instrumental in making available a 60-credit course program. In addition, the professional must work for two years under supervised conditions to gain experience in a mental healthcare setting before they are allowed to apply for a license. There are 48 states within the union that provide a license to PC's. The public recognizes the need for these professionals due to the efforts of the AMHCA. PC's may also find employment with insurance companies, mental health organizations, and in national professional alliances. The AMHCA works diligently to expand the public awareness of the work performed by PC's.

Mental health awareness efforts
Mental health awareness efforts are ongoing. The AMHCA has designed Mental Health Counseling Awareness Week to help the public recognize the need for sound mental health practices. The Mental Health Counseling Awareness Week program provides various educational materials. One awareness tool is the development of a mental health awareness stamp. The stamp is promoted by Dr. Wayne Meyerowitz. The concentration of the mental health awareness efforts are on prevention and wellness programs for the public held in the community. Prevention and wellness programs look favorably on the role of the mental health counselor as a holistic provider of services. Holistic care involves looking at a client's physical, mental, and social conditions in providing treatment recommendations. The holistic care model contrasts with the more limited focus of traditional mental health care.

Professional identity
AMHCA is an organization for mental health counselors with membership totaling about 5,600. The AMHCA

diligently ensures that professional counselors work under a set of standards and obtain the best training available. The AMHCA established ongoing educational opportunities for its members, including an annual conference. The AMHCA publishes a newsletter entitled The Advocate, and a quarterly scholarly journal entitled The Journal of Mental Health Counseling. AMHCA lobbies politically to get legislative and policy issues passed that make a positive impact on the work of mental health counselors. Presently, there is no national standard for counselors. Each state's licensure and title for the mental health counseling position is different. The differences in each state lead to misidentification and misunderstandings.

Public policy
The AMHCA's director of public policy and legislation is Beth Powell. She works in a full time position to promote and reach the AMHCA's political objectives, which include the reimbursement of mental health counseling services from Medicare and other plans under the Federal Employee Health Benefits Plan (FEHBP). The AMHCA is also interested in stopping discriminatory referral practices of doctors and administrators under CHAMPUS/TRICARE insurance. The AMHCA desires to establish laws that give mental health counselors the status of independent providers operating in Navy Family Service Centers and other military established health care. The AMHCA concentrates its attention on the privacy of mental health patients through regulation. The AMHCA strives for patients' confidentiality rights as a legislative issue.

State legislation
The AMHCA's political objectives have reached the state level. States that do not have independent licensure and accreditation legislation have adopted the

licensure laws promoted by the AMHCA. The AMHCA works diligently to provide protection under the law for counselors that use its testing instruments for assessment purposes. The AMHCA tries to ensure that reimbursement for the work performed by mental health counselors is legislated. The AMHCA is lobbying for the designation of mental health counselors as providers in the Medicaid guidelines. Lobbying is still necessary because the AMHCA's efforts to obtain the designation failed in the 2004 Medicare law revisions. However, the AMHCA will continue to work on behalf of mental health counselors to make this designation a reality in future revisions.

Collaborative relationships

AMHCA's efforts are collaborative and impact a multitude of organizations. The mutually concerned organizations are: The American Association of State Counseling Boards; Divisional Affiliate of the American Counseling Association; Canadian Counseling Association; Capitol Area Rural Health Roundtable; Consumer Coalition For Health Privacy; Council for the Accreditation of Counseling and Related Programs; Mental Health Liaison Group; Mental Health Policy Roundtable; National Coalition on Mental Health and Aging; National Health Council; National Quality Caregiving Coalition of the Rosalynn Carter Institute; Patient Access to Specialty Care Coalition; and the Prevention Coalition. The advantages of collaborative relationships are two- fold: The community gains a more thorough understanding of mental health care needs, and mental health counselors are accepted as a vital component of the mental health providers and delivery system.

Future of counselor credentialing

The efforts of the AMHCA have had a profound effect upon the licensure laws for counselors in the mental health field. Counselor education programs have applied more exacting standards to their courses. Managed care options in the insurance industry have also changed the MHC provider's standing within the profession. This change has benefited the equality that mental health counselors desire to be accepted by other professionals. Legislation was passed that helped them gain equal standing. The credentials and licensure laws will continue to change as government bodies are influenced by the efforts of AMHCA. The twenty-first century promises to be one in which more opportunities are presented to the MHC's who have achieved the appropriate credentials required in their state of operation. New counseling professions will emerge as the need for more versatile counselors arises.

Technological Literacy

Advancements in technology

Gutenberg invented moveable type in the fifteenth century. Bell invented the telephone and Marconi the radio in the nineteenth century. The twentieth century brought computers, the World Wide Web, cell phones, and a wide range of other technological advancements. Cars can assist drivers and anticipate accidents. These advancements have resulted in a change in almost every professional field of study. Mental health professionals can expect to see these technological advancements applied in a number of ways. Clients have new ways to access services. Counselors and clients may find new formats for interaction. Management procedures may change to support the technological structures. Training may be altered or delivered via different formats or systems. The latest research may increase in comprehension and availability. The mental health counselor will need to be competent in technological literacy and the applications of technology in the field.

Technological literacy

Technological literacy can be described as the ability to comprehend the use of technology and to select the appropriate applications used in a variety of systems. The person who is technologically literate will be able to make an informed decision about the use of technology in a given area. The technologically literate person will have the basic skill level that is needed in a variety of technological environments. The technologically literate counselor will be able to access technology at work, at home, and in the community environment. The technologically literate counselor will understand that there are certain security risks associated with the use of technology, and will be able to make sound judgments about ethical dilemmas that can arise through the use of technology. The technologically literate counselor will be able to critically examine new advancements for their potential counseling uses.

Appropriate competency levels

The Association for Counselor Education and Supervision (ACES) started the ACES Technology Interest Network in 1997. The network has three initiatives that involve the following: A set of technological competencies for mental health counselors; an established Web site; and counselor education programs in a web-based format. These initiatives evolved from consultation with counselor educators on a global scale. The proposed competencies were introduced to the American Counseling Association World Conference in Indianapolis in the spring of 1998. Twelve competency standards were approved at that time. These twelve

competencies are subject to updates by the ACES Technology Interest Network. Updates will be needed as interaction increases through Web-based technologies. Chat rooms, bulletin boards, instant messaging, blogs, listservs, virtual offices, video conferencing, electronic meetings, and email communications allow a variety of formats for interaction.

There were twelve competency levels approved at the American Counseling Association World Conference in 1998. The first competency level states that the counselor will use productivity software. This use will allow the counselor to create web pages, group presentations, letters, or reports as needed. The second competency level states that the counselor will use audiovisual equipment. This use will allow the counselor to operate audio recorders, projection equipment, video conferencing equipment, and playback units as required. The third competency level states that the counselor will use computerized statistical packages. This will help the counselor create statistical reports. The fourth competency level states that the counselor will use computerized testing, diagnostic, and career decision-making programs. This will allow the counselor to provide information and assistance to clients in a less expensive and more easily accessible format.

The fifth competency level states that the counselor will use e-mail communications. This will allow the counselor to communicate cheaply on a professional level by utilizing e-mail technological systems. The sixth competency level states that the counselor will be able to find counseling-related information on the Internet related to careers, employment opportunities, educational programs, training programs, financial assistance, scholarship opportunities, treatment methodologies, and social/personal issues. The seventh competency states that the counselor will subscribe to, participate in, and sign off counseling listservs, as appropriate. This ensures that the counselor understands the techniques to access and protect the listservs available to counselors. The eighth competency states the counselor will access CD data bases that contain counseling-related information. This will allow the counselor access to information that is needed in the profession.

The ninth competency states that the counselor will comprehend legal and ethical codes and apply those codes to their Internet use for delivering counseling services. This is necessary to protect the client and to ensure legal care for the client. The tenth competency states that the counselor will comprehend advantages and disadvantages associated with the Internet. This is needed to prevent unforeseen complications that can arise when using a complex system. The eleventh competency states that the counselor will use the Internet for continuing education purposes. This is needed to ensure that the counselor can access education and training as it becomes available and will keep the counselor's competency and skill levels up-to- date. The twelfth competency states that the counselor will evaluate the information gleaned from the Internet for its quality.

Consultation, collaboration, and shared decision-making

The counselor must be able to collaborate and work with a wide group of people through technologically-based systems. The counselor can access others through electronic devices like the Internet. E-mail is used on a day- to-day basis by many individuals. Electronic communications can be accomplished on global scales. In the discussion group format, units are formed to talk about topics regarding specific activities, goals, or projects. In the data collection and organizational activities format, databases are used to organize, share, and retrieve information. Information can be given in the form of references, curriculum projects, research papers, and an exchange of contact information. In the document or file sharing format, the capability exists to allow each person in the group to work on a project at the same time, in synchronous collaboration.

Communication

In synchronous communication, real time is incorporated to allow users to accomplish text chats with each other. Some real time applications allow videoconferencing. When documents are involved, annotations systems (such as in Microsoft's Word) can be employed to allow the users to comment and edit the project. Online communication brings people together in an electronic format. A network of colleagues is formed to alleviate some of the isolation counselors experience. Inclusion is promoted. Asynchronous communication is a sharing of ideas at different times. This can be a benefit to the counselor who needs an opportunity to reflect on new ideas. An additional benefit is found in the sharing of solutions within the collaborative community. Online collaboration can save time and money. It is easily accessible and increases productivity, as the counselor doesn't have to leave his own office.

Netmeeting or Click to Meet is a communication format that allows conferencing to be conducted on the Internet and corporate intranet. This tool incorporates audio, video, and text communication. The user can exchange information in various ways. Graphics are exchanged on an electronic whiteboard. Files can be transferred. Instant Messenger allows users to send real time messages to each other and to authorized buddies. Authorized buddies are the people on the list provided by the user. A Usenet newsgroup is a free service that allows a global discussion. Newsgroup users can post their messages via this system. Blogs are a journal format that is kept on the Internet. Blogs are updated by the individual who started the blog or maintains the blog. Postings to blogs are done in chronological order. These can be maintained by persons with little or no technical expertise.

Web counseling

Web counseling is a new format for mental health counselors. There is a mixture of perceptions about how web counseling is performed, but there is no formal definition for this structure. Some think that this is not a viable way to accomplish counseling, because there is limited body language visible on a Web cam. There is no research to answer the questions that arise concerning the virtual environment and any possible negative effects that may occur from Web counseling. Nor is there any research on its possible benefits. Some fear that online personalities differ from personalities encountered in real life. Others fear that generalization of coping strategies may not allow them to materialize in the life of the client. Some counselors are taking a "wait and see" approach until this new field becomes more formally defined. Some see cyber or Web counseling as beneficial as a supplemental tool to face-to-face counseling sessions, and are embracing this new structure.

Web counseling may be able to increase efficiency and accessibility for persons seeking counseling services. An individual with physical disabilities may find that this medium is more accessible. Others may find that this medium is less intrusive upon their privacy, especially if it is by text alone. These clients may be more comfortable in disclosing private thoughts and feelings in the virtual environment. Counselors can provide electronic file transfers or links that connect clients to available research, or other information. Counselors can seek help from colleagues in collaborative efforts. Assessment, instruction, and informational resources are available via the Internet. Virtual environments give counselors and clients a forum to answer questions, gain social support, and conduct virtual counseling sessions. Marriage and family counseling can be conducted with clients from different parts of the globe. Supervision can be conducted through anecdotal evidence shown in e-mails. Increased communication between student counselor and supervisor counselor can be accomplished.

Disadvantages of web counseling
There are disadvantages of web counseling with respect to security failures and poverty. Encryption and security measures can fail, increasing the risk that confidentiality is breached. Counselors must provide all possible and reasonable security measures in an effort to protect their clients. The counselor and the client may not be proficient in their computer skill levels. Keyboarding, electronic file transfers and other computer skills are required. Geographical factors may be ignored. Natural disasters in one part of the country may not be so readily understood in other parts of the country. Community or cultural events may be ignored. Therefore, the counselor should research

- 139 -

the client's locale to anticipate geographical factors that may be of significance to the client. Research documents the digital divide separating rich from poor, and old from young, populations in America. The division among socioeconomically disadvantaged groups may be widened if the counselor fails to realize the resentment of underserved individuals.

Certification and licensure issues have yet to be regulated in the virtual environment. Virtual environments may not be conducive to building trust, concern, and authentic working relationships between client and counselor. The client's identity cannot be established with verification procedures in the virtual environment. Clients could potentially disguise their gender, race, or other pertinent details about their life. Ethical standards as they apply to Web counseling have yet to be established. The fluidity of the Internet and the changes that can occur in technology may have future implications on mental health service delivery that have yet to be realized. Therefore, training and educational programs may not be effective in preparing the mental health counselor to conduct Web counseling. There is an increase in online issues, like compulsive shopping, gambling, pornography, online marital affairs, online bullying, online stalking, and hatred-based web sites.

Political Activists

Political issues

The United States has a political system with a listening ear for the issues that are important to its citizens. One way that this political system works is for individuals to speak out about the issues that are significant to them. A wide spectrum of communication systems are available to help in this endeavor. The individual may present this issue to others through speeches, telephone calls, emails, or Web sites. The AMHCA recognizes the need to bring issues important to mental health counselors to light, and works jointly with the American Counseling Association (ACA) to send lobbyists to Washington to represent mental health counselors. As early as 1982, the AMHCA had managed to enlist the services of a renowned lobbyist to represent its interests in the political arena.

MHC's were taught how to represent themselves as political advocates and lobbyists in the grassroots campaigns set up by the AMHCA. The AMHCA and the ACA have worked diligently to establish a network that is competent in issuing timely e-mails, written correspondence, phone calls, and face-to-face communications to promote its political agenda. The successes of the lobbying efforts have been critical in the licensure legislation set up in the majority of states. Only two states remain uncommitted in this issue. Therefore, it is expected that the AMHCA and the ACA will turn their efforts to equality issues for the mental health counselor. The problem of recognition exists on the corporate level. Private corporate third party payers and some insurance companies have yet to recognize the high standards and expertise that exist in the mental health counselors' professional credentials.

Recognition of the Mental Health Counselor

The MHC received limited recognition in the early 1980's. This limited recognition originated from the efforts of the Office of Civilian Health and Medical Program for the Uniformed Services (OCHAMPUS), who refused to recognize the MHC as the fifth core service provider. This recognition would have placed MHCs on the same level as psychiatrists, psychologists, clinical social workers, and psychiatric nurses if it had been successful. Opponents found the lack of a universal licensure or certification system for MHCs to be problematic. However, the managed care programs have helped this process. The managed care systems' demand for licensed mental health counselors caused the states to appropriately respond by passing licensure legislation. Recognition can now be given to the counselor in forms of reimbursement payments for services rendered. This battle for recognition continues to be a concern.

Legislative process

The legislative process begins with a proposed bill. This proposed bill must be assessed to determine what strategies are applicable to get the bill to pass and become law. The bill must be presented to the legislature. This calls for some consideration about the most receptive body. Some bills do well in the House of Representatives, and other bills are more suited to the Senate. Still others perform well in both the House and the Senate. The political representative who is chosen must be the best advocate for the particular cause. Special interest groups may help promote the bill through legislative contacts, after it has been presented to the legislative body. Lobbyists work to establish relationships with key committee members. The bill must go through the committee before it can be voted on.

Passing a bill

Most bills that are introduced to a legislative body never make it out of committee. The bill that does make it out of committee must still be given support by the majority of the legislative body to be approved. The approved bill can then be sent to the executive branch of the government. The executive branch on the state level is the governor. The executive branch on the national level is the president. The executive branch representative has the responsibility of signing the bill into law. The executive branch is subject to lobbying efforts. The executive branch may veto or reject a bill. The legislative process is expensive and time-consuming. The AMHCA sees it as their responsibility to take on this complex process to ensure that MHC's are recognized and credentialed by each state.

Lobbyists

The unpaid lobbyist works to influence the political entities and representatives who have the power to pass a bill. The mental health counselor assigned as a lobbyist creates a rapport with elected government officials face-to-face, and develops it through telephone call, letters and e-mail correspondence. The intended result of this diligent communication effort is to remind the official about issues that are important to the mental health counselor. The face-to-face visit can be accomplished during visits to the official's office in the home state. This setting gives the official a chance to connect with his constituents and to engage in conversation on key issues.

Mental health professionals may frown on a relationship that is built on campaign contributions as ethically suspect. However, the time- honored tradition of donating money to a candidate's election campaign is effective in gaining the attention of elected government officials. The government official takes a donation to mean that you are a member of his group and you support his position as a representative for your state. This puts you in a privileged and influential position. A campaign donation may be enough for you to gain faster access into the government official's office. Any relationship you build should be given attention to maintain it. Keep up your communication efforts, even when you do not have a lobbying agenda in place.

Votes and financial backing

Politicians are elected on the basis of how many votes they receive from their constituents. This means that the politician finds great worth in the power of the voter. Constituents who are part of an organized group can mean a great many votes on re-election day. The politician will pay attention to the lobbyist who represents large numbers of constituents. The Political Action Committees (PAC) had a strong influence on the political system in the past. However, today this influence has diminished. PAC and many lobbying committees are careful to keep a low profile because of the negative attitudes that voters have about paid lobbyists and large corporations. MHC lobbyists do not have much in the way of financial resources, but do have the grassroots support of other MHC voters that are responsible for electing government officials into office.

Grassroots efforts

Grassroots efforts are the hard work that goes into the communication process of the MHC's network of supporters. The network is developed through e-mail communication or telephone trees that connect the members with each other. The connection among the members can be centralized to one state or it may be on a national level. E-mail communication and listservs have advanced these efforts immensely. The communication system is activated whenever there is a bill that requires attention. The members receive

a request to take action. The actions to be taken often involve letter writing campaigns. The members receive advance training in the art of persuasive letter writing. This well organized communication system has been effective in gaining the support of members in the legislative body. Participants in this system recognize the importance that their vote makes to the elected official.

Communication

The importance of communicating in succinct terms cannot be overstated. The unpaid lobbyist must make his or her point quickly and succinctly to be heard. Otherwise, the unpaid lobbyist risks "the brush off", or is not understood by the official. The best way to present your issue is through brief telephone calls, short telegrams, or notes. The notes should be written by hand on paper that bears your personal letterhead. E-mails are not as effective. Your communication should clearly state how the bill will make a positive impact on the voting constituents. Keep your client's needs at the forefront of your mind. Represent these needs accurately to your elected government official. The official needs to understand how the bill will improve mental health counseling services for the client.

Timing

Timing is another issue that should be addressed in the life of an unpaid lobbyist. Activate the communication network system among your fellow MHC supporters whenever there is a vote in front of a legislative committee. The support of other MHC's within the organized network should impact this vote in a positive way. The bill cannot go to the floor for a vote by the larger body of legislators until it is passed by the committee. The tree needs to be activated again when the bill comes up for a vote on the floor. This is a critical time, as the vote must pass to go on to the next step in the legislative process. The final stop is at the executive branch. This is also a critical time for the communication network to make their opinions known to their elected governmental leader.

Professional group membership

The ACA and the AMHCA are organizations that represent the professional and political interests of the mental health counselor. These two organizations can do this due to their large numbers of members, which give pause to the elected officials when they work together to influence the political system. Numbers are triumphant in giving the group influence in the political arena. Membership funds are used to facilitate these labors. The group counts on volunteer service to lend a hand to their legislative undertakings. One issue at hand is the realization of full parity for all MHC's. State officials, federal officials, private insurance companies, and managed care personnel must be made to understand. Lobbying is of paramount importance in changing the minds of these stakeholders.

Research & Counseling

Counselor-client relationships

The counselor goes into the mental health field for a variety of reasons, but should bear in mind that the counseling field primarily involves relationships with clients who cannot find solutions to their problems independently. The counselor may have a strong interest in research design, data collection methods, research variables, and the reliability and validity of assessments. These elements are tied to the relationship that the counselor

builds with his client. The approach utilizes theory, research, and practice. Theory is the rules and techniques that have been discovered in study and in the life experience of individuals. Research involves an assessment of the information compared to the results of other studies. Practice describes how therapy and decisions are applied for the client's well being.

Counselor and researcher

All counselors today receive training in how to apply theories and methods that have been discovered through research. The counselor learns how to evaluate the clinical interventions that have been applied in therapy. The counselor remains objective in his examination of the data. The counselor maintains ethical procedures and is accountable for his actions. This means that the counselor is careful to document his work. The counselor is competent in his use of terminology and can make a sound interpretation of the research obtained. The counselor and the researcher work for the client's benefit. The client must not be harmed. The counselor and the researcher recognize that the client has a choice to determine his or her own actions. The counselor and the researcher are fair and loyal to the client. Both desire to help the client develop steps that will assist in the solution of the problem.

The researcher uses different terminology than the counselor does. However, this is semantics. The researcher commonly refers to hypothesis, data, and tests of significance. The counselor uses different words that have similar meanings like hunches, client provided information, and case conceptualizations. The mental health counselor is careful to identify the problems that the client is trying to convey in his conversation. The client

- 143 -

will work with the counselor in the collaborative formulation of goals. Implementation of the goals follows this procedure. The client must be evaluated as he or she progresses through the intervention. Termination occurs when therapy ends. The client and counselor participate in a summary interpretation that is a restatement of the progress made. This can provide the basis to help the client come to future conclusions and to make informative decisions.

Researcher's steps in helping clients

The researcher takes different steps than the counselor in helping the client. The first research step is to identify the problem with a series of questions. These questions are used to formulate a research design. The research design will utilize the goals that are essential to the researcher's investigation process. The treatment or interventions that will be applied are considered in the choice of measuring instruments to be used. The interventions are implemented so that the researcher can collect data on the various interventions and results of each. The data is then evaluated to determine the desired outcome. The data is interpreted in accordance with prescribed criteria. The conclusions that are reached are used to help increase the knowledge that the research was used to develop. Counselors may use knowledge gleaned from previous research to help a client with his or her problem.

Positivistic research

Positivism is a scientific method that can be applied in social science research. The researcher uses the method to make predictions about what he thinks may happen in the future. The researcher takes care in designing experiments that can be disproved or supported by observations of the conditions that occur.

The research is accomplished by comparing groups. The numerical data obtained is taken from random samples of a population. The numerical data is compared to the group findings. Positivistic research investigates causality by comparing the group members in one group with another group. The variables that are different in each group are known as variable X or variable Y. Typically, variable X refers to an independent variable. Variable Y is known as the dependent variable that can be changed with the application or the withdrawal of variable X.

Post positivism

The belief of those researchers who support post positivism is that truth cannot be fully revealed. The post positivist will collect data and perform methodical examinations of the data. These examinations help the researcher to develop a probability about the results. Probability is defined as a prediction which is founded on hypothesized truths that are generally believed. The post-positivism researcher does not deal in absolutes. Instead, the researcher will apply statistical tests that will support their hypothesized and inconclusive information. They refrain from making an assertion about the absolute truth of an answer to the problem. The researcher will state a number of close approximations to the truth based on quantitative research. Quantitative refers to the quantity or the amount which is described in numerical terms of measurement. Qualitative research is different, in that it uses narrative forms of data.

General methodological issues

The counselor may read a number of research materials in his search to find a possible solution for his client's problem.

The research may be quantitative or qualitative. The counselor should be able to identify the methodology used in the research. Laboratory research may be used, in contrast to field research. The difference is found in the setting of the experiments conducted. The researcher controls the setting and the variables found in the setting as much as he can. Laboratories are more easily controlled than a field setting. In controlling the variables, the researcher may seek to standardize the implementation of the treatment applied in a counseling session. Another control may be found in external issues like temperature, light, and noise. The mental health counselor will find field research to be more applicable to real life than laboratory work.

Lab research, field research, and validity

Lab research has a high internal validity value because it is more easily controlled in terms of the cause and effect relationships of the variables applied under specific conditions. It also eliminates other explanations that can be attributed to a change in the results. However, lab research does have a low external validity, in that generalization to other people, places, or time frames may not be so easy to accomplish. Generalization means that the action can be repeated in other situations. Field research is more easily accomplished because it is done in a natural setting or environment. The researcher will travel to the field of study. Field research demonstrates low internal validity because of the lack of control over external variables. Field research has high external validity because it can be generalized to other situations and settings.

Research designs

Quantitative research design
Quantitative research designs include experimental, quasi-experimental, and descriptive research. The experimental research designs are described in two methods. The between-group method is one in which there is a control group and an experimental group that are both being observed. The experimental group is the one to which the treatment is applied. The treatment is known as the manipulation of the independent X variable. The control group will receive no such treatment. This allows the researcher to compare the results of the two groups. The results are compared in relation to data obtained in the pre-test and the post test. The pre-test provides the standard of comparison that indicates a change occurred after the treatment was applied. The post test-only control group refers to the data collected after the experimental group has been subjected to the dependent variable. The post test-only control group is only compared at the end of the treatment, not beforehand.

The researchers who collect data from both control groups use it to create an average that is used in the comparison of the data. Both groups are used to collect this data. The comparison is used to determine whether or not the hypothesis was supported. However, there is one difference in the pre-test/post test control group, in that its comparisons are made before and after the treatment is applied, while the post test-only group is only compared at the end. The pre-test/post test control group is used to compare distinctions in the experimental group's average scores and the control group's average ratings. The pre-test comparisons may identify group similarities. The Solomon four-group design uses all four groups. This gives the added benefit of comparing the effects of the pre-test by comparing the pre-test groups with those who did not receive the pre-test.

Factorial designs

Factorial designs are described as what happens when two or more independent variables are used simultaneously. The comparison is made to determine how the independent variable affects the dependent variable. The comparison is also made to determine how a combination of the two affects the dependent variable. This can provide a comparison that is useful for assessing differences found in different populations, like males versus females. The therapy and the gender would be the independent variable x. This comparison may also be appropriate for the evaluation of outcomes versus a change in the client. The clients are used to appraise improved quality of life versus a comparison that can be done to contrast the client's quality of life to other clients. This evaluation of the outcome versus an evaluation of the change can be useful to the counselor in addressing a factorial design in his approach.

Within-subject designs

The within-subject designs found in the quantitative research design are based on the participant. The participant forms his own control group of one. Every participant is exposed to all aspects of the treatment applied. The evaluation is done to determine the change in the single person, not the entire group. The crossover-within-subjects design is: (a) randomly assigned; (b) given a pre-test; (c) exposed to the same type of treatment known as TRT 1; (d) given a post test to determine the result of the treatment; (e) after the post test, the subject is switched or crossed over to a second treatment which is known as TRT 2; (f) the subject is given another post test to determine the result of the second treatment. The Latin

Square Design uses more than two treatments and expands the number of groups that a researcher uses for a single study.

Latin Square Design

The Latin Square Design has three separate groups of subjects. Each group will receive three different treatments. These treatments will be given in a counterbalanced fashion. The researchers will collect the data in between each treatment that is given. The groups are labeled as Group One, Group Two, and Group Three. For explanation purposes we will begin with Group One's exposure to treatment 1 or TRT 1. Group Two is exposed to treatment 2 or TRT 2. Group Three is exposed to treatment 3 or TRT 3. Each group is subjected to a post test after exposure to the treatment. Then, Group One is exposed to TRT 2. Group Two is exposed to TRT 3. Group Three is exposed to TRT 1. Each group is again subject to a post test to measure the effects of the treatment received in this design.

Finally, Group One is exposed to TRT 3. Group Two is exposed to TRT 1. Group Three is exposed to TRT 2. The groups receive a post test to measure the effects of the final treatment received. The researcher examines the effects of each treatment. The researcher examines the sequential effects of the treatments received. This type of procedure may be applied to an individual receiving counseling. However, the difference would be made in determining which treatment was most effective with an individual client after trying three types of treatments. This differs from the Latin Square Design that has three separate groups of subjects. It is similar, in that the individual client will receive three different treatments, just as each control group did. The researchers and the counselor will both collect the data in between each treatment that is given.

Quasi-experimental research design

The quasi-experimental research design utilizes an independent variable that is subject to manipulation by the researcher. The researcher is concerned with the examination of cause and effect relationships between the variables that are being studied in the research design. The quasi-experimental approach is most useful when subjects are not available for random assignments into groups. The researcher is confined to studying groups that are already formed. These are known as intact groups. The quasi-experimental research design is appropriate for use in intact groups found in school systems or clinical settings. Using three intact groups can allow two treatment groups and one control group. This use can solve an ethical dilemma that arises when treatment is withheld from certain parties within a study. The researcher is not faced with assigning members to the group, as they are selected at random. Therefore, the researcher is not forced to face an ethical decision.

Non-randomized, pre-test/post test control group design

The non-randomized, pre-test/post test control group design is a derivative of the quasi-experimental design. The pre-test/post test control group is used to compare distinctions in the experimental group's average scores and the control group's average ratings. The subjects of this research are not given random assignments into a group. This can cause a condition known as non-equivalent groups, which exhibit distinctive qualities that are unlike other groups. The pre-test comparisons may identify group similarities or distinctive differences in the groups. However, when too many differences exist within the groups, the researcher may have difficulties in interpreting the data collected. The groups are used to collect data. The researcher must use prudent decision making processes when making these interpretations. One solution to the problem of non-equivalent groups can be found in the cohort research design.

Cohort design

The cohort is formed from students within a school setting who follow a set course path. The students in the cohort exhibit similarities that may be attributed to characteristics, career goals, or other shared interests. The cohort participants share similar environments or settings. The researcher will test the effects of a variable on the cohort group. Some variables that have been applied include new curricula and performance levels. One example of this is found in the application of a mathematics curriculum applied to ninth grade students. The students receive a pre-test and a post test to measure their performance levels. The next year, another group of students receive the same pre and post tests, and the same curriculum. A comparison is made of the results obtained from both cohort groups. This will be used to determine the effects of the new curriculum on mathematics performance in students.

Single-subject design

Single-subject designs are associated with the clinical-research models of the modern age. Counselors prefer this design for a variety of reasons attributed to the descriptive qualities that are found in the client-counselor relationship. This can be used to target behaviors. Groups can include couples, families, small groups, or organizations. The target behaviors are referred to as dependent variable Y. The dependent variable Y is used for numerous data collections over an extended time frame. The researcher measures the dependent variable Y, which is the targeted behavior being observed, prior to the application of the treatment. The treatment will be known as the independent variable X. The researcher will also take data during application of the treatment. An AB design is referred to as a single-subject design. The baseline is known as Phase A. The treatment is known as Phase B.

AB design

The AB design is a single-subject design utilized when researchers need to take multiple measurements. The measurements are gleaned during observations of the subjects. The observations occur in Phase A and Phase B. Phase A is the baseline for the study. The data collected in Phase A is used to determine the current level of functioning in subjects before any treatment or intervention is given. In Phase B, data is collected to determine the functioning levels of subjects during treatment. The baseline and the treatment data collection are used to make a comparison to expose changes in the target behaviors. The baseline must be a stable component to allow the comparison to be made. The ABAB design is given to denote the withdrawal/reversal design. This design introduces the baseline, then treatment, which is followed by a withdrawal or reversal of the treatment, and ends with treatment.

ABAB design and descriptive design

The ABAB design is given to denote the withdrawal/reversal design. This design introduces the baseline, then treatment, which is followed by a withdrawal or reversal of the treatment, and ends with treatment. If the behaviors return after treatment is withdrawn or reduced, then it is assumed that the treatment has a causal relationship on the targeted behavior. If the target behavior does not return, then the researcher cannot establish a cause and effect relationship between the treatment and the targeted behavior. That means that the variables do not have a cause and effect relationship that can be established. There may be other variables that resulted in the change in the targeted behavior. Descriptive design alludes to the variables in a study. Variables are dependent or independent within a study. Variables can be manipulated or controlled within a study.

Survey research

Survey research is used to illustrate, clarify, or investigate variables in a research study. Counseling research depends on the client's sharing specifics, opinions, and mannerisms. Descriptive survey research is conducted to gain essential data on issues of concern. One might address the frequency of an issue. Explanatory survey research is used to explain why an issue happens. The researcher may make notes of the variables that may be attributed to the issue. Exploratory survey research is used to examine aspects of an issue that have not been given much attention. Data can be gleaned from questionnaires, mailed surveys, telephone interviews, or face-to-face interviews. Longitudinal research describes the same groups of people being questioned over a lengthy time frame. Cross-sectional research describes many different people are questioned at once. There are difficulties that can arise when using a survey. Researchers may have unrelated variables that produce invalid or unreliable results.

Ex Post Facto Designs

Ex post facto is a Latin term which means "after the fact". The research is conducted after the variables have already been introduced into the picture. The researcher is trying to establish how the dependent variable has been influenced by the independent variable. The variables are not manipulated by the researcher, due to the inherent nature of the variable. These variables include components like gender, personality types or traits, or other inherent qualities. Typically, a client's file will have information that can be used in the Ex post facto design. Correlation studies involve the establishment of relationships with the use of statistical data. The Pearson correlation yields a numerical coefficient in the range of +1.0 to -1.0 to describe whether or not a relationship has been supported by the statistical data collected: 0.70 = high correlation; 0.30—0.69 = moderate correlation; and -0.3—+0.3 = low correlation.

Qualitative research designs
Qualitative research designs include action research, feminist inquiry, critical theory, ethnography, grounded theory, and case study. A researcher uses inductive reasoning to investigate problems, design research studies, accumulate data, and generate a hypothesis. Qualitative researchers are highly concerned with providing trustworthy research. This begins with the collection of credible data. The research should be characterized by internal validity, which cuts down on mistakes. The research should be characterized by external validity that is transferable or generalizable to others. The research does not follow a standardized plan. The research is carried out on the basis of the subjective experiences that the participants share. The researcher also makes subjective judgments about the data collected. The data has dependability qualities and is found to be reliable for use. The research can be confirmed through parallel research studies that apply like research methods. This is known as confirmability.

Ethnography

Ethnography is based on culturally relevant data that is seen as a social interpretation of the world. This research is based on relationships that are observed. These relationships may be founded within the contextual confines of the sub-culture being observed. The research is also based on the relationships that the observer has with the observed subjects in the study. The research is based on the setting where the observations are conducted. The research is slanted in the perspective viewpoint of the observer and the observed subject. The observer and the observed subject share interpretations of the results. The research also considers the reader or the consumer of the study who will use the research. Ethnography is rarely used in counseling sessions, due to its intensive field research component. This can be a time-consuming endeavor. However, ethnography is successfully used in the field of anthropology.

Grounded theory and case studies

Grounded theory involves the use of data that can describe connections between theory and what happens in real life. Data can be analyzed to find patterns or themes. These patterns or themes help the researcher to define the real life data that has been collected. Grounded theory provides the researcher with a theoretical link that gives evidence that the theory is plausible in its explanation of a real world phenomenon. Case studies are used to provide qualitative data to support the findings of an investigation. The study usually begins with interviews, observations, videotaping, analysis of documents, or surveys. The researcher records his or her observations. Researchers do not develop a close relationship with the subjects being observed in the study. The reader can experience the setting and the problem readily by becoming involved in the story that is told in the research study.

Ethics

The mental health counselor is obligated to uphold ethical standards. The nature of the work presents the counselor with ongoing challenges that test the counselor's ethical positions about a problem. Counselors not only have to consider the ethical position they should take when a problem presents, but must also consider how the solution will be of benefit to the client. The client cannot be damaged from the solution. Therefore, the consequences of the solution should be weighed carefully. The other consideration the counselor must reflect on is the tendency for most counselors to do nothing when an ethical issue is involved. This tendency may be due to the fact that the counselor feels unsure of just how to proceed in the situation, or it may be that the counselor is reluctant to proceed.

Ethics and curricula

It was not until after 1990 that ethics courses were incorporated into the mental health counselors' graduate degree programs. The American Psychological Association played an important part in the 1970's to change the curricula offered in doctoral programs, by requiring colleges to teach ethics. This requirement was necessary before the college could be granted accreditation privileges. Those in the field prior to 1990 had to depend upon their supervisors' ability to both model and train in ethical procedures and conduct. This was an inefficient method for a number of reasons. The supervisor may not have been aware of the ethical code that applied to a given situation. The supervisor may not have had a good understanding of sound ethical principles. Instruction in ethical principles should not be the sole responsibility of the clinical supervisor.

Code of Ethics

The first attempt to supplement the mental health professionals' degree programs was instruction in the Code of Ethics. The Code was taught to those entering the profession after 1990 as counselors, social workers, or psychologists. The Code gave specific solutions to specific problems; however, the Code had ambiguous interpretations in areas not specifically spelled out. The ambiguity is seen in the way that the Code does not specify the meaning of exact terms. The National Board for Certified Counselors sought in 1997 to provide a less ambiguous wording for the Code of Ethics, so it is no longer seen as abstract rules that do not apply to real situations and real people. Problem-solving models and appreciation for the philosophical basis of each code has been applied to the more comprehensive ethical courses available in colleges today.

Koocher and Keith-Spiegel's problem-solving model

There are nine steps used in the problem-solving model designed by Koocher and Keith-Spiegel in 1998:
- Step 1: Determine the ethical problem
- Step 2: Review the ethical guidelines available that pertain to the problem at hand, including possible solutions that have previously worked with other clients
- Step 3: Peruse the impact that other sources may have on the decisions that should be made to resolve the problem

- Step 4: Consult with trusted professionals about the problem and possible solutions
- Step 5: Assess the human rights and civil liberties of the client, which may be impacted by the solution to the problem, and consider possible consequences of the solution for the problem at hand
- Step 6: Create a number of avenues that may be explored in the solution to the problem
- Step 7: Evaluate the possible consequences that can be the result of each solution applied to the problem at hand
- Step 8: Make a decision about one solution to be implemented
- Step 9: Follow through with the decision that was made

Koocher and Keith-Spiegel's approach can be applied to many ethical dilemmas that a counselor faces in his or her daily professional life. This model is currently in use in the instruction of ethical principles in degree programs throughout the country. It is important to note that this model does offer the counselor the opportunity to keep a professional relationship between himself and his client.

Multiple relationships

In 1974, Arnold Lazarus was a renowned psychotherapist who supported multiple relationships in his ethical decision-making model (multi-modal therapy). Lazarus thought that the client could benefit from the development of a therapeutic and social relationship with the counselor. In 1993, M.C. Gottlieb responded with his own five-step model.
- Step 1: Consider the element of power, where the client feels inferior to the counselor and may find a long-standing relationship harmful
- Step 2: Consider the duration of the relationship by predicting how the relationship and the balance of power may change over time
- Step 3: Consider the clarity of termination, which involves compatibility between the client and the counselor, and consequences that can occur when the client and counselor roles are conflicting and harmful
- Step 4: Gain the perspective and advice of a professional associate
- Step 5: Present the relationship change to the client, and give him or her time to make a decision about this change in the relationship.

Some multiple relationships are expected. For instance, the small town phenomenon describes a situation in which the therapist may have to come into contact with clients within the social structures of a community. A small town therapist may belong to the same religious organization as a client. The small town therapist may find that his clients live in the same neighborhood, or have children in the same school as his own. The small town therapist may belong to the same charitable organizations or attend the same functions.

Kant's categorical imperative and Mill's utilitarianism

One foundational philosophy developed by Immanuel Kant was his categorical imperative. Deontological perspectives deal in universal truths, where everyone receives equal treatment. Therefore, when a counselor believes that privacy should be part of his service, then that privacy is applied to all clients in every situation. There is no room for

- 151 -

exceptions to the rule. Likewise, there is no need to consider consequences in this philosophy, as all people are treated equally. The Golden Rule is rooted in deontology. Utilitarianism was presented by John Stuart Mill. He believed that the consequences had to be looked at in relation to the resulting outcomes. The overall goal is to create as many constructive and positive consequences as possible for the majority of the people.

Tarasoff vs. the Board of Regents of the University of California

John Stuart Mill proposed that the utilitarian should break confidentiality when it benefited the majority of the people. In 1976, a lawsuit was brought to the California Supreme Court to contest the deontological perspective against the utilitarian perspective. In the case of Tarasoff versus the Board of Regents of the University of California, the courts supported the utilitarian perspective on breaking confidentiality for the good of the majority. The court allowed that keeping confidentiality in this case could have caused injury to others. However, some mental health counselors do tend to believe that confidentiality should be an absolute right of the client. The virtue ethics philosophy holds that people with high ethical standards have the ability to make good ethical judgments. This philosophy is also known as value ethics or principle ethics. Lazarus' decision making model is based on the virtue ethics philosophy.

Virtue ethics

The mental health counselor can find that having a strong philosophy of virtue ethics can assist him in his work. Virtue ethics helps the counselor to be motivated to make the best decision for his client. Virtue ethics helps the counselor to understand his responsibility to act in a positive manner and to implement an ethical solution to a problem. Virtue ethics helps the counselor in his appraisal of possible consequences that can arise in a given solution. The counselor with a strong philosophy in virtue ethics has a strong moral character. Virtue ethics is based on beneficence and nonmaleficence, which are the basis of the Hippocratic Oath that states, "First, do no harm." This means that the counselor works to help the client and does not want any damage to come to his client. The decisions that are made in counseling must not disregard the principles maintained in virtue ethics.

Many HMO's and other third party influences may cause the counselor to question whether virtue ethics principles are being followed in the client's care. The counselor may believe that the client is in need of more sessions that are not covered under the client's insurance policy. The counselor can follow a series of actions to maintain the virtue ethics principles, known as beneficence and nonmaleficence. The counselor may appeal to the insurance company for additional sessions. The counselor may also continue to see the client at a reduced price, giving additional sessions at an affordable rate, or issue a referral to the client to seek free services from a government agency or reputable charity. These actions reflect a sense of caring for the client that follows ethical guidelines.

Virtue ethics is based upon beneficence and nonmaleficence. Care and compassion takes the principles behind beneficence one step further. In 1982, Gilligan described caring as a bonding process that created a sense that the counselor had the ability to understand and to identify with how the client was feeling. Gilligan also proposed that the counselor was able to react quickly and favorably in meeting the needs of the client. Gilligan went on to state that the counselor exhibited a compassionate and concerned commitment to his client. The counselor performs these acts of caring in a professional manner. The counselor should not try to practice counseling methods that fall outside his scope of expertise and training. The counselor may violate an ethical principle by not realizing his own incompetence in an area. Some violations occur out of arrogance, over- involvement, or control issues with the client.

Virtue ethics are essential in the role that the mental health counselor performs. However, a note of caution: No one source can be trusted to maintain a virtue ethics perspective. Therefore, supervisors, ethical codes, decision-making models, utilitarian perspectives, and deontological perspectives should all be understood and reviewed when making ethical decisions. The mental health counselor should seek to internalize sound virtue ethics principles. The mental health counselor recognizes the virtue ethics and seeks to live by those ethics in all areas of life. The mental health counselor seeks to gain additional education and training to ensure that he gains competency in a variety of areas. The mental health counselor seeks out an ethical support group. The mental health counselor seeks to establish sound ethical philosophies that reflect virtue ethics principles.

Competence

Competence is the ability to do something to a compulsory set of standards. However, this denotes the most basic level of competency. In the mental health counselor's role, competence must be reached at its uppermost levels. This regard for excellence in performance levels follows the perspective held in virtue ethics. Therefore, the mental

health counselor takes on a life-long commitment to achieving competency levels in his profession. In 1996, Pope and Brown proposed that there were two types of competence to be achieved. The first type involves intellectual competence, which consists of education and training. The second type involves emotional competence. The counselor is self-aware of prejudices held, emotional stability, and competence levels. The counselor seeks professional supervision and referrals when it is necessary.

Justice and accountability

The mental health counselor is aware of his role in providing his clients with a fair program of treatment. Fairness involves the same equal treatment of all clients, as each receives a fair amount of the counselor's time and attention. The virtue of justice may be violated when the counselor is in denial, or when the counselor tries to rationalize his actions. Accountability is part of the virtue ethics philosophy. This means that the counselor takes responsibility for his actions and that of others in his field. Unethical behavior in others can be handled professionally and emphatically. Confrontations need to be approached with respect and a sense of fair play. The goal of the confrontation is to achieve a positive result. The counselor should role-play or rehearse confrontations to ensure that possible responses and consequences can be responded to on a professional level.

Respect

The mental health counselor provides his clients with respect. Respect involves accuracy in reporting details, loyal devotion, honesty, confidence, reliability, keeping promises, and valuing the client's personal independence. The counselor relays to the client an accurate representation of the counselor's role, the client's rights, confidentiality rights, and any negative consequences that can result in a prescribed treatment plan. A handout and simple explanation does not ensure client understanding. The client and legal guardians must give informed consent before treatment can be applied. Clients with a legal guardian must have the guardian's consent to the therapy. Informed consent involves confidentiality in the counselor-client relationship. Confidentiality is maintained in individual counseling sessions, unless the client is a danger to himself or others. This harm must be identified by method and time. Confidentiality is not assured in a group setting or in cases of child abuse.

Self-knowledge

Self-knowledge is an area in which a counselor should make a daily assessment. Some psychoanalytically-trained therapists must undergo mental health counseling therapy as part of their training. This is not always the case, however. Self-knowledge is essential in developing competency in an area. Competency is a considerable part of value ethics. Self-knowledge is also supported by supervisory personnel in the field. Peers or colleagues can be sought out to gain advice on ethical dilemmas. Some counselors violate virtue ethics by becoming too absorbed in the client's problem. Caring and compassion is taken to unhealthy emotional levels. One condition that can arise from this violation is post traumatic stress disorder. The counselor has the tendency to develop hypervigilance in response to stressful situations that arise on a daily basis. The counselor may experience burnout or withdraw from his family. The counselor may also experience physical or emotional symptoms.

Self-care

The mental health counselor should take care of his or her own needs, to ensure an ongoing ability to do the job. Self-care should be attended to on a daily basis. The wise counselor will seek out psychotherapy, coaching, exercise, meditation, hobbies, and healthy relationships with others. Psychotherapy is useful in helping the therapist realize areas in which he or she may be deficient. Training may be needed in a specific area. Psychotherapy can help the therapist to target character issues that can have a negative impact on virtue ethics. Coaching is useful in helping the therapist target career or family goals. Coaching can be achieved via the phone or secure internet connections. Exercise programs are beneficial, but should be scheduled as a fun and rewarding part of the day. Meditation can be utilized, in the form of transcendental meditation, yoga, or breathing exercises.

The wise counselor develops hobbies, and healthy relationships with others. Hobbies and a wide range of interests help the counselor to remain stimulated on an intellectual and emotional level. These activities can give the counselor a zest for life and help him to refocus his attention. Family and friends provide the counselor with social and emotional outlets. These outlets can help the counselor reduce feelings of isolation that can lead to burnout. Peers or colleagues can be supportive in our work environments. These supportive groups can provide needed opportunities for socialization in the work setting. Overall, the mental health counselor should approach self-care needs as priorities in his daily life.